Anthrop·

THE POWER OF LAW IN A TRANSNATIONAL W

THE POWER OF LAW IN A TRANSNATIONAL WORLD

Anthropological Enquiries

Edited by
Franz von Benda-Beckmann, Keebet von Benda-Beckmann
and Anne Griffiths

Berghahn Books
New York • Oxford

Published in 2009 by

Berghahn Books

www.berghahnbooks.com

©2009, 2012 Franz von Benda-Beckmann,
Keebet von Benda-Beckmann, Anne Griffiths

First paperback edition published in 2012.

Library of Congress Cataloging-in-Publication Data

The power of law in a transnational world anthropological enquiries / Edited
by Franz von Benda-Beckmann, Keebet von Benda-Beckmann and Anne
Griffiths.
  p. cm.
Includes bibliographical references and index.
ISBN 978-1-84545-423-4 (hbk.) -- ISBN 978-0-85745-615-1 (pbk.)
  1. Legal polycentricity. 2. Law and globalization. 3. Law and anthropology.
I. Benda-Beckmann, Franz von. II. Benda-Beckmann, Keebet von. III. Griffiths,
Anne M. O.

K236.P683 2009
340'.115—dc22

2008053764

British Library Cataloguing in Publication Data

A catalogue record for this book is available from the British Library

Printed in the United States on acid-free paper.

ISBN: 978-0-85745-615-1 (paperback)   ISBN: 978-0-85745-616-8 (ebook)

Contents

Acknowledgements

This volume is the second publication that has resulted from a series of conferences organized by the School of Law, Edinburgh University, and the Max Planck Institute for Social Anthropology in Halle/Saale, Germany, on the development of the anthropology of law. The first volume, *Mobile People, Mobile Law: Expanding Legal Relations in a Contracting World*, appeared in 2005 with Ashgate. We thank the Max Planck Institute, the Economic and Social Research Council (U.K.), the British Academy (U.K.) and the Wenner-Gren Foundation for Anthropological Research (U.S.) for their financial support. We are deeply indebted to Astrid Finke and Jacqueline Cottrell, who worked on the manuscripts written by non-native speakers, to Margaret Beechey and Myra Reid for their work in organizing the conference, and to Gesine Koch, Sung-Joon Park, Cornelia Richter, Philipp Humpert and Titus Rebhann for preparing the manuscript.

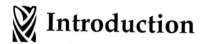

Introduction

THE POWER OF LAW
Franz von Benda-Beckmann
Keebet von Benda-Beckmann
Anne Griffiths

Law is a source for constituting and legitimating power. It defines and validates positions and relations of power of persons or organizations over other persons, organizations and resources. It lays down in general terms which exercises of power are permissible or prohibited. It can be actualized in social interaction when the exercise of power is rationalized and justified with reference to law.[1] Of course, other means for constituting and legitimating power and exercising social control coexist and compete with legal ones. These include moral and ethical standards as well as naked, unabashed power based on the command and exercise of physical force. Yet even autocrats exercising power on the basis of 'might is right' often feel the need to legitimate their position through reference to a higher and more noble source. The 'legal certification of power' (F. von Benda-Beckmann 2005: 3) is therefore a resource much sought after in local, national and transnational arenas.

Earlier discussions on the relationship between law and power and the function of law for preventive and reactive social control situated law primarily in a national context.[2] Over the last decades law has become an important factor in transnational relationships and is far less exclusively tied to a particular national state than before. National law is often made in response to transnational developments urging homogenization and assimilation. At the same time, it has become increasingly clear that the degree to which transnational developments reach out to local levels and how they are dealt with locally varies greatly. Moreover, the idea of legal pluralism drawing attention to the possibility that there may be sources of law other than the nation state has become far more widely accepted than it was only a few decades ago. Besides state-internal constellations, 'global' legal pluralism is a subject of intensive debate.[3] In an earlier publication, we have explored some of these transnational dimensions of 'mobile law and mobile people' (F. von Benda-Beckmann, K. von Benda-Beckmann and A. Griffiths

2005). The present volume explores some of the connections between law and power, taking account of these new configurations.

The volume is organized around three sets of issues. The essays in the first section, on the *Power of Law as Discourse: Claims to Legitimacy and Higher Morality*, focus on power differentials entailed in the strategic use of legal discourses. Law plays an important part in creating, producing and enforcing meanings of concepts such as 'justice', 'authority' and 'rights'; and in instantiating notions of 'legality' that may be invoked by different social actors in their construction of hegemonic and counter-hegemonic discourses. Such discourses not only operate on a rhetorical or ideological level but may also serve to underpin the actual use of force or violence to achieve their ends. The second section – *At the Intersection of Legalities* – focuses on how different actors make and maintain law in a whole variety of settings that represent very diverse constellations of power as they navigate their way through the plural legal orders they encounter. Finally, the chapters in the third section – *Religion as a Resource in Legal Pluralism* – explore the impact that religion may have on law, especially under conditions of legal pluralism where it may be employed to extend state control, or alternatively, to create a space for autonomy from such control. Rather than pitting religion against the state, the authors highlight the need for a more concrete understanding of the specific contexts in which religion is invoked, displaying the complex relationship that exists between it and other intrastate regulatory frameworks, such as customary law, that make up the sources of legal authority on which people and institutions may draw.

Exploring these interconnections demands an understanding of the analytical complexities that inhere in the relationship between law and power. We will, therefore, briefly address this relationship and the challenges that it poses for a study of the power of law before we turn to a more detailed discussion of the issues that the contributors raise.

Understanding Law and Power

In our understanding, 'law' is a cover term that encompasses a wide range of legal phenomena. Legal orders or single rules may be rooted in different sources of legitimacy, such as age-old tradition, religion, the will of the people, or agreements between states. The coexistence of such legal forms in the same social field (however defined) is generally called 'legal pluralism'.[4] The kinds of law discussed in this volume include the formal laws of states and international laws and conventions

(Greenhouse, Nader, Baxi, Griffiths and Kandel), human rights (F. von Benda-Beckmann), regulatory regimes that include bureaucratic forms of governance such as executive orders (Greenhouse) or the project law of development organizations (Weilenmann), as well as civil servants' and NGOs' supervision of diplomatically determined international agreements (Cowan) and fisheries quotas in Canada (Wiber and Kearney). They also include traditional or neotraditional ethnic and religious legal orders (Whitecross, K. von Benda-Beckmann, Pirie).

What emerges from this perspective are the different actors who are engaged in contestations over who has the power and authority to generate law and construct its meaning. This is especially pertinent in plural legal constellations where there may be contestation over what is the 'correct' law in particular contexts. The actors engaged in these processes not only include national states acting as sovereign law makers or in concert with other states in the construction of international law, but also national or transnational nongovernmental organizations, 'law merchants',[5] epistemic communities,[6] self-regulatory networks, traditional and religious authorities and local communities. The power struggles in which they are engaged often reflect asymmetrical power relations among parties and among legal orders. This affects the ways in which law's legitimacy is constituted and reconfigured through social processes that frame both its continuity and transformation over time.

The contributions to this volume thus endorse a view of legal pluralism that rejects any idea of a single site of legal sovereignty embodied in the state. Such a legal anthropological perspective challenges conventional, doctrinal approaches to law that present it as a concept, universal across time and space, that can only derive its legitimacy and validity from the state and that represents a system of law that is coherent and uniform. It also challenges anthropological and sociological conceptions of law that directly tie law to the state and thus reproduce within their own conceptual approach the normative hierarchy between legal orders as defined by lawyers and state law. In so doing, the authors undermine stereotypical depictions of the global, the state and the local, and their relationships with one another that are founded on a bounded, hierarchical and stratified notion of law. Such a depiction of law obscures our understanding of the significance of legal orders and the power that they exercise as a form of social control. Today, it is commonly accepted that states are far from homogeneous and must be viewed as heterogeneous entities that are not only enmeshed in international domains but are also engaged in negotiating their relationship with, and control over, citizens and others who fall within their jurisdictions.

This creates a considerable amount of legal pluralism within state legal structures, namely state legal pluralism, an aspect of legal pluralism that has been relatively under-researched (Merry 1988; Woodman 1998). Taking account of this phenomenon therefore requires a re-examination of the role of the state in the context of intersections between transnational capital, civil society, nongovernmental actors, other states and international organizations (Benda-Beckmann et al. 2005). Several contributions demonstrate the various ways in which states may become destabilized by patterns of global legal interaction that erode the boundaries between domestic and international law, and between internal and external juridical authorities (McGrew 1998). Some contributors focus on states' attempts to extend their power both at home (Whitecross) and abroad (Nader, Baxi) through ideological assertions about the rule of law, or even through war. Others explore the complexities that arise within states where different, coexisting forms of law are selectively prioritized and implemented by local communities in different ways, in order to marginalize control by central government (Pirie) or when disputing parties seek redress before a court (K. von Benda-Beckmann).

This perspective also challenges conventional notions of the relations between law and power. With many authors following Weber (1956), we find it useful to characterize power as a potentiality or probability. In Giddens's words it is a 'sub-category of transformative capacity, where transformative capacity is harnessed to actors' attempts to get others to comply with their wants' (1979: 93). Power thus understood is relational, relative and always embedded in social relationships. Any field of social relations and networks is (amongst others) a power field.[7] Power and power differentials thus concern not only the relations between government and governance agents and their subjects or citizens, but also family relationships and relationships within organizations, as well as property relations. What power 'is', how its potential is mobilized and with what consequences, varies depending on the layer of social organization we look at, that is, whether we examine power as inscribed into general legal rules and institutions, or as an element in ideologies, or in social relationships, or in the actual social interactions that are structured by them, which reproduce and change them.[8]

At the legal-institutional level law defines relations and positions of power of persons or organizations over persons, organizations and other resources in terms of general rights and obligations. These often encode power asymmetries, as Starr and Collier (1989: 6f.) pointed out, but they may also prescribe formal equality, for instance between women and men, or commercial entities and states. In plural legal orders, more than one set of interpretive legal constructions define power and its relationship with positions of authority, often in contradictory ways. Thus one legal order may locate supreme authority in the state's sovereignty, while religious legal orders may assign supreme authority to religious leaders. Yet another form of ordering may allocate such power to customary or traditional authorities. However, legal rules and institutionalized frameworks are not the only means for ascertaining power relations. In a more general, less structured way most societies have one or more ideologies about power. While ideological notions of power often become inscribed in legal frameworks, they are never completely captured or transformed by them. As a result, the way in which power is deployed in terms of these general ideologies may vary considerably from the way in which it operates in more legally institutionalized frameworks.

At another level it is also necessary to acknowledge that power features in actual social relationships and networks. Ideological or legal constructions of power relations are not necessarily mirrored in actual power relationships. The actual power relationships between states, for instance, do not represent the notion of equality embedded in the concept of sovereignty and international law. Gender equality prescribed in law often does not correspond to the distribution of power in actual social relationships between men and women. In fact, as Balbus (1977) observed decades ago, the formal legal equality that exists often obscures social, economic and political inequalities between citizens. The potential of power becomes manifest in social interaction. By tracing interactions and their intended and unintended consequences we can see how power works and the dynamics it may engender. Arts (2003) and others have shown that given its multifaceted nature it is useful to distinguish different types of power, that is, sets of activities through which power is exercised that include decisional power, discursive power and regulatory power.[9]

As Foucault (1980) has emphasized, techniques of exercising power and exercising control should not simply be looked for in the unequal relations between state and citizens in some kind of command-obey-sanction model, but also in the increasingly important realms of disciplinary power and techniques of power through the management of the population, often referred to as 'governmentality'.[10] In different types and techniques of social interaction, the relations of power become instantiated in social practice, are reproduced, maintained or changed and become the context for further interactions. Historically grown and sedimented patterns of power relationships affect interactions, creating waves of interdependence in turn. Any interaction occurs in a context of which actual power relations, legally institutionalized legitimate power positions and ideological conceptions of power are part (see Holy 1999). They form power potentials that can be actualized in social practices of exercising power. The power encoded in general legal regulations and inscribed into actual social relations and into the rights and obligations to command, urge, follow, obey and submit entailed in these constructions, is just one among many sources of potential power.[11] In order to mobilize the power positions encoded in legal regulations or in existing social relationships, actors must therefore be able to draw on other sources of power.

The increasing opening up of the national state due to global connections on the one hand, and internal differentiating factors on the other, has forced both analysts and actors involved in power struggles to shift from a too-exclusive focus on the national state and its law towards alternative legal orders and other actors engaged in lawmaking. Within a world that is increasingly characterized by legal pluralism, each of the component legal orders has lost its self-evident pre-eminence. As a consequence it is harder to establish which legal order acquires precedence over another. This is not an entirely new phenomenon, for it required considerable efforts on the part of scholars and activists to convince states of the validity of traditional legal orders.[12] Prioritizing legal orders today continues to create dilemmas and opportunities for contestation, given the lack of consensus on how relationships between competing legal orders are to be determined, a problem that has become more pronounced in recent years given the far greater range of actors involved in creating and remodelling constellations of legal pluralism.[13]

Power of Law as a Discourse:
Claims to Legitimacy and Higher Morality

The chapters in this first part focus on the power of law as a system of representation and meaning through the study of discourse and its claims to legitimacy and a higher morality. They examine how law is used to create, produce and enforce meanings and relationships pertaining to civilization, rationality, equality, justice and due process. They stress the cultural significance of law through examining discourses concerned, for example, with development, democratization and the rule of law. The essays show that such legal discourses and the claims for higher morality entailed in them are used in order to establish the superiority of a particular kind of law over others. By focusing on the power differentials entailed in the strategic use of legal discourses, these chapters analyse some of the contradictions entailed in hegemonic discourses of law. Hegemonic states seek to enforce central Western legal concepts and values upon states that seem to lack these, while at the same time legitimating the unilateral and often illegal use of violence by reference to a higher moral order, thereby undermining the same legal values they seek to impose upon others. In doing so, they pitch an idealistic view of Western law and democracy against a stereotyped negative view of states that are seen as a source of threat and instability.

Much discursive energy is used to define the dominant law as the 'normal' legality. Religious and traditional 'ethnic' laws are usually presented as alternative or counterhegemonic legalities (Santos and Rodríguez-Garavito 2005). Which legal order then is considered to be the 'normal' legality, and which one the 'alternative' legality, will largely depend on the historical moment in time and on the eyes through which one beholds the normative and empirical power differential between legal orders and their constructions of power. Islam in particular is demonized as epitomizing violence and terror. The reference to the higher morality is then used to legitimize violence. Narratives of violence and terror themselves have become central epistemic concepts in legitimating violence by hegemonic states that is often beyond the law. They underline the extent to which powerful actors, such as states or international organizations, feel compelled to legitimate their actions by reference to a higher morality in order to strengthen their position, while also drawing attention to the ways in which less powerful actors appeal to those same higher values in order to question or subvert the very legitimacy that is imposed on them. In this process rhetorical claims may be employed to support the expansion of state control through discourses of democracy that have been used to disenfranchise and delegitimate other forms of legal ordering and political organization. The essays thus try to understand how discourses that refer to higher morality and claims to legitimacy are powerful resources in political struggles for hegemony, the effect of which undermines the very premises upon which hegemony is claimed.

By spotlighting the implementation of the Military Order in the U.S., Greenhouse examines the implications for the way in which ethnographers may theorize the neoliberal state and 'rethink the ethnography of power from a standpoint of executive power'. In her chapter she illustrates the uncoupling of the American state from democratic engagement in its bypassing of judicial and legislative guarantees through its recourse to executive orders, for the Military Order that was issued did not require the consent or cooperation of other branches of government to establish its existence. In analysing this development Greenhouse adopts a novel ethnographic approach that focuses on the debate that the order itself generated in the U.S. Thus her emphasis is not on the traditional domains of anthropology of law as it developed in the twentieth century, namely dispute processes, courts and 'trouble cases'. Instead she explores the terms of the order 'in larger terrains of discursive circulation and opposition' that are not accessible from the text itself.

This involves employing a new methodology that is based on two main interpretative resources that she terms 'discursive trails' and 'career pathways'. The first picks up on commentaries in the media, especially those that promote the Military Order; the second follows the career pathways of the commentators themselves in order to elucidate the broader context of values in which the Military Order should be understood. The commentaries provide valuable supplements to official documents by providing evidence of the wider meanings at play in policy documents. They bridge public and private sectors and illustrate how 'contemporary hegemonic discourse circulates – not just top-down but also, strategically, from disparate political communities of the private sector into the state'. This is important in a context where executive power is dominant and where representation occurs 'at the level of competition over signs of authority and legitimacy, rather than in actual deliberative arenas like legislatures and courts'.

What becomes clear is that, read from its advocates' perspective, the Military Order links terrorism to urban violence as related sites of tension among competing agents of federal, local, military and civilian control. In discussing the ways in which international law is seen as 'constituting a real and immediate threat to U.S. national interests' that will eliminate the unilateral use of military force, Greenhouse highlights the transnational production of domestic politics. She makes an important contribution to our understanding of how transnationalism selectively empowers the executive in relation to other branches of government and other levels of government within a country's jurisdiction. In addressing this somewhat ignored aspect of law in the context of debates on transnationalism and globalization, Greenhouse demonstrates how states do not wither away but rather shows 'the extent to which neoliberal states, through their executive branches, retain their option on strong forms of power even in the case of transnational alliances'.

In analysing how law forms part of discourse, Nader focuses on 'law as a terrain of political struggle' and pushes scholars to consider 'how law really works in the service of power and empire' and how the rule of law and of democracy discourse 'works in the service of political, military and economic power in Iraq'. She explores the continuity of such discourse, from the past as part of an imperial and colonial project, to the present where 'the rule of law' continues to underpin the 'Euro-American civilizing project'. Her analysis shows the way in which culture is mobilized to lay the foundation for an ideological vision of the world in which an idealized version of Western law is juxtaposed against other legal systems, such as Islamic law, and accorded moral superiority over them. In her discussion Nader is critical of the role that legal scholars have played in this process and of 'how scholarship is implicated in contemporary U.S. foreign policy in the Islamic World'. Reviewing Weber's typologies of law, and the work of scholars such as Rosen and Schacht, she argues that the continuing stereotyping of Islamic law forms part of an essentialist, orientalist perspective depicting 'the anarchy of the Arab way of life'. Such stereotyping of Islamic law goes hand in hand with a most idealized representation of Western law. Such representations are of interest to ethnographers 'because of their use in shaping hegemonies or counter-hegemonies'.

Understanding the contexts that underpin these representations of law is important, for as Nader notes, 'law practice today is constructed internationally within the inequalities of the contemporary international economic system'. For Nader, this raises questions about how illegalities associated with 'lawlessness and plunder' (demonstrated by the war in Iraq) become changed into legalities. She points to the way in which military force has 'allowed for the disorganization of competing legal controls in Iraq'. Another example is provided by the interim constitution, which according to ordinary legal principles cannot be termed a 'constitution' due to the undemocratic process through which it was established. Nader also refers to Executive Orders in the U.S. 'passing for law', unless challenged, although their creation has bypassed the other two branches of government. Finally, she draws attention to the 'state of exception' that represents an extension of executive power that 'has potential to transform democracies into totalitarian states'.

What her chapter highlights is the ways in which law and legitimacy, legalities and illegalities 'are all intertwined in a transparent study of law practices set in the grand scheme of geopolitics'. Under these conditions Euro-American law, which is so dominant in geopolitics, can, through its 'positional superiority', give rise to the legalization of illegal acts that not only subvert local law but also deny the very existence of legal pluralism. Such a state of affairs not only opens up the possibility of law 'as a system of discontrol', but also raises issues about how far the frontiers of illegality can be pushed 'before we understand the threat of such ruptures to the very definition of legality and the rule of law'.

For Cowan, who examines supranational engagement with minority protection and rights in Europe, linkages between national and international domains are significant. They raise questions about how practices and relations beyond the state 'are also implicated in the creation of populations' and 'the reformulation of relations between states, subjects and the "international" in certain key moments'. These key moments include the decade following the First World War and the role of the League of Nations, and the post-1989 situation involving states applying for membership of the European Union as part of the enlargement process. What emerges is an asymmetry of power relations, reflecting a double standard of selective supervision with regard to selective enforcement of these rights among states. In her analysis Cowan stresses 'two unequally structured interactions involving a supranational body and minority state on the one hand, and between minority states and their own minorities on the other'. These conjunctions, which are concurrent and interlocking, create a situation where the state is 'simultaneously subordinate and superordinate', raising questions about the nature and scope of state sovereignty and its limits.

From an anthropological perspective, what is important is to acknowledge the array of actors involved in this supranational or international supervision and to analyse 'their varying positions, interests, identifications and indeed, fantasies'. Cowan highlights how powerful states in the EU use the concept of minority, group and human rights to 'supervise' other, less powerful states on the European periphery that seek international recognition and membership in the EU. Her paper shows how minority rights and the governance of difference are used to provide the rationale and focus for the supranational supervision of states in way that represents 'the "indirect rule" of a new liberal imperialism'. Her chapter traces how such political/legal categories as 'minorities', 'states', 'nations' and nationalities became 'reified, actualized, negotiated, differentiated and consolidated in the process, including the encounter between the various kinds of actors at this institutional site'. Looking behind the scenes, Cowan draws specific attention to the important role played by NGOs in the supervision process and highlights the need to unravel 'the institutional practices of accountability' that are a feature of the 'ever-proliferating audit process' integral to the harmonization of laws and institutions of the European Union. In conclusion, Cowan argues that it is not enough merely to retheorize 'the state' and its relation to 'the local', 'the global' and the international; rather, 'we need to consider its multiple forms and degrees of sovereignty, legitimacy and autonomy, as well as the ways that the meaning of intra-state "difference" is being reconceptualized and contested in the contemporary moment'.

Working at the level of global discourse, Baxi interrogates the use of terms such as 'war on terror' and 'war of terror' and the implications of the rhetoric they embrace, which has spawned a 'globalization of fatwas'. In stressing the need to understand that terrorism is not 'a single casually coherent phenomenon' and the need to understand 'terror' outside a state-centred perspective, he questions how we may 'achieve understandings of "reasonable pluralism" in a world made infinitely violent by pre- and post-histories of 9/11'. Like Greenhouse and Nader, he acknowledges 'the destruction of substantive international law as a source of pluralism'. While recognizing the need for pluralist perspectives that generate discussion above the level of 'Manichaean discourse' associated with the 'clash of civilizations', he questions how legal pluralist traditions of learning and research may 'begin to ethnographically engage the consequentialist claims that justify feats of state terrorism as jurisgenerative', for, as he notes, behind every system of violence 'lie congeries of unsanctioned violence'. Just as Nader points to legalities and illegalities being antagonistic yet functionally connected elements, so Baxi observes that the distinction between violence sanctioned by the law and violence beyond the law is often illusory. For example, the White House and Whitehall may unilaterally determine the meanings of international law. Thus pre-emptive war may be justified under an innovative doctrine of regime change. The notion of an 'unreasonable veto' may be introduced into the Security Council of the UN and the normative regimes of military occupation and international humanitarian law may be rewritten.

Baxi is critical of anthropologists and studies in legal pluralism for having 'insufficiently addressed ethnographies of terror'. Indeed, he challenges them 'to more reflexively address their location in the new moments of "terror" already constituted'. This would require an investigation into, and an understanding of the presentation of, many histories of terror. This is necessary because the languages of terrorism determine both the 'subjects' and 'their supporting predicates' that determine 'the sequence of response'. Given the propagandist use of terms such as 'terror', 'anthropology as intervention ought to put into question the epistemic violence of terror narratives' in order to deconstruct their mythic power. This would, in his opinion, create 'a first step towards curbing such violence in future'. This is necessary because the central question in his view is not so much 'our preferred ways of understanding legal pluralism but rather how these leave intact the structures of global violence and the carriers of costs of legal pluralism'. Thus he highlights the discrepancy in discourse 'that celebrates in the

very first years of this century the Golden Jubilee of the Universal Declaration of Human Rights at the same time that it ushers in an era of its
recessional futures'.

All these contributions raise questions about how discourses of legitimation are constructed and the powerful role that law plays in upholding or negating the authority of those who act, at whatever level
they operate, from a transnational domain to a local enclave. The polar-
ization that ensues from an essentializing rhetoric that is used to create
categories of difference (e.g. to separate out Euro-American law from
Islamic law) forms the subject matter of Franz von Benda-Beckmann's
chapter, where he examines the limitations placed on human rights discourse when it is reduced to debates upholding universalist or cultural
relativist perspectives. He argues that such a focus has resulted in a
conflation of empirical and ideological assertions as to whether human
rights exist universally or should exist universally. The former and the
latter have become rolled into one so that the tensions between ethnographic research on the one hand, and political and moral evaluation
on the other, continue to have an impact upon the debate.

Franz von Benda-Beckmann argues that the tensions between universalism and relativism are often presented as an international or
intercultural problem between 'our' Western rights and 'their' Third
World culture, or 'our culture' and 'their rights'. As a consequence little
attention has been given to the fact that both human rights and culture
in most parts of the world coexist with a variety of legal forms, and that
the major contemporary struggles that really concern people are not so
much between 'Western human rights' and 'Third World cultures' but
between different laws and cultures within states. In his view the rights
versus/as/to culture paradigm has remained pervasive even after the
deconstruction of culture as a homogeneous whole and the development of more refined analytical understandings of the concept (as in
Cowan, Dembour and Wilson 2001). This translates the political assertion of the superiority of human rights law as law over culture into a
corresponding conceptual inequality, denying the analytical status of
(nonstate, nonhegemonic) law to the alternative legalities.

The proposed analytical understanding of culture therefore must
be accompanied by an analytical understanding of law and legal pluralism. This will show that the main conflicts may be between human
rights and a plurality of law in states, including state law, and a population's 'culture' or cultures, however homogenous or heterogeneous
these may be. Thus the anthropologist's role is to make a clear distinction between empirical and normative assertions about the universal-
ity/relativism of human rights 'as a precondition for systematic and

comparative research'. Such an approach, with its close attention to specification and analysis of the variability of social and cultural organization, will provide 'more nuanced attitudes towards the tensions between analytical description and moral evaluation' that will provide for more informed debate on the issue.

At the Intersection of Legalities

Given the relational aspects of power that are highlighted in the volume, the contributors underline the asymmetries that exist between parties not just in terms of their unequal social relations but also in terms of the legal orders to which they lay claim, thereby documenting who has the power to construct and reconfigure law's legitimacy in particular contexts. In these processes, despite the increasing dominance of the law of states in many regions of the world and the increased proliferation of inter- and transnational law, nonstate legal orders not only continue to exist but are revitalized, or reinvented, or simply gain importance as actors seize the opportunity to reshape the legal landscape in which they operate by reconfiguring the legal spaces to which they have access.[14] Paradoxically, state law itself may strengthen its legitimacy by drawing on other normative orders.

Plural legal situations provide different repertoires of legitimate power relations and their political and economic relations of dependence, opening up opportunities for 'idiom shopping' and 'forum shopping' as well as for shopping behaviour by courts and other authorities (K. von Benda-Beckmann 1981, Spiertz 1991). Thus social actors may draw selectively and often quite indiscriminately upon the various types of law as suits their needs – but only as far as they are able to. In such processes, legal constructions of legitimate power can be mobilized against each other, but they can also be combined to improve the level of legitimation.[15] In this way 'our legal life is constituted by an intersection of different legal orders', as Santos noted, and legal pluralism represents different economies of scale that give rise to what Santos (1987: 298) terms 'porous legality or legal porosity' that represents 'interlegality'. The chapters in this section discuss ways in which actors navigate these intersections from the highest transnational down to the local level.

The first three essays in this section discuss the role of these other players in relation to state agencies. The chapters show that the involvement of these other actors tends to increase the multiplexity of legal orders because they act either as (self-appointed) supervising institutions, or as lawmakers that to a considerable extent stand outside the state. The chapters furthermore discuss some of the implications for the ways in which states negotiate their relationships with their subjects or citizens and address how various actors respond to the tensions involved in these processes. They point at the contradictions that ensue from these fragmented and multi-focal state structures that at the same time are deeply implicated in wider legal and political structures.

The asymmetry of power relations is a theme picked up by Wiber and Kearney in their chapter on the regulation of the fishing industry in Canada. This has come about through the changes wrought by alterations in the technology of fishing involving the increased capitalization of costs and the ceding of greater control to processing companies. In the Canadian government's attempts to deal with the depletion of fish stock and to regulate the industry, the federal government has introduced a system of individual transferable quotas. Such a system derives from technical epistemic communities (that is, communities of experts that are spread across the globe) that are extremely influential and have played a central role in creating regulatory frameworks and blueprints for fisheries management and administrative law in this area all over the world.

However, through their ethnographic study of fishers in the inshore sector of the Nova Scotia Fundy region, Wiber and Kearney point to an alternative means of regulation, evolved by local communities in the area, that involves a community-based management system. The advantage of this system is that it is able to take account of the specificities of local knowledge of ecological conditions and socioeconomic realities allowing for a wide diversity of production practices that are ignored by inflexible, programmatic plans put forward by epistemic communities that do not encourage 'local solutions to local problems'. Yet such solutions provide more broadly based, inclusive networks 'that affect wider environmental areas, develop common values and manage conflict among a wider set of users according to a fairer set of rules'.

The study details the ways in which a state-centric approach to regulation creates barriers to sustainable management where this is not part of the dominant privatization regime. The authors argue that what is needed is a real institutional matrix for the management of natural resources that involves 'significantly under-theorized institutional elements' at both the 'micro and macro level'. This involves an acceptance of pluralism that engages with 'significant levels of legal pluralism' that take account of the interconnection and discontinuities that form part of 'the total legal landscape'. Thus government and state bureaucrats, at federal and provincial levels, should remain part of a process that becomes more inclusive by acknowledging the wider legal landscapes (including local practices) within which the negotiation of fishing rights takes place.

Weilenmann also discusses competition over regulating powers among local, national and transnational actors, but focuses on examples in which the state agencies are in a weak position. On the basis of a case study from Burundi, he demonstrates how in some developing countries the rule of law and territorial control is often contested by powerful development agencies and NGOs that could be said to achieve a 'quasi-state status' in their sponsorship of programmes aimed at promoting good governance, justice and human rights. This is achieved through the bureaucratic mechanism of what he terms 'project law' that governs international aid. Such law comes into being at two levels. The first concerns those legal rules that guide the planning and the conceptualization phase of a development project and that monitor and transfer project responsibilities to local implementing organizations. At this stage, regulation is often based on procedures developed by bilateral or multilateral development agencies that are frequently derived from those agencies' own national legal systems. This sets the framework for the second stage, where project law represents those rules that are formed by project personnel during the implementation process and interaction with target groups. Such a process undermines any real involvement on the part of local actors as their participation is prescribed according to the conditions set by the donor agency.

The power wielded by international development agencies and NGOs is well acknowledged. What Weilenmann's anthropological perspective brings to the discussion is a more nuanced understanding of how such power is constructed at different levels. This involves an analysis of the chains of translation that are traced from the policy-making agenda of the executive board, to the rules of negotiation that are framed by the international project personnel, through to the practices of local partner organizations, such as Burundian NGOs. His analysis demonstrates how a development-related topic changes its interpretation and has methodological consequences as a result. The analysis of the whole process of translation activity reveals the different circumstances that different actors use to legitimate their competing claims, as well as the strategies they employ in drawing on competing legal sources, such as customary, state and religious law. These bodies of law are often ignored due to the way in which project law operates, by stealth, in evading ordinary processes of democratic control.

As Weilenmann points out, development projects have had considerable political impact on the social life of developing countries. This is cause for concern, given the constraints under which project law operates, particularly the limited spatial, temporal and institutional validity that is built into each individual project. Project law has 'the potential to fragment the prevailing legal and political orders in recipient countries in such a way as to weaken their rule of law'. The cumulative, fragmented field of competing normative systems to which project law of the various development agencies gives rise may have a destabilizing effect. Weilenmann suggests that greater transparency would allow for alternative options for action and for greater local participation, which would render the processes more democratic.

The issue of transparency and competing normative orders is raised in Griffiths and Kandel's chapter on managing communication in Scottish children's hearings. Their analysis examines how the United Nations Convention on the Rights of the Child and the European Convention on Human Rights and Fundamental Freedoms are put into operation and interpreted in the local domain of hearings in Glasgow that deal with children under sixteen who are in need of compulsory measures of supervision. At the opposite end of the spectrum from Weilenmann, they highlight the asymmetric power relations of the actors involved and explore how local actors respond to international and national regulation that governs intervention in the lives of children. Such intervention involves balancing principles of welfare and autonomy at a number of levels. The authors demonstrate how what is intended to represent a transparent and open forum in fact represents a more complex and concealed process of communication that derives from partial silence and half-told truths.

This arises because of the composition of the 'local' domain, where the different interests, agendas and normative conceptions of all the local actors, while overlapping in some respects, may also compete with one another in shaping the hearing's process. While panel members, who are authorized to make decisions about what is in the best interest of the child at hearings, strive for greater participation and disclosure, children and their families are often wary of saying too much for fear of what the consequences will be. Children balance their obligations at hearings with the informal codes of neighbourhood and family that order their lives outside the hearing. As a result, in an attempt to resist intrusion into their lives, many children's participation is centred on strategies of silence, compliance, and autonomy and defiance. Panel members are aware of the problems that exist in fostering communication and strive to interpret their legal remit in a way that meets the needs of these local actors through interpretive strategies that they employ in dealing with legislation.

It is not only the divergent perceptions of children, families and panel members, that are at stake, however. Other officials involved in the process may find themselves balancing the system's formal legal requirements with the regulatory demands and policies of the bureaucracies they work with while fulfilling their job descriptions. Griffiths and Kandel demonstrate how the best interests of the child as promoted by legislation may conflict with the institutional demands placed on social workers who may have to accommodate other priorities in their job. As a result the constraints of their position may entail a degree of secrecy. What emerges in navigating this universe is that holding back information that doesn't suit you, and emphasizing what does, proves for all concerned to be a much more powerful tool than transparency and openness in providing for management and control of the process. What takes place in hearings must, therefore, be viewed in the context of the varying demands placed on them through the differing institutional roles and professional affiliations of those who service them. As a number of contributions to this volume also stress, governance through bureaucratic management is a tool that may well be at odds with, or counteract, the formal power of law in certain circumstances.

Religion as a Resource in Legal Pluralism

In the work on legal pluralism, the role of religious law has not figured as prominently as has that of customary law or transnational law. While there have been a number of studies of religious courts, these have tended to have a somewhat limited focus, one that ignores the larger political context within which such courts are located, which is what the chapters in this section address.[16] In the more general literature, religion is often depicted in opposition to the state, as a means for critiquing state power or abuse, or as an alternative moral order that may be called on to undermine state authority. Thus religion becomes imbued with positive or negative attributes depending on the role that is ascribed to it, as the chapters in the first section demonstrate. Discourses about Islam, for example, are often presented in an inherently negative way when set against and contrasted with the highly valued principles of democracy and the rule of law associated with Western legal discourse. Rather than engaging with emotive rhetoric, the chapters in this section adopt a more impartial view. They approach the subject from a perspective that treats religion as one of a number of normative orders that exists in the mix of intrastate regulatory frameworks on which people and institutions may draw. Their aim is to demonstrate the different ways in which religion may be perceived and the varying objectives for which it may be invoked.

These studies make it clear that the role of religion and religious law must be examined in terms of the specific contexts in which it is invoked, paying careful attention to who is calling upon religion and for what purposes. To acquire a complete understanding of what this entails, it is necessary to take account of the whole range of normative orders that exist within the field of study, of which religion forms only one part. For Whitecross this involves examining the new 'Western'-inspired laws introduced by the state of Bhutan. In this case, the state itself invokes religion in order to enhance legitimacy of changes within the state legal system that have little to do with religion or religious law. In the chapter by Keebet von Benda-Beckmann, however, it is the Indonesian state law and its judicial system and customary law that is at stake. In this context the Indonesian state attempts to exert its power to enhance the role of religion not by prescription or prohibition, but by offering Muslim citizens the option of bringing their inheritance disputes to the Islamic court. In Pirie's essay religion is primarily viewed in relation to local normative orders that exert a powerful influence among communities where the state legal system is somewhat remote and inaccessible. In this situation religious officials are called on to manage disputes where local customary institutions are unable to do so. Surprisingly, however, these officials do not apply religious norms to the cases that come before them but invoke customary law. Just as Whitecross demonstrates how the state may find it advantageous to draw on religious norms to create legitimacy for the introduction of Western-style laws that they fear would not be accepted by the population otherwise, so the Republic of Indonesia has instituted Islamic courts in order to broaden its jurisdiction, while at the same time containing Islamic legal aspirations.

These chapters highlight the complex manoeuvres that are employed to reach certain objectives and form a counterpoint to earlier discussions where the hegemonic force of the state and its law was underlined. They draw attention to the limits that may be placed on state power to determine the nature and scope of local law and the roles of those that apply it. They show the variety with which religion can be implicated in the other available orders: invoking religious institutions or functionaries does not necessarily also include the demand that religious norms should govern the problematic issue in question; in the same way, appeal to state organizations does not rule out that religious norms may be selected to determine the outcome despite being applied by state institutions.

From the perspective of the state, Whitecross demonstrates how Bhutan has, since the mid 1970s, been engaged in attempts to legitimate its new programme of law reform by reference to Buddhist principles. These are used to create an image of Bhutanese law backed by centuries of tradition, when in fact such law incorporates many new terms that derive not from Buddhism but from Western legal terms and concepts, especially those associated with Anglo-American legal systems. Thus the state attempts to align contemporary court practices and legal principles with Buddhist teachings. In doing so it is actively engaged in promoting a highly publicized modernization programme among the heterogeneous peoples living in Bhutan that will appeal to the international community and donor agencies, while at the same time promoting 'a reified view of Bhutanese cultural values' for its domestic audience.

In this way the state simultaneously stresses its openness to change while underlining its role in upholding traditional and uniquely Bhutanese cultural practices. The establishment of a particular vision of the moral basis of law is achieved symbolically, through the very architecture of new court buildings and through the visual imagery of a ritual dance associated with religious festivals. A similar function is performed in the text put out by the Royal Court of Justice, in which it is stated that 'Bhutanese laws have evolved over the centuries as a reflection of culture and lifestyle of people'. In forging links with the past, any discussion of how modern law codes and practices differ from those of the earlier legal system is omitted, especially with regard to the separation of administrative and judicial powers that were vested in provincial governors. Thus the projected reality, which creates a spectacle that builds on cultural symbols and meanings as part of the spectacle, seeks to make any changes appear indigenous and firmly rooted in the cultural, moral and religious values of Bhutan.

In this process two audiences are addressed, for while the 'Western'-inspired codes of court procedure reflect links with transnational law, within the confines of the court itself its spatial organization, its temporal routines and its linguistic codes all represent an attempt to present 'justice' and the operation and function of the courts in recognizably Bhutanese terms, in order to legitimate the judiciary and enhance public confidence in the formal legal process. Whitecross concludes by observing that despite the state's attempts, the majority of people at whom this spectacle is aimed do not 'recognize law in its Buddhicized version being presented by the courts and its personnel'. Instead they continue to view law as secular and retain 'a deep scepticism about its claims to impartiality' and to 'the equality of those appearing before the courts'.

Courts are also the focus of Keebet von Benda-Beckmann's chapter, which explores the shifts that are occurring within legal pluralism in Indonesia. In this case, the state legal system reflects an ongoing balancing act between three types of symbolic universes that encompass the state, religion, and local customs and customary law known as *adat*. Through a comparative study of two different regions in Indonesia, the Gayo Highlands of Central Aceh and West Sumatra, she analyses the different role that is accorded to religion and religious law in inheritance matters where state legislation explicitly allows citizens free choice between courts and legal orders. In the Gayo Highlands, Islamic courts are used rather frequently, while among the Minangkabau in West Sumatra, hardly any inheritance cases are contested in Islamic courts. Keebet von Benda-Beckmann suggests that the different patterns of court use can be understood only if the analysis addresses the way different actors are implicated in the reconfiguration of the three legal systems and proposes a comparative analysis in three steps. The first step considers the character of kinship and inheritance rules. The second step examines the position of courts and judges within the two regions, as part of the state legal system yet with a certain amount of autonomy regarding the relative role of customary and religious law. In the third step of her analysis she points to the two regions' different processes of incorporation into the colonial and national state and the significance that access to and control over resources plays in the construction of regional identity.

Thus, she argues, the difference in use of courts cannot be accounted for simply on the basis of differences in substantive rules of kinship, property and inheritance. In order to fully appreciate the differential use of Islamic and civil courts it is necessary to take account of the different histories of the two regions' incorporation into the colonial and postcolonial state, along with the current relationships that exist between the regions and central government. This reveals that whereas in Central Aceh Islam was mobilized as a basis for regional autonomy; this was not the case in West Sumatra, where the focus of discussion on Islam centred on the moral and legal, rather than political, role that it should play among Minangkabau. The chapter thus underlines the importance of analysing regional developments from a comparative and historical perspective that combines analyses at the micro-local level of courts with analyses of the intersection of national, regional and transnational arenas. As Keebet von Benda-Beckmann demonstrates, courts play a pivotal role here. They 'are especially illuminating because they serve as a prism through which the power of the state to change the disputing behaviour of its citizens may be observed, by changing the options that are available to such citizens, by giving them an element of choice rather than by formally prescribing or prohibiting certain behaviour'.

Pirie addresses the question of religion from another angle, exploring the contexts in which religious functionaries are called on to manage disputes among two local Tibetan communities in Ladakh, India, and Amdo, China. In her study, Pirie demonstrates how moral and religious norms do not necessarily coincide but may be differentiated from one another in the regulation of everyday life. She highlights the ways in which both communities, despite their location in states that adhere to markedly different ideologies of law and government, have succeeded in maintaining a considerable degree of autonomy over local legal processes. In Ladakh, such processes are centred on the internal management of the community through the *yulpa*, which exercises the ultimate political and judicial authority in the village.

Within this context, which draws on a local moral universe based on agreement in which all forms of violence are condemned, disputes present a problem for the whole community and require a form of conflict resolution that is based on reconciliation. While Buddhist monks are highly respected within this community, there is no evidence that they have ever been allowed to interfere in village politics or processes of conflict resolution. As a consequence, the authority of respected religious practitioners is confined to a distinct ritual and cosmological sphere. While Ladakhis accord Buddhist monks the utmost respect, they never 'made any explicit link between their moral judgments and any aspect of their religious or cosmological practices'.

By contrast, the pastoral group of Amdo, whose property tends to be mobile, has an ideology of revenge and group loyalty that requires individuals to display anger and aggression in response to incursions on property. Here major disputes arise between villages or encampments, and external mediators are often called in to negotiate a resolution when the council of tribal headmen is unable to use its authority to restrain and resolve violence. Those engaged in this external intervention may include senior monks from local monasteries. Buddhist lamas are viewed as being at the pinnacle of this system, able to resolve conflict that is beyond the capabilities of local mediators because they are perceived as a reincarnation of Buddhist deities who possess special powers to assist souls in the afterlife. This potent and charismatic authority gives them the power to overcome the nomads' norms of violent retribution. However, although the nomads in Amdo endow their senior religious leaders with the ultimate judicial authority, this is not to say that such authority is based on Buddhist morality, for *lamas* settle the nomads' disputes according to local norms of revenge and compensation. Like the Ladakhis, the nomads of Amdo retain their own set of norms for conflict resolution that are independent of religious principles and never make any references to Buddhist morality when discussing their approach to conflict resolution. Thus in both cases morality and religion operate in different spheres.

Reconstituting Power and Law in a Transnational World

In exploring the relationship between law and power and the forms that it takes, the contributors to this volume demonstrate how state law is not the only source of power mobilized in a whole variety of social fields that transect local, national and transnational domains. Indeed, they highlight the importance of legal pluralism in providing a repertoire on which social actors can draw in constructing discourses of legitimacy that may be used to promote and justify multiple forms of intervention, action and policy-making in many different arenas. As a result, plural legal situations provide different repertoires of legitimate power relations and their political and economic relations of dependence that not only can be mobilized against each other but also may be combined or accumulated. Given the relational aspects of power that are highlighted in the volume, the contributors underline the asymmetries that exist between parties, not just in terms of their unequal social relations but also in terms of the legal orders to which they lay claim, thereby documenting who has the power to construct and reconfigure law's legitimacy in particular contexts. They underline the transformative capacities of power as it operates at a number of levels, including those of ideology, legal rules and institutions, and social interactions that arise from and reconfigure social relationships.

Some chapters focus on the power of law as a system of representation and meaning through the study of discourse and its claims to legitimacy and a higher morality. They emphasize the extent to which powerful actors, such as states or international organizations, feel compelled to legitimate their actions by reference to a higher morality in order to strengthen their position, while also drawing attention to the ways in which less powerful actors appeal to those same higher values in order to question or subvert the very legitimacy that is imposed on them. In this process rhetorical claims may be employed to support the expansion of state control through discourses of democracy that have been used to disenfranchise and de-legitimate other forms of legal ordering and political organization. What these chapters illuminate is the way in which actors choose from and combine elements from available legal resources in the light of emerging reconfigurations and the productive dimensions of new international practices. They highlight the profound implications that such developments have for the construction and consolidation of both political-legal categories – 'minority', 'majority', 'state', among others – and the ratification or denial of particular instantiations.

At another, more instrumental level, contributors to the volume focus on the ways in which social actors operate in situations of legal pluralism under very diverse constellations of power. In doing so they examine the various ways in which power is configured in different social settings and how it is accommodated, adapted, ignored or resisted by the numerous participants through playing one legal order off against another to varying effect. They provide data on how law is mobilized from an array of perspectives, including the strategies employed in the selection and use of differing normative orders that meet with varying degrees of success. They demonstrate that comparative evaluations of legal orders have no universally accepted foundation for ranking these but involve skilful theorizing, pragmatic considerations and sometimes even violent political struggles. What emerges from these chapters is the extent to which state law must increasingly respond to transnational developments, while at the same time acknowledging the ways in which local constituencies respond to these developments. In the case of the latter, a heterogeneity is demonstrated that highlights the uneven and often contradictory effects of globalization.

The contributors' observations disclose how states and their varying populations are enmeshed in horizontal and vertical legal relationships that crosscut one another both within and beyond territorial borders. In these processes, despite the increasing dominance of the law of states in many regions of the world and the increased proliferation of inter- and transnational law, nonstate legal orders not only continue to exist but are revitalized or reinvented as actors seize the opportunity to reshape the legal landscape in which they operate by reconfiguring the legal spaces to which they have access. Paradoxically, state law itself may strengthen its legitimacy by drawing on other normative orders. Such processes allow for new forms of governance that challenge the law's hegemony (as pronounced by states) through establishing alternative legalities of power.

Notes

1. For discussions of the concept of power, see Weber (1956); Bachrach and Baratz (1970); Lukes (1974); Foucault (1980); Giddens (1984); Wolf (1990);

Hindess (1996); Arts (2003); Nuijten (2003). For discussions of power and law see Moore (1970); Turk (1978); Starr and Collier (1989: 7); Lazarus-Black and Hirsch (1994); Nader (1997); A. Griffiths (1997); McClure (1997); Santos (2002); F. von Benda-Beckmann (2005).

2. A useful overview of the many meanings of social control is given in J. Griffiths (1996: 763ff.) Law has frequently been defined as one specific mode of social control backed by the sanctioning power of the state or some other third-party agency: see Hoebel (1954); Schwartz (1954); Black (1976); Gibbs (1981, 1982); J. Griffiths (1984).

3. See Michaels (2005); Merry (2006); Berman (2007).

4. For overviews and elaboration of this term, see J. Griffiths (1986); Merry (1988); Tamanaha (1993, 2000); Woodman (1998); K. von Benda-Beckmann (2001); F. von Benda-Beckmann (1992, 2002); A. Griffiths (2002).

5. Lawyers who travel the world, usually on behalf of governments, development organizations or multinational law firms, to introduce their law to countries that are in the process of legal reform; see Dezalay and Garth (1996).

6. See Wiber (2005), who uses this term to refer to a network of persons spread across the globe who share and promote a particular form of knowledge. See also Haas (1992); Maher (2002).

7. We employ the field-metaphor here because it points at sets of social relationships and interactions that are not closely bounded. This can also be understood as semi-autonomous social field in Moore's (1973) sense, or as 'force field' (Nuijten 2003, 2005).

8. See F. von Benda-Beckmann (2005). Bachrach and Baratz (1970) wrote about the 'two faces' of power, 'basically power as structured in institutions and power instantiated in social interaction'. Nuijten (2005) distinguishes three types of power relations that partly overlap with these distinctions, namely power as strategic games, government or institutional power, and domination and structural power.

9. Arts (2003), as quoted in Büscher and Dietz (2005: 5–6).

10. See McClure (1997). It should be noted, however, that Foucault's realms of disciplinary power and governmentality are also constituted and legitimated by law.

11. Turk (1978), e.g., distinguished political, economic, ideological and diversionary power and the control over direct physical violence.

12. See Bruns and Meinzen-Dick (2000); F. von Benda-Beckmann (2006); Faundez (2006); Wollenberg, Anderson and López (2005); Weilenmann (this volume).

13. See e.g. Michaels (2005); Merry (2006); Berman (2007).

14. See Mamdani (1996); Rouveroy van Nieuwaal and Ray (1996); F. von Benda-Beckmann, K. von Benda-Beckmann and Turner (2007); Davidson and Henley (2007).

15. Turk (1978) has talked about law as a 'weapon in social conflict', and Vel (1992) characterized the plurality of coexisting legitimations of powers as an 'arsenal'. See Moore (1970); Tigar and Levy (1977); K. von Benda-Beckmann (1984); Scott (1985); F. von Benda-Beckmann (1990, 2002, 2005); Wiber

(1993); Nader (2002); F. von Benda-Beckmann and K. von Benda-Beckmann (2006); Eckert (2006).
16. See e.g. Dwyer (1979); K. von Benda-Beckmann (1984); Rosen (1989); Hirsch (1998); Bowen (2003); Shehada (2005).

References

Arts, B. 2003. 'Non-state Actors in Global Governance: A Power Analysis'. Paper presented at the 2003 ECPR Joint Sessions, Workshop 11. Edinburgh, March 28–April 2.

Bachrach, P. and M.S. Baratz. 1970. *Power and Poverty*. New York: Oxford University Press.

Balbus, I.D. 1977. 'Commodity Form and Legal Form: An Essay on the "Relative Autonomy" of the Law'. *Law and Society Review* 11: 571–88.

Benda-Beckmann, F. von. 1990. 'Ambonese Adat as Jurisprudence of Insurgency and Oppression', in R. Kuppe and R. Potz (eds), *Law and Anthropology, International Yearbook for Legal Anthropology, Volume 5*. The Hague, Boston, London: Martinus Nijhoff, 25–42.

———. 1992. 'Symbiosis of Indigenous and Western Law in Africa and Asia: An Essay in Legal Pluralism', in W.J. Mommsen and J.A. de Moor (eds), *European Expansion and Law: The Encounter of European and Indigenous Laws in 19th- and 20th-century Africa and Asia*. Oxford, New York: Berg Publishers, 307–25.

———. 2002. 'Who's Afraid of Legal Pluralism?' *Journal of Legal Pluralism* 47: 37–82.

———. 2005. 'Pak Dusa's Law: Thoughts on Law, Legal Knowledge and Power', *The Journal of Transdisciplinary Environmental Studies. Special Issue Power, Development and Environment* 4(2), (http://www.journal-tes.dk).

———. 2006 'The Multiple Edges of Law: Dealing with Legal Pluralism in Development Practice', in C.M. Sage and M. Woolcock (eds), *The World Bank Legal Review, Volume 2 – Law, Equity and Development*. The Hague: The World Bank and Martinus Nijhoff, 51–86.

Benda-Beckmann, F. von and K. von Benda-Beckmann. 2006. 'Changing One Is Changing All: Dynamics in the Adat-Islam-State Triangle', in F. von Benda-Beckmann and K. von Benda-Beckmann (eds), *Dynamics of Plural Legal Orders. Special Double Issue of the Journal of Legal Pluralism and Unofficial Law Nrs. 53–54/2006*. Berlin: Lit, 239–70.

Benda-Beckmann, F. von, K. von Benda-Beckmann, and A. Griffiths (eds). 2005. *Mobile People, Mobile Law: Expanding Legal Relations in a Contracting World*. Aldershot: Ashgate.

Benda-Beckmann, F. von, K. von Benda-Beckmann, and B. Turner. 2007. 'Umstrittene Traditionen in Marokko und Indonesien', *Zeitschrift für Ethnologie* 132: 15–35.

Benda-Beckmann, K. von. 1981. 'Forum Shopping and Shopping Forums: Dispute Processing in a Minangkabau Village', *Journal of Legal Pluralism* 19: 117–59.

———. 1984. *The Broken Stairways to Consensus: Village Justice and State Courts in Minangkabau. Verhandelingen van het Koninklijk Instituut voor Taal-, Land- en*

Volkenkunde. Vol. 106. Dordrecht, Leiden, Cinnaminson: Foris Publications, KITLV Press.

————. 2001. 'Transnational Dimensions of Legal Pluralism' in W. Fikentscher (ed.), *Begegnung und Konflikt – eine kulturanthropologische Bestandsaufnahme.* Munich: Verlag der Bayerischen Akademie der Wissenschaften, C.H. Beck Verlag, 33–48.

Berman, P.S. 2007. 'Global Legal Pluralism', *Southern California Law Review* 80: 1155–237.

Black, D. 1976. *The Behaviour of Law.* New York: Academic Press.

Bowen, J.R. 2003. *Islam, Law and Equality in Indonesia: An Anthropology of Public Reasoning.* Cambridge: Cambridge University Press.

Bruns, B.R. and R.S. Meinzen-Dick (eds). 2000. *Negotiating Water Rights.* London: Intermediate Technology Publications.

Büscher, B. and T. Dietz. 2005. 'Conjunctions of Governance: The State and the Conservation-development Nexus in Southern Africa', *The Journal of Transdisciplinary Environmental Studies, Special Issue Power, Development and Environment* 4(2), (http://www.journal-tes.dk).

Cowan, J.K., M.-B. Dembour and R.A. Wilson. 2001. *Culture and Rights: Anthropological Perspectives.* Cambridge: Cambridge University Press.

Davidson, J.S. and D. Henley (eds). 2007. *The Revival of Tradition in Indonesian Politics: The Development of Adat from Colonialism to Indigenism.* London and New York: Routledge.

Dezalay, Y. and B.G. Garth. 1996. *Dealing in Virtue: International Commercial Arbitration and the Construction of a Transnational Legal Order.* Chicago: University of Chicago Press.

Dwyer, D.H. 1979. 'Law Actual and Perceived: Sexual Politics of Law in Morocco', *Law and Society Review* 13: 739–56.

Eckert, J. 2006. 'From Subjects to Citizens: Legalism from Below and the Homogenisation of the Legal Sphere', in F. von Benda-Beckmann and K. von Benda-Beckmann (eds), *Dynamics of Plural Legal Orders. Special Double Issue of the Journal of Legal Pluralism and Unofficial Law Nrs. 53–54/2006.* Berlin: Lit, 45–75.

Faundez, J. 2006. 'Should Justice Reforms Projects Take Non-state Justice Systems Seriously?' Perspectives from Latin America', in C.M. Sage and M. Woolcock (eds), *World Bank Legal Review, Volume 2 – Law, Equity and Development.* The Hague: The World Bank and Martinus Nijhoff, 113–39.

Foucault, M. 1980. 'Two Lectures', in M. Foucault, *Power/Knowledge: Selected Interviews and Other Writings 1972–1977,* ed. C. Gordon. New York: Pantheon House, 78–108.

Gibbs, J.P. 1981. *Norms, Deviance and Social Control.* New York: Elsevier.

————. 1982. *Social Control: Views from the Social Sciences.* Beverly Hills, CA: Sage.

Giddens, A. 1979. *Central Problems in Social Theory: Action, Structure and Contradiction in Social Analysis.* London: Macmillan Press.

————. 1984. *The Constitution of Society.* Oxford: Polity Press.

Griffiths, A. 1997. *In the Shadow of Marriage: Gender and Justice in an African Community.* Chicago, London: University of Chicago Press.

————. 2002. 'Legal Pluralism', in R. Banakar and M. Travers (eds), *An Introduction to Law and Social Theory.* Oxford-Portland, OR: Hart Publishing, 289–310.

Griffiths, J. 1984. 'The Division of Labor in Social Control', in D. Black (ed.), *Toward a General Theory of Social Control*. New York: Academic Press, 37–70.

——. 1986. 'What Is Legal Pluralism?' *Journal of Legal Pluralism* 24: 1–50.

—— (ed.). 1996. *De Sociale Werking van Recht: Een Kennismaking met de Rechtssociologie en Rechtsantrolopologie*. Nijmegen: Ars Aequi.

Haas, P.M. 1992. 'Introduction: Epistemic Communities and International Policy Coordination', *International Organizations* 46: 1–35.

Hindess, B. (ed.). 1996. *Discourses of Power: From Hobbes to Foucault*. Oxford: Blackwell.

Hirsch, S.F. 1998. *Pronouncing and Persevering: Gender and the Discourses of Disputing in an African Islamic Court*. Chicago Series in Law and Society. Chicago: The University of Chicago Press.

Hoebel, E.A. 1954. *The Law of Primitive Man*. Cambridge, MA: Harvard University Press.

Holy, L. 1999. 'Contextualisation and Paradigm Shifts', in R. Dilley (ed.), *The Problem of Context*. New York and Oxford: Berghahn Books, 47–60.

Lazarus-Black, M. and S.F. Hirsch. 1994. *Contested States: Law, Hegemony, and Resistance. After the Law*. New York: Routledge.

Lukes, S. 1974. *Power: A Radical View*. London: Macmillan.

Maher, I. 2002. 'Competition Law in the International Domain: Networks as a New Form of Governance', *Journal of Law and Society* 29: 111–36.

Mamdani, M. 1996. *Citizen and Subject: Contemporary Africa and the Legacy of Late Colonialism*. Princeton, NJ: Princeton University Press.

McClure, K.M. 1997. 'Taking Liberties in Foucault's Triangle: Sovereignty, Discipline, Governmentality, and the Subjects of Rights', in A. Sarat and T.R. Kearns (eds), *Identities, Politics and Rights*. Ann Arbor: The University of Michigan Press, 149–92.

McGrew, A.G. 1998. 'Global Legal Interaction and Present-day Patterns of Globalization', in V. Gessner and A.C. Budak (eds), *Emerging Global Certainty: Empirical Studies on the Globalization of Law*. Aldershot: Ashgate, 325–45.

Merry, S.E. 1988. 'Legal Pluralism', *Law and Society Review* 22: 869–96.

——. 2006. 'Anthropology and International Law', *Annual Review of Anthropology* 35: 99–116.

Michaels, R. 2005. 'The Re-state-ment of Non-state Law: The State, Choice of Law, and the Challenge from Global Legal Pluralism', *The Wayne Law Review* 52: 1209–59.

Moore, S.F. 1970. 'Politics, Procedures and Norms in Changing Chagga Law', *Africa* 40: 321–44.

——. 1973. 'Law and Social Change: The Semi-autonomous Social Field as an Appropriate Subject of Study', *Law and Society Review* 7: 719–46.

Nader, L. 1997. 'Controlling Processes: Tracing the Dynamic Components of Power', *Current Anthropology* 38(5): 711–37.

——. 2002. *The Life of the Law: Anthropological Projects*. Berkeley, Los Angeles, London: University of California Press.

Nuijten, M. 2003. *Power, Community and the State: The Political Anthropology of Organization in Mexico*. London: Pluto Books.

——. 2005. 'Power in Practice: A Force Field Approach to Natural Resource Management', *The Journal of Transdisciplinary Environmental Studies*.

Special Issue Power, Development and Environment 4(2), (http://www.journal-tes .dk).

Rosen, L. 1989. *The Anthropology of Justice: Law as Culture in Islam. Lewis Henry Morgan Lecture Series.* Cambridge: Cambridge University Press.

Rouveroy van Nieuwaal, E.A.B. van and D.I. Ray. 1996. *The New Relevance of Traditional Authorities to Africa's Future. Special Issue of the Journal of Legal Pluralism* 37–38.

Santos, B. de Sousa 1987. 'Law: A Map of Misreading. Toward a Post-modern Conception of Law', *Journal of Law and Society* 14: 279–302.

———. 2002. *Toward a New Legal Common Sense: Law, Globalization, and Emancipation,* 2nd ed. Toronto: Butterworths.

Santos, B. de Sousa and C.A. Rodríguez-Garavito. 2005. 'Law, Politics, and the Subaltern in Counter-hegemonic Globalization', in B. de Sousa Santos and C.A. Rodríguez-Garavito (eds), *Law and Globalization from Below: Towards a Cosmopolitan Legality.* New York: Cambridge University Press, 1–26.

Schwartz, R. 1954. 'Social Factors in the Development of Legal Control: A Case Study of Two Israeli Settlements', *The Yale Law Journal* 63: 471–91.

Scott, J.C. 1985. *Weapons of the Weak: Everyday Forms of Peasant Resistance.* New Haven, CT, and London: Yale University Press.

Shehada, N. 2005. *Justice without Drama: Enacting Family Law in Gaza City Shari'a Court.* The Hague: Institute of Social Studies.

Spiertz, H.L.J. 1991. 'The Transformation of Traditional Law: A Tale of People's Participation in Irrigation Management on Bali', *Landscape and Urban Planning* 20: 189–96.

Starr, J. and J. Collier (eds). 1989. *History and Power in the Study of Law: New Directions in Legal Anthropology.* Ithaca, NY, and London: Cornell University Press.

Tamanaha, B.Z. 1993. 'The Folly of the "Social Scientific" Concept of Legal Pluralism', *Journal of Law and Society* 20: 192–217.

———. 2000. 'A Non-essentialist Version of Legal Pluralism', *Journal of Law and Society* 27: 296–321.

Tigar, M.E. and M.R. Levy. 1977. *Law and the Rise of Capitalism.* New York, London: Monthly Review Press.

Turk, A.T. 1978. 'Law as a Weapon in Social Conflict', in C. Reasons and R.M. Rich (eds), *The Sociology of Law: A Conflict Perspective.* Toronto: Butterworths, 213–32.

Vel, J.A.C. 1992. 'Umbu Hapi versus Umbu Vincent: Legal Pluralism as an Arsenal in Village Combats', in F. von Benda-Beckmann and M. van der Velde (eds), *Law as a Resource in Agrarian Struggles, Wageningse Sociologische Studies, vol. 33.* Wageningen: Wageningen University, 23–43.

Weber, M. 1956. *Wirtschaft und Gesellschaft.* Cologne: Kiepenheuer und Witsch.

Wiber, M.G. 1993. *Politics, Property and Law in the Philippine Uplands.* Waterloo (Canada): Wilfried Laurier University Press.

———. 2005. 'Mobile Law and Globalism: Epistemic Communities versus Community-based Innovation in the Fisheries Sector', in F. von Benda-Beckmann, K. von Benda-Beckmann and A. Griffiths (eds), *Mobile People, Mobile Law: Expanding Legal Relations in a Contracting World.* Aldershot, Hampshire: Ashgate, 131–51.

Wolf, E.R. 1990 'Facing Power: Old Insights, New Questions', *American Anthropologist* 92(3): 586–96.

Wollenberg, E., J. Anderson, and C. López. 2005. *Though All Things Differ: Pluralism as a Basis for Cooperation in Forests*. Situ Gede, Sindang Barang, Bogor Barat: CIFOR (Center for International Forest Research).

Woodman, G.R. 1998. 'Ideological Combat and Social Observation: Recent Debate about Legal Pluralism', *Journal of Legal Pluralism* 42: 21–59.

POWER OF LAW AS DISCOURSE

Claims to Legitimacy and Higher Morality

1

THE MILITARY ORDER OF 13 NOVEMBER 2001

An Ethnographic Reading

Carol J. Greenhouse

The Military Order of 13 November 2001 – a legal linchpin of the Bush administration's war on terror – claimed new judicial powers for the executive branch for purposes of prosecution, trial, sentencing and appeal in cases involving noncitizens charged with terrorism (The White House 2001a). The legality of the order was immediately contested, first in the press and on the Internet by representatives of citizens' rights organizations, and soon thereafter in Congressional hearings. Subsequently, a series of lawsuits arising from the government's handling of detainees brought elements of the order to the United States Supreme Court. The contest continues in a variety of public and private arenas. What can ethnographers of law learn from this modern trouble case, beyond the particulars of the order and its immediate context in the events of that autumn?[1]

To be sure, those particulars are engaging for anyone interested in the early history of the war on terror as it unfolded in the United States. But that history is not my main concern here. Rather, I am interested in the extent to which the Military Order (like other elements of the war on terror in the United States and elsewhere) challenges us to rethink the ethnography of law from the standpoint of executive power, while simultaneously revealing something of the nature of those challenges. The value of that theoretical and methodological project extends beyond the war on terror, and beyond the United States.

In the twentieth century, the anthropology of law developed primarily in relation to judicial arenas, and it remains well adapted to courts and other processes involving representation and dialogue in a wide range of settings, formal and informal, private and public – e.g. interpersonal disputing, community deliberation and parliamentary legislation. In such settings, the 'ecology of law' (Collier 1975) can be imagined as the connection between legal processes and the wider social spheres in which they are embedded – through the self-identity and self-expression of their participants, the social histories of their needs and wants, and the concepts and behaviours construed as normative practices (among other things). The very notion of the trouble case, as formulated by Llewellyn and Hoebel (1941) in the midst of world war, was keyed to the circumstances of unmediated access to law, in turn theorized as an expression of collective social and moral norms. Indeed, the intellectual traditions of legal anthropology also support the premise of embeddedness also 'working' the other way, given the production of law itself through social processes.[2] Since the 1980s, ethnographers have continued these traditions through concepts of legal discourse and legal consciousness, generalized references to the sociocultural contexts of law, along with law's sources and effects. This framing tends to presuppose that law's discursive force is hegemonic, and, conversely, that law's hegemony is itself discursive – an indirect means by which the idea of state control is internalized and realized (Abrams 1988; Mitchell 1991).

In contrast to the scenarios of law making and receiving implicit in these theoretical and methodological traditions, the legalities of the war on terror in the United States have not been produced in deliberative or discursive arenas of the kind that legal anthropologists have traditionally studied. Even when it has involved constitutionally required legislative or judicial action, the war on terror has developed primarily as an *executive* initiative, to which the other branches of government have consented wholly or in part (e.g., the USA PATRIOT Act and the advance authorization for the use of military force in Iraq). The Military Order is noteworthy because it requires neither the consent nor the cooperation of the other branches – it is an executive order.

By definition, an executive order is an expression of executive power purely in its own terms, and this makes it a valuable artifact for methodological reflection.[3] But as an artifact, it is an opaque one – the self-enclosure of its textual form resisting contextualization, literally and figuratively. In this chapter, my effort is precisely to develop an ethnographic approach to the problem of contextualizing the Military Order. I suggest by demonstration that context emerges ethnographically from the debate that the order itself generates – those adjacent texts adding historical depth and political valence to its terms, and thereby situating them in larger terrains of discursive circulation and opposition not accessible from the text itself. In effect, this is a method of 'thick description' (Geertz 1973: chap. 1) – rekeyed to the demands of a novel ethnographic situation.

My approach involves two main interpretive resources, which, taking them together, I call *discursive trails*. The first trail involves the commentary on the Military Order (hereafter 'the order') immediately prior to its promulgation and then in the days, weeks and months following, as commentators debated its means and ends. I focus on that debate, giving emphasis to proponents' contributions – since they claimed to speak for the White House, in the figurative sense of allying themselves with the administration. The advocacy of the order contributed to its normalization, in that while the order itself emphasized the crisis nature of the newly declared war on terrorism, its proponents defended it in terms that extended to the routine workings of federal institutions under normal circumstances. Those extensions are, I suggest, key features of the ethnographic context of the order. I also draw on public commentary in the months immediately following the promulgation of the order (November 2001 through February 2002, when the first wave of reaction drew to a close).[4]

The second discursive trail involves the commentators themselves, or rather, their career lines, as pathways along which their various professional commitments can be aligned as evidence of discursive continuities over time as well as diverse circumstances (commentaries are listed in the Appendix).[5] In this chapter, I concentrate on two career lines, chosen for the thickness of their dossiers in relation to the war on terror as well as the length of their association with Republican administrations. I focus on career lines rather than personal motives, intentions or interests, since the former leave a public record and the latter can only be grounds of speculation.

I prefer to work from discursive trails, rather than some more generalized notion of discourse, in order to retain the form and content of contestation within government as well as in the wider social fields in which ideas of 'stateness' (Hansen and Stepputat 2001) circulate. The commentators whose texts I draw on in this chapter are, in fact, specialists in creating and bridging discursive opposition by means of tactical arguments that lean heavily (and iconically) on previous or ongoing antagonisms in other domains. This process is colloquially known as *spin*. This is what makes the texts of the administration's allies and surrogates useful as guides to contextualization. As we shall see, they themselves argue by means of strategic contextualization.

Before proceeding along these lines, let us step back for a moment to take stock of the wider debate by reviewing the general features of the public commentary on the Military Order over the course of the long winter of 2001–2002.

Evaluating the Military Order of 13 November 2001

The commentaries unfold around the following main issues:

1. All of the commentaries situate the Military Order squarely in the middle of wider judgments as to the efficacy of the institutions of American government. Every commentary begins with a reference to terror; every commentary compares military tribunals to the federal courts.

   Specifically, advocates of the military tribunals almost always make a constitutional argument alongside claims as to the relative inadequacy of the federal court system in relation to the anticipated demands of terrorist prosecutions. They refer to the need for security (protecting prospective civilian court personnel and juries from terrorist acts as well as restricting public access to evidence and investigative techniques). Even more emphatically, they claim that courts and Congress are inefficient in ways that military tribunals would improve upon (by easing evidentiary and procedural rules). Critics of the tribunals point to successful prosecutions and convictions of terrorists in civilian courts, but advocates point to the same trials – of the 1993 World Trade Center bombers and the trial of the men charged with the bombing of Pan Am 103 – as examples of the failures of the civilian court system.[6]

   The efficacy argument similarly tends to be the more prominent among those who identify themselves as proponents of the tribunals. They portray the federal courts as encumbered by rules of evidence and other procedure that they characterize as complications or outright barriers to terrorists' prosecution and conviction. Advocates also point to appeals processes as inordinately time consuming. At the same time, commentators disagree as to whether the tribunals are a supplement to the federal courts, or a substitute. Some proponents take the position that the tribunals provide a salutary shunt around Congress – implying that the length of the debate over the USA PATRIOT Act showed Congress to be incapable of timely action.[7]

2. The language of the Military Order draws a bright line between citizens and noncitizens, establishing military tribunals for the prosecution of noncitizen detainees accused of terrorist acts. Most proponents of the Military Order emphasize this distinction as a way of deflecting critics' concerns over the implications of the tribunals for Americans' civil liberties.[8] Most of the critics focus on the vulnerability of marginal populations (Muslims, new immigrants) to suspicion, and the high stakes in arrest.

Some proponents deftly sidestepped the jurisdictional issue through caricature – substituting an American celebrity for Osama bin Laden. Senator Mitch O'Connell (R-KY) imagined the federal court alternative as 'a repeat of the O.J. Simpson trial, complete with grandstanding by defense lawyers' (Lewis 2001). Stewart Baker, former general counsel of the National Security Agency, said: 'I don't think anyone wants to see Osama bin Laden brought before a court here to be defended by Johnnie Cochran' (Myers and Lewis 2001).[9] Attorney General Ashcroft expanded on this image in more general terms: 'Now, when we come to those responsible for this, say who are in Afghanistan, are we supposed to read them the Miranda rights, hire a flamboyant defense lawyer, bring them back to the United States to create a new cable network of Osama TV or what have you … ?' (*New York Times* 2001). We shall return to these and other allusions to Los Angeles, the setting of the Simpson trial.

3. Indeed, the commentary on military tribunals – ostensibly reserved for noncitizens – consistently reterritorializes them, usually by reference to previous military commissions on American soil. For example, Robert Bork, a federal judge and former nominee to the United States Supreme Court, argues that the Military Order does not go far enough, citing precedent for extending the jurisdiction of such tribunals to citizens (Bork 2001). Rivkin et al. discuss what they claim is one such precedent – the 1862 military commission that sentenced over three hundred Dakota Sioux to death by hanging in the aftermath of a raid against white settlers in Minnesota, ignoring the fact that the Dakota were not citizens of the United States at the time (Rivkin, Casey and Bartram 2001, cf. Chomsky 1990). Other commentators refer to President Roosevelt's Executive Order 9066 (19 February 1942), compelling the internment of Japanese and their Japanese American children – sometimes as evidence of the legality of military tribunals, even for citizens.[10]

4. On both sides, the commentary draws on longstanding debates over the efficacy of the civil justice system, federalism and separation of powers – specifically the efficacy of the judiciary as viewed retrospectively across the era of rapidly expanding civil rights lawmaking in the 1960s and 1970s. While civil rights never come under critical attack per se, the premise of these commentaries is that the courts are currently encumbered by procedural rules. The advocates of military tribunals present the modern judiciary as hampered by civil rights concerns (including law covering police arrests and criminal procedure) that might interfere with the processing of the (presumptively)

guilty. The critics of military tribunals cast that same history in a different light, drawing distinctions between processing, prosecution and punishment of the accused.[11]

5. The main difference among commentators involves the question of whether the 'war on terror' is war in the legal sense – and whether the constitutionality of the military tribunals would depend on this.[12] This issue is discussed below.

Following the Tribunals' Discursive Trails

The discursive trail of the military tribunals begins some time before 13 November 2001. As early as 20 September 2001, George J. Terwilliger III expressed support for a military or executive tribunal for the prosecution of Osama bin Laden, should coalition forces succeed in capturing him.[13] In the same interview, Terwilliger advocated extending the president's authority to defend national security 'to use even more aggressive techniques than they have so far' (McGraw 2001): 'I don't think that the investigation ought to be … bound by the rules of criminal procedure, the rules of evidence or available lawful investigative techniques that are part of a criminal investigation […] I think the authority to investigate and … to obtain evidence … is much greater than that' (McGraw 2001; brackets indicate added ellipses.)

Terwilliger, now a partner at the law firm of White and Case, is former Deputy Attorney General and Acting Attorney General under former President G. H. W. Bush, and he also served in the Reagan White House.[14] In the private sector, he often appears on the news or the worldwide web as a commentator on matters related to criminal prosecution and anti-terrorism. He testified in favour of the tribunals at the Congressional hearings on this military tribunals issue (United States Senate Judiciary Committee 2001). He is lead author of an undated memorandum distributed by the Federalist Society, recommending military commissions as an appropriate response to the demands of prosecuting terrorists. 'International terrorism is a matter of national security, rather than merely criminal law enforcement' is the title of one section, in which he cautions against 'the over-judicialization of political and policy issues'. His larger argument in the memorandum addresses the issue of the president's emergency powers and the flexibility of the Fourth Amendment under certain circumstances. He emphasizes that a corollary to the president's 'plenary power' in relation to establishing military commissions and border controls in the United States is the potentially global scope of its investigative powers through 'any truly independent assistance or information offered by other nations without regard to the methods or sources by which it was obtained' (Terwilliger et al. n.d.).

I take Terwilliger's memorandum as a telling example since his career yields a long discursive trail. During his years in the Justice Department, he was involved in several high-profile cases involving the FBI – at Ruby Ridge (where he was involved in planning the rules of engagement), Los Angeles (where he coordinated the prosecutions in the aftermath of the violence there in 1992), and in Panama (where he was involved in planning Operation Just Cause, the mission that resulted in the capture of Manuel Noriega). Each of these situations involved elements that have parallels in the present war against terrorism – in particular, for our purposes, the coordination of state and federal prosecution of individuals arrested during the violence in Los Angeles (arising in part from the simultaneous engagement of city police and California National Guard, federalized during the emergency). For this reason, I draw on the record of the 1992 violence in Los Angeles and its aftermath, to probe the connections between the rationales for military tribunals and earlier partisan debates over domestic civilian prosecution.

In Los Angeles, beginning on the afternoon of 29 April 1992, five days of violence followed the acquittal of four white policemen charged with the beating of Rodney King, an African American. The beating had been caught on videotape, and circulated widely – immediately becoming an object of media commentary and discussion in other quarters. Almost immediately, the question emerged as to whether the violence was domestic or foreign – and planned or spontaneous. Law enforcement officers took seriously the possibility that it was the work of a conspiracy, possibly involving radical Muslims and 'even certain Colombians and Iraqis' (Mike Davis, quoted in *CovertAction* Information Bulletin 1993: 147).The violence was a response to the jury verdict on 29 April. The Los Angeles Police Department (LAPD) was unable to establish order, and the California National Guard was called up to assist. Federal troops were deployed on the streets of Los Angeles for two days, 1 and 2 May. The violence ended on 3 May. On 6 May, the president sent a team of fifty federal officials to oversee a federal investigation of 'riot-related violence' and to coordinate arrests (Wines 1992). That team was headed by Terwilliger, whom the New York Times referred to as 'an architect of the Justice Department's response to the riots' (Wines 1992). In the course of six days, there were 5,002 arrests, mostly by the LAPD (Webster and Williams 1992: 26).

For two weeks, Los Angeles was occupied by over ten thousand federal troops. Coordination between the federal troops and the LAPD was highly problematic (Webster and Williams 1992). As coordinator of federal prosecutions, Terwilliger in effect had to disentangle law enforcement and military personnel, so as to establish the appropriate court jurisdiction for each of the individuals under arrest. He has long been a champion of the values of speed and finality in the federal prosecution of violent offenders, developing approaches that eliminate litigation from the law enforcement process and freeing law enforcement from oversight.[15]

In this regard, Terwilliger's extensive career can be read as the context for his advocacy of military tribunals. From an ethnographic standpoint, it is also evidence of the broader context of values in which the Military Order should be understood. In other words, the order can be read not just as a response to the extremity of the immediate post-9/11 period, but also as an extension of other, far older situations at home and abroad. The main links to those other situations – particularly Los Angeles – are to be found in the order's emphasis on clean lines of jurisdiction, swift prosecution, and finality. To put this differently, the order – as read from the vantage points its advocates supply – links terrorism to urban violence as related sites of tension among competing agents of federal, local, military and civilian control.

Federalism and Democracy – 'or something like that'

The 2001–2002 debate over the Military Order crosscut the conventional lines between Democrats and Republicans, liberals and conservatives, in part because what was at stake was not a particular policy or social issue, but – as most commentators acknowledged – the working structure of government and the parameters of its flexibility *as functions of presidential power.* George Terwilliger drew this very connection in a symposium on crisis leadership: 'People will not follow those whom they don't believe, particularly in life-and-death circumstances ... Leadership needs to tell the truth to people. There may be issues of timing, of when you tell people things. But it is a crime against democracy to affirmatively mislead people about critical events, unless withholding information is necessary to prevent further bloodshed or violence *or something like that,* and even that should be viewed as temporary' (quoted in CIAG 2000; emphasis added).

In this section, then, I turn to commentary on military tribunals that focuses specifically on presidential power in relation to the other branches of government and international law – following a discursive trail that leads through the portfolio of coauthors David B. Rivkin and Lee A. Casey.[16] Their joint professional dossier anticipates policy commitments on the part of the Bush administration in certain key areas. Most notably for our purposes, the Casey-Rivkin memorandum on 'Bringing Al-Qaeda to Justice' – posted a week prior to the publication of the Military Order – undertakes an assessment of the options for trying Al-Qaeda members under the military justice system, in either courts-martial or military tribunals (Rivkin, Casey and Bartram 2001). In this particular memorandum, they make no recommendation for or against military tribunals, but spell out the advantages of the military justice system 'from the government's perspective'. The positives include exclusion of the public, speed and protection of 'highly sensitive intelligence material'. As negatives, they anticipate that Al-Qaeda defendants will press for civilian trials, and that there might be diplomatic repercussions. They recommend a formal declaration of war by Congress as the surest means of avoiding a negative test at the Supreme Court, given what they regard as the court's softening in favour of increasing due process guarantees. The rest of the article advocates classification of Al-Qaeda members as 'unlawful combatants' and assesses the possibility of avoiding a court challenge on the grounds that the United States is in 'a state of war' with the Taliban, as sponsors of Al-Qaeda. The Military Order was published the following week, declaring a 'state of war' and categorically refusing appeal to civilian judicial institutions. The same authors' article on 'unlawful belligerency' – a new category of offense integral to the Bush administration's public rationale for establishing a detention center at Guantánamo – appeared a few weeks later (Casey, Rivkin and Bartram 2001).

The Rivkin-Casey dossier includes position papers on a wide range of issues, broadly connected by the issue of U.S. autonomy in international affairs. Their essay of 2001 on 'Europe in the Balance' argues that the U.S. should distance itself from Europe, on the grounds that European Union is a premodern feudal state, inappropriately positioned to influence the U.S. 'For far too long', they write, 'we have been conceding the moral high ground to the Europeans' (Casey and Rivkin n.d.).[17] In their 2001 testimony before the U.S. Senate Foreign Relations Committee, they take the view that the Anti-Ballistic Missile (ABM) Treaty is no longer valid, on the grounds that the Soviet Union no longer exists. Since (they continue) the president cannot – in effect – create a new treaty partnership with the Russian Federation and other former Soviet states without Senate ratification, the treaty should be scrapped. They recommend that the ABM Treaty be considered null and that its renewal proceed from new negotiations with the ratification of the Senate (Nuclear Age Peace Foundation 1999). The White House announced the withdrawal of the United States from the ABM Treaty on 13 December 2001 (The White House 2001b).

Their article titled 'The Rocky Shoals of International Law' (Rivkin and Casey 2000/2001) argues that 'international law constitutes a real and immediate threat to U.S. national interests'. They object to a '"new" international law [that] purports to govern the relationship of citizens to their governments, affecting such domestic issues as environmental protection and the rights of children. Among other things, it would: nearly eliminate the unilateral use of military force' (Rivkin and Casey 2000/2001). Their critique of international law follows an earlier article vigorously recommending that the U.S. refuse to join the International Criminal Court: 'The fundamental rights secured by the Constitution – rights successfully defended by Americans on battlefields around the world – can be summed up as follows: The American people govern themselves, and they have a right to be tried in accordance with the laws enacted by their elected representatives and to be judged by their peers and none other. The Rome ICC treaty, in concept and execution, is utterly antithetical to these rights. It should be opposed by the United States with all the vigor it has mustered, throughout its history, to fight similar threats to the fundamental values of the Republic' (Casey and Rivkin 1999). On the domestic front, separately or together, they oppose abortion and the Clinton administration's health care reform proposal, the latter on the grounds that it enlarges the federal government at the expense of personal liberty (Rivkin 1994).

The significance of these extracts in relation to the military tribunals is their demonstration – in the aggregate – of where the tribunals are situated on the political horizon formed by the tensions between sovereignty, transnationalism and internationalism. In contrast to the intensity of the crisis discourse in 2001–2002, the war on terror emerges in this light as but another assertion of presidential leadership in the interest of U.S. autonomy, fully rehearsed in ongoing partisan debates over the nature and limits of presidential power in a range of domestic and foreign affairs.

The Transnational Production of Domestic Politics

The line between domestic and foreign can take the form of jurisdictional ambiguity – as it did in Los Angeles in 1992 and has done in relation to the war on terror since 2001 – even when no border intervenes.

In the context considered in this essay, transnationalism emerges along two horizons: first as a discursive compression of the foreign and domestic, making them difficult to distinguish (e.g. as in usages of such words as 'alien' or 'terrorist'), and second as a series of executive alliances across national governments. The most vivid example of the former is the conflation of O.J. Simpson and Osama bin Laden – offered in jest by early commentators, but a sign of what was to come when citizens were brought into detention (notably in the Hamdi and Rasul cases, among others). As we have seen, an important rehearsal for that very compression came eight years earlier, in the context of the violence in Los Angeles in 1992 – when citizens were initially imagined to be foreigners or foreign agents, and the respective jurisdictions of the military and local police were left in doubt. The general conclusion to this part of the discussion is that, in practice, citizenship and foreignness continually confront and meld into each other.[18]

With respect to the second horizon of transnationalism on the international front, it is clear that the mesh of transnational legality does not just hang vertically from the top down; it also stretches laterally, along parallel tracks.[19] The most striking parallel to the order was in Britain, where, on 12 November 2001, Prime Minister Tony Blair's government proposed a bill to Parliament creating expanded arrest and detention powers, invoking a suspension of Article 15 of the European Convention of Human Rights (Hoge 2001a, 2001b). Among the other main coalition countries, other parallels can be found in the extent to which the politicization of new security measures at the national level pressured local political organizations, weakening them at least temporarily. In Spain, the transnational war on terror had the effect of adding to President Aznar's political arsenal against the ETA, which his strongly centrist party parlayed into a broad attack on Basque nationalists (including the moderate nationalists who dominate the Basque Country's parliament).[20] In Italy, too, the war on terror fuelled a context in which executive power expanded to fill the widening gap between national and transnational (i.e. European) governance paradigms (see Greenhouse 2005b.) In the months immediately following the initiation of the war on terror, Prime Minister Berlusconi's winning political strategy involved resisting the European Union while actively supporting President Bush. In the early electoral cycles after 2001, in both Spain and Italy, opposition to the ruling party fragmented, splitting centrists and anti-globalization groups; however, subsequent realignments later defeated the parties that were in power in 2001.

While a full comparative discussion of the domestic consequences of the war on terror is beyond the scope of this essay, even these brief

observations indicate where and how transnationalism selectively empowers executives relative to both other branches of government and
other levels of government within their home countries.[21] This issue
is relatively unexplored in scholarship on the political dimensions of
globalization (for influential formulations, see Sassen 1996; Held and
McGrew 2002: chaps. 2 and 3; Beck 2005: chap. 3). It also supplements
anthropological accounts of law in contexts of transnationalism and
globalization. These tend to focus on the experiential aspects of legality in everyday life, as well as on the problematics of national states in
relation to nonstate actors (domestic and transnational): e.g. in circumstances of mobility, including institutional coordination and flows of
ideas (Ong 1999; F. von Benda-Beckmann, K. von Benda-Beckmann,
and A. Griffiths 2005), the articulation and circulation of human rights
(Jean-Klein and Riles 2005; Goodale 2006; Merry 2006) and the reconfiguration of legal authority in relation to neoliberalization and privatized
forms of power (Comaroff and Comaroff 2004).

Conclusion

Read in its own terms, the Military Order of 13 November 2001 is a
response to a unique event, its applicability limited to specific circumstances that exclude citizens and that do not compromise the normal
powers of the judiciary or Congress. The ongoing legal disputes involve
these very questions. It was the broader meanings of the order that the
United States Supreme Court put at the center of two landmark opinions arising out of the Guantánamo detentions.[22] As noted at the outset,
the legal contest continues over those rulings and related matters.

What can we learn from an ethnographic reading of the order, beyond the troubled circumstances of its making and implementation? I
draw two main lessons. First, notwithstanding the ease of dismissing
from the ethnographic frame conspicuously partisan activities such as
'spin' or 'loyal opposition', commentaries such as the ones I have drawn
on here are valuable supplements to official documents, as they provide evidence of the wider meanings in play in policy documents. They
bridge the public and private sectors and in the process illustrate how
contemporary hegemonic discourse circulates – not just top-down, but
also, strategically, from disparate political and moral communities of
the private sector into the state. The institutional and discursive means
of such uptake are especially relevant to the ethnography of law in contexts where executive power is dominant, i.e. where representation occurs at the level of a competition over signs of authority and legitimacy,
rather than in actual deliberative arenas.[23]

Second, more generally, this trouble case has implications for the way ethnographers might theorize neoliberal states. My general thesis in this regard is that the war on terror illuminates aspects of state power that earlier scholarship on globalization in peacetime tended to understate or miss – that is, the extent to which neoliberal states, through their executive branches, retain their option on strong forms of power even in the face of (indeed, *by means of*) transnational alliances (see Ong 2003; Aman 2004; cf. Appadurai 1996; Sassen 1996). In contrast to earlier assessments of the fate of the nation state confronted with globalization, states do not fade away under the pressure of transnational forces. Perhaps their conventional means of describing and ascribing value to relationality are called into question (Perry and Maurer 2003: xi–xii), but as we have seen, transnationalism is not *outside* state government. Rather, it constitutes a pragmatic and conceptual register for leveraging power between national and local governments as well as between national governments – a process in which national executives are prominent actors by virtue of their administrative and law enforcement powers.

Neoliberal governmentality is extraordinarily flexible in this regard, in part because it entails broad scope for state alignment with (or delegations by contract to) private-sector entities. Indeed, in the current environment, states in a sense operate as if they *were* a private sector relative to each other, as national executives have an interest in working through each other's institutions (e.g. among the countries of 'the coalition') even when they do not otherwise share common goals (e.g. in the interrogation of detainees suspected of terrorism). The main relevance of this observation for purposes of this discussion is that different institutions of state government are involved in transnationalism in different ways. The sphere of the transnational tends to marginalize courts, and even more so, legislatures. This much is well established (as noted above); however, the consequent gains in executive power are less well remarked. Further, by virtue of this very effect, the state-citizen bond is potentially destabilized specifically in relation to criminalization (particularly to the extent that law enforcement – an executive function in the United States – develops separately from judicial and legislative guarantees of civil liberties).

The expansion of executive power along these lines in the United States by no means begins with the war on terror (see Flaherty 1996; Aman 2004); however, the Military Order explicitly consolidates presidential power in novel terms, particularly in assigning judicial powers to the president. This observation brings us full circle, back to the order itself. Read as a text, the order invokes the citizen-foreigner distinction as a central premise. However, read in context, the order subordinates this distinction to the more prominent divide between presidential power – reinforced as transnational power – and the powers of the other (domestic) branches of government. This message emerges from the commentaries and their discursive trails. In the process of defending the order, the commentators in effect specify this subordinate and moveable citizenship as the contingency of a normal, even desirable, state of affairs. From the wider perspective of ethnography, it is by this route that executive power – as theoretical object – is profoundly connected to our concerns (both methodological and ethical) with the conditions of everyday life.

Appendix

Principal commentaries consulted (in addition to those cited in the References section)

American Bar Association Task Force on Terrorism and the Law; Report and Recommendations on Military Commissions, 4 January 2002. Electronic document: http://www.abanet.org/leadership/military.pdf (accessed 4 May 2005).

Baker, M.M. 2001. Fools, Drunkards, & Presidential Succession. The Federalist Society. National Security White Paper. Electronic document: http://www.fed-soc.org/Publications/Terrorism/presidentialsuccession .htm (accessed 4 May 2005).

Davies, F. 2001. Commentary from Dean Kmiec. Originally published: the Miami Herald, 28 October 2001. Electronic document: http:// www.law.cua.edu/faculty/Kmiec/ commentary.htm (accessed 4 May 2005).

Edgar, T. 2001. Memorandum re President Bush's Order Establishing Military Trials in Terrorism Cases. American Civil Liberties Union 'In Congress' Memorandum, 29 November 2001. Electronic document: http://www.aclu.org/congress/l112901b.html (accessed 2 December 2001).

Grigg, W.N. 2001. 'America under Siege', New American 17(21). 8 October 2001. Electronic document: http://www.thenewamerican.com/ tna/2001/10-08-2001/ vol7no21_america.htm (accessed 4 May 2005).

———. 2002. 'Terror Tribunals'. New American 18(01). 14 January 2002. Electronic document: http://www.thenewamerican.com/artman/ publish/article_903.shtml (accessed 4 May 2005).

Heritage Foundation. 2001. 'The Daily Briefing Extra: On Military Tribunals ...' Electronic document: http://www.heritage.org/dailybriefing/ dbextra/extra 011217.htm (accessed 30 January 2002).

Holmes, K.R. and Meese III, E. 2001. 'The Administration's Anti-Terrorism Package: Balancing Security and Liberty', *Heritage Foundation Backgrounder* 1484, 3 October 2001. Electronic document: http://www .heritage.org/library/backgrounder/bg1484.html (accessed 23 February 2002).

Neas, R.G. 2001. 'Statement Concerning the Senate Judiciary Committee's Hearings on Civil Liberties'. People for the American Way Press Release, 28 November 2001. Electronic document: http://www.pfaw .org/news/press/2001-11-28-347.phtml (accessed 3 December 2001).

New York Times. 'Justice Deformed: War and the Constitution'. 2 December 2001. Section 4, 14.

Orenstein, J. 2001. 'Rooting out Terrorists Just Became Harder', *New York Times,* 6 December 2001, A35.

Ratner, Michael. 2001. 'Moving Towards a Police State or Have We Arrived? Secret Military Tribunals, Mass Arrests and Disappearances, Wiretapping & Torture'. Electronic document: http://www .humanrightsnow.org/policestate.htm (accessed 3 December 2001).

Rychiak, R.J. 2001. *Humberto Alvarez-Machain v. United States*: The Ninth Circuit Panel Decision of 11 September. The Federalist Society. National Security White Paper. Electronic document: http://www.fedsoc.org/Publications/Terrorism/ninth.htm (accessed 30 January 2002).

United States Senate. Committee on the Judiciary. Hearings on Department of Justice Oversight: Preserving Our Freedoms While Defending Against Terrorism. Electronic document: http://judiciary.senate .gov/hr120301f2.htm (accessed 4 December 2001).

United States Senate. Committee on the Judiciary. Hearings on the Department of Justice and Terrorism. Electronic document: http://www .nytimes.com/library/politics/ 011207ashcroft-text.html (accessed 6 December 2001).

Williams, P. 2001. 'This Dangerous Patriot's Game'. Originally published in *Observer* of London, 2 December 2001. Reprinted: Common Dreams News Center, 3 December 2001. Electronic document: http:// www.commondreams.org/views01/1202-01.htm (accessed 3 December 2001).

Acknowledgements

I am very grateful to the editors as well as Annelise Riles, Martha Mundy, Laura Nader, Alfred Aman, Alexander Smith and Jennifer Gaynor for their critical readings of this essay or related work – though responsibility for any errors of fact and interpretation remain my own. The discussion of the Military Order draws on material originally presented in Greenhouse 2005a.

Notes

1. The 'trouble case' is Llewellyn and Hoebel's (1941) blanket term for conflicts and their emergent demands for legal action (formal or informal) – as evidence of the cultural context of law.
2. The history of legal anthropology in these terms is well covered, most recently, by Nader (2002), Starr and Goodale (2002) and Moore (2005).
3. I borrow the term 'artifact' from Pottage (2004: 11–24).
4. The metaphor of the trail – as directive, limited and limiting – is intended here also as acknowledgement of zones of silence and – as Mitchell urges us to consider – 'the unspeakable and unimaginable' as 'turns in the stream of discourse, swerves in the temporal unfolding of speech and spectacle' (2005: 297).
5. I borrow the concept of career lines from Weber (1978: 963), discussed in Greenhouse (2005a).
6. For a contrasting view, compare interviews reported in Bumiller and Myers (2001) and Weiser (2002).
7. United States Senate (2000). For full text, see http://www.epic.org/privacy/terrorism/hr3162.html (accessed 4 May 2005).
8. The list of principal commentaries is included as Appendix A.
9. Simpson had been charged with the murder of his wife and her friend; Cochran was his lawyer. At the conclusion of the lengthy trial – which was covered live on television – Simpson was found not guilty by the jury.
10. On *Korematsu* as a positive precedent, see Glaberson (2001).
11. Robert Bork: lawyer, former federal judge, nominee to Supreme Court; Lee A. Casey: lawyer, former Office of Legal Counsel, Department of Justice, under former President George H. W. Bush; Orrin G. Hatch: lawyer, U.S. Senator (R-UT); Edwin M. Meese III: lawyer, former Attorney General under President Reagan; Michael J. Nardotti, Jr.: lawyer, U.S. Army (ret), former Judge Advocate General; Pierre-Richard Prosper: lawyer, Ambassador-at-Large for War Crimes Issues, former assistant U.S. Attorney in Los Angeles; David B. Rivkin, Jr.: lawyer, former legal advisor to the counsel of the president (Reagan and G. H. W. Bush) and deputy director, Office of Policy Development, U.S. Department of Justice; Cass R. Sunstein: lawyer, academic; George J. Terwilliger III: lawyer, former deputy Attorney General and acting Attorney General under former President Bush.
12. On war, see Rivkin, Casey and Bartram (2001); cf. Turner (2001).
13. Stephen Brill reports that Terwilliger was a proponent of the 'unlawful enemy combatant' designation as well as military tribunals (Brill 2003: 125–26). With former Attorney General Robert Barr, Terwilliger had 'brief conversations with people in the White House but never attended a meeting' (Brill 2003: 220). Brill reports that Terwilliger called Timothy Flanigan

(in the Office of Legal Counsel) 'to suggest the military commissions' (Brill 2003: 221).

14. Terwilliger was lead attorney for the George W. Bush campaign in the Florida election cases in November and December 2000; see White and Case (2001).

15. In 2000, for example, Mr. Terwilliger testified before House Judiciary Committee's Subcommittee on Crime, reporting on 'Operation Triggerlock', a Justice Department initiative to streamline prosecution of 'the most dangerous armed chronic offenders': 'We aimed to maximize the bang for the taxpayer's buck by going after "the badest [sic] of the bad." ... These cases [about 7,000] did not overburden the federal judiciary with lengthy trials. They were simple cases, the only relevant question being. "Does the accused have the prior conviction and did the accused possess a gun?"' (United States House of Representatives 2000).

16. Casey and Rivkin are partners in the Washington, D.C., law firm of Baker and Hostetler.

17. Their reference to Europe as premodern seems to anticipate Secretary of Defense Rumsfeld's reference to 'old Europe' in the context of building a coalition for war in Iraq (United States Department of Defense 2003).

18. The point is not limited to the United States. See the recent *American Ethnologist* forum on the elisions of racism, anti-Semitism and Islamophobia in Europe (Dominguez 2005).

19. I borrow the images of horizontality and verticality in this context from Spencer's discussion of the ethnography of postcolonial politics (1997: 8). Spencer uses the terms as metaphors to evoke the spill-over effects of politics (along the horizontal) and hierarchies of representation (along the vertical).

20. Ultimately, its uses of that power over the succeeding two years (to flout the majority of Spaniards opposed to the war in Iraq, police the Basques, curtail employees' rights and control immigration) contributed to the dramatic defeat of the *Partido Popular* (PP) in the national elections of March 2004 (see Grimond 2004).

21. Among European coalition partners, these political gains were seriously compromised by the popular reaction against the advance to war in Iraq, as subsequent elections (i.e., after 2003) have confirmed – but that is another story.

22. Hamdi et al. v. Rumsfeld (03-6696) and Rasul et al. v. Bush (03-334).

23. In theory, in such circumstances 'everything is at least potentially political' (Schmitt 1996: 22) – which is to say, the condition of what Schmitt calls the 'total state' (1996: 22) is met.

References

Abrams, P. 1988. 'Notes on the Difficulty of Studying the State', *Journal of Historical Sociology* 1(1): 58–89.

Aman, A.C., Jr. 2004. *The Democracy Deficit: Taming Globalization through Law Reform*. New York: New York University Press.

Appadurai, A. 1996. *Modernity at Large*. Minneapolis: University of Minnesota Press.

Beck, U. 2005. *Power in the Global Age*, trans. Kathleen Cross. Cambridge: Polity Press.

Benda-Beckmann, F. von, K. von Benda-Beckmann, and A. Griffiths (eds). 2005. *Mobile People, Mobile Law: Expanding Legal Relations in a Contracting World*. Aldershot: Ashgate.

Bork, R. 2001. Having their day in (a military) court. National Review Online. Originally published: National Review, 17 December 2001. Electronic document: http://www.nationalreview.com/17dec01/bork121701.shtml (accessed 26 October 2008).

Brill, S. 2003. *After: How America Confronted the September 12 Era*. New York: Simon and Schuster.

Bumiller, E. and S.L. Myers. 2001. 'A Nation Challenged: The Presidential Order; Senior Administration Officials Defend Military Tribunals for Terrorist Suspects', *New York Times*, 15 November 2001, B6.

Casey, L.A. and D.A. Rivkin, Jr. n.d. 'Europe in the Balance', *Policy Review*, no. 107. Electronic document: http://www.policyreview.org/jun01/casey_print. html (accessed 4 May 2005).

———. 1999. The International Criminal Court vs. the American People. Heritage Foundation Backgrounder Executive Summary no. 1249, February 5, 1999. Electronic document: http://www.heritage.org/library/backgrounder/ bg1249es.html (accessed 11 December 2001).

Casey, L.A., D.B. Rivkin, Jr., and D.R. Bartram. 2001. 'Unlawful Belligerency and Its Implications under International Law. The Federalist Society'. National Security White Paper. Electronic document: http://www.fedsoc.org/Publica- tions/Terrorism/ unlawfulcombatants.htm (accessed 4 May 2005).

Chomsky, C. 1990. 'The United States-Dakota War Trials: A Study in Military Injustice', *Stanford Law Review* 43: 13–96.

Collier, J.F. 1975 'Legal Processes', *Annual Review of Anthropology* 4: 121–44.

Comaroff, J. and J. Comaroff. 2004. 'Policing Culture, Cultural Policing: Law and Social Order in Postcolonial South Africa', *Law & Social Inquiry* 29(3): 513–45.

CovertAction Information Bulletin. 1993 . 'Uprising and Repression in L.A.: An Interview with Mike Davis', in R. Gooding-Williams (ed.), *Reading Rodney King, Reading Urban Uprising*. New York: Routledge, 142–54.

Critical Incident Analysis Group (CIAG). 2000. 'Threats to Symbols of Ameri- can Democracy 8. Reflections on Leadership'. Electronic document: http:// faculty. virginia.edu/ciag/threats_leaders.html (accessed 3 December 2001).

Dominguez, V. (ed.). 2005. '*AE* Forum: Exclusionary Projects and Anthropo- logical Analysis' *American Ethnologist* 32(4): 497–537.

Flaherty, M.S. 1996. 'The Most Dangerous Branch', *Yale Law Journal* 105(7): 1725–839.

Geertz, C. 1973. *The Interpretation of Cultures: Selected Essays*. New York: Basic Books.

Glaberson, W. 2001. 'Support for Bush's Anti-Terror Plan', *New York Times*, 5 December 2001, B6.

Goodale, M. (ed.). 2006. 'In Focus: Anthropology and Human Rights in a New Key', *American Anthropologist* 108(1): 1–83.

Greenhouse, C.J. 2005a. 'Hegemony and Hidden Transcripts: The Discursive Arts of Neoliberal Legitimation', *American Anthropologist* 107(3): 356–68.

———. 2005b. 'Nationalizing the Local: Comparative Notes on the Recent Restructuring of Political Space', in R. Wilson (ed.), *Human Rights in the 'War on Terror'*. Cambridge: Cambridge University Press, 184–208.

Grimond, J. 2004. 'From A to Z', in J. Grimond (ed.), *Special Section: A Survey of Spain, The Economist* 371(8381): 5–7 (26 June–2 July 2004).

Hansen, T.B. and F. Stepputat. 2001. *States of Imagination: Ethnographic Exploration of the Postcolonial State*. Durham, NC: Duke University Press.

Held, D. and A. McGrew. 2002. *Globalization/Anti-Globalization*. Cambridge: Polity Press.

Hoge, W. 2001a. 'A Nation Challenged: London; Britain Moves to Expand Arrest Powers', *New York Times*, 13 November 2001, B5.

———. 2001b. 'Official Says Resisting Bill on Terror Puts Britain at Risk', *New York Times*, 10 December 2001, A13.

Jean-Klein, I. and A. Riles (eds). 2005. 'Symposium: Anthropology and Human Rights Administration: Expert Observation and Representation after the Fact', *Political and Legal Anthropology Review* 28(2), 173–315.

Lewis, N.A. 2001. 'A Nation Challenged: The Hearings; Justice Dept. and Senate Clash over Bush Actions', *New York Times*, 29 November 2001, B7.

Llewellyn, K. and E.A. Hoebel. 1941. *The Cheyenne Way: Conflict and Case Law in Primitive Jurisprudence*. Norman: University of Oklahoma Press.

McGraw, S. 2001. 'What If Bin Laden Is Caught?' Electronic document. http://www.lexisone.com/news/nlibrary/b092001a.html (accessed 3 December 2001).

Merry, S.E. 2006. *Human Rights and Gender Violence: Translating International Law into Local Justice*. Chicago: University of Chicago Press.

Mitchell, W.J.T. 1991. 'The Limits of the State: Beyond Statist Approaches and their Critics', *American Political Science Review* 85(1): 77–96.

———. 2005. 'The Unspeakable and the Unimaginable: Word and Image in a Time of Terror', *Journal of English Literary History* 72(2): 291–308.

Moore, S.F. 2005. 'Certainties Undone: Fifty Turbulent Years of Legal Anthropology, 1949–1999', in S.F. Moore (ed.), *Law and Anthropology: A Reader*. Oxford: Blackwell Publishing, 346–67.

Myers, S.L. and N.A. Lewis. 2001. 'A Nation Challenged: The Tribunals; Assurances Offered about Military Courts', *New York Times*, 16 November 2001, B10.

Nader, L. 2002. *The Life of the Law: Anthropological Projects*. Berkeley: University of California Press.

New York Times. 2001. 'United States Senate Judiciary Committee Hearings. Subject: The Department of Justice and Terrorism. Testimony of Attorney General John Ashcroft', 6 December 2001. Electronic document: http://www.nytimes.com/library/politics/011207ashcroft-text.html (accessed 4 May 2005).

Nuclear Age Peace Foundation. 1999. 'Statement of David B. Rivkin and Lee A. Casey on the Legal Status of the ABM Treaty before the Committee on Foreign Relations United States Senate'. Electronic document: http://www.nuclearfiles.org/menu/key-issues/missile-defense/history/rivkin-casey_statement-abm-status-htm (accessed 7 December 2001).

Ong, A. 1999. *Flexible Citizenship: The Cultural Logics of Transnationality.* Durham, NC: Duke University Press.

———. 2003. 'Zones of New Sovereignty in Southeast Asia', in R.W. Perry and B. Maurer (eds), *Globalization under Construction: Governmentality, Law, and Identity.* Minneapolis: University of Minnesota Press, 39–69.

Perry, R.W. and B. Maurer. 2003. 'Introduction', in R.W. Perry and B. Maurer (eds), *Globalization under Construction: Governmentality, Law, and Identity.* Minneapolis: University of Minnesota Press, ix–xxi.

Pottage, A. 2004. 'Introduction: The Fabrication of Persons and Things', in A. Pottage and M. Mundy (eds), *Law, Anthropology, and the Constitution of the Social: Making Persons and Things.* Cambridge: Cambridge University Press, 1–39.

Rivkin, D.B., Jr. 1994. 'Health Care Reform vs. the Founders'. Originally published in the *Wall Street Journal,* 29 September 1993. Republished by Future of Freedom Foundation at http://www.fff.org/freedom/0294f.asp (accessed 4 May 2005). [Ed note: Rivkin is misspelled 'Rivkind' on website.]

Rivkin, D.B., Jr., and L.A. Casey. 2000/2001. 'The Rocky Shoals of International Law', *The National Interest,* no. 62. Electronic document: http://www.nationalinterest.org/issues/62/Rivkin-Casey.html (accessed 30 January 2002).

Rivkin, D.B., Jr., L.A. Casey, and D.R. Bartram. 2001. 'Bringing Al-Qaeda to Justice: The Constitutionality of Trying Al-Qaeda Terrorists in the Military Justice System'. The Heritage Foundation. Legal Memorandum 3, 5 November 2001. Electronic document: http://www.heritage.org/library/legalmemo/lm3.html (accessed 2 December 2001).

Sassen, S. 1996. *Losing Control? Sovereignty in an Age of Globalization.* New York: Columbia University Press.

Schmitt, C.1996. *The Concept of the Political,* trans. G. Schwab. Chicago: University of Chicago Press.

Spencer, J. 1997. 'Postcolonialism and the Political Imagination' (Malinowski Memorial Lecture 1995), *Journal of the Royal Anthropological Institute (N.S.)* 3(1): 1–19.

Starr, J. and M. Goodale. 2002. 'Introduction. Legal Ethnography: New Dialogues, Enduring Methods', in J. Starr and M. Goodale (eds), *Practicing Ethnography of Law: New Dialogues, Enduring Methods.* New York: Palgrave Macmillan, 1–10.

Terwilliger, G., C. Theodore, G. Shawn, D. Blumenthal, and R. Parker. n.d. 'The War on Terrorism: Law Enforcement or National Security?' National Security White Papers. The Federalist Society. Electronic document: http://www.fed-soc.org/Publications/Terrorism/militarytribunals.htm (accessed 2 December 2001).

Turner, R.F. 2001. 'The War Powers Resolution: An Unnecessary, Unconstitutional Source of "Friendly Fire" in the War against International Terrorism?'

The Federalist Society. National Security White Paper. Electronic document: http://www.fed-soc.org/Publications/Terrorism/warpowers.htm (accessed 30 January 2002).

United States Department of Defense. 2003. 'Secretary Rumsfeld Briefs at the Foreign Press Center'. News transcript, 22 January 2003. Electronic document: http://www.defense link.mil/transcripts/2003/t012232003_t0122sdfpc .html (accessed 21 April 2006).

United States House of Representatives. 2001. Committee on the Judiciary, Subcommittee on Crime, Legislative Hearing on H.R. 4051, 'Project Exile: The Safe Streets and Neighborhoods Act of 2000', 6 April 2000. Electronic document: http://www. house.gov/judiciary/cr040600.htm (accessed 7 January 2002).

United States Senate. 2000. 'Uniting and Strengthening America by Providing Appropriate Tools Required to Intercept and Obstruct Terrorism' (USA PATRIOT Act) Act of 2001. HR 3162, 107th Congress, 1st Session. 24 October 2001.

United States Senate Judiciary Committee. 2001. 'Hearings. Department of Justice Oversight: Preserving Our Freedoms While Defending Against Terrorism', 4 December 2001. Electronic document: http://judiciary.senate.gov/ te120401f2-terwilliger.htm (accessed 5 December 2001).

Weber, M. 1978. *Economy and Society: An Outline of Interpretive Sociology*, trans. Ephraim Fioschoff et al., ed. G. Roth and C. Wittich. Berkeley: University of California Press.

Webster, W.H. and H. Williams. 1992. 'The City in Crisis', a Report by the Special Advisor to the Board of Police Commissioners on the Civil Disorder in Los Angeles, 21 October1992.

Weiser, B. 2002. 'Ex-Prosecutor Wants Tribunals to Retain Liberties', *New York Times*, 8 January 2002, A13.

White and Case. 2001. 'George J. Terwilliger III'. Electronic document: http:// www.white case.com/terwilliger_george.html (accessed 3 December 2001).

The White House. 2001a. Military Order of 13 November 2001. 'Detention, Treatment, and Trial of Certain Noncitizens in the War against Terrorism', 66 F. R. 57833. Electronic document: http://www.whitehouse.gov/news/ releases/2001/11/2001113-27.html (accessed 4 May 2005).

———. 2001b. 'ABM Treaty Fact Sheet: Statement by the Press Secretary', Announcement of Withdrawal from ABM Treaty. Electronic document: http:// www.whitehouse.gov/news/releases/2001/1220011213-2.html (accessed 4 May 2005).

Wines, M. 1992. 'Bush and Justice Dept. Step up Response to Riot', *New York Times*, 6 May 1992, A24.

2

LAW AND THE FRONTIERS OF ILLEGALITIES

Laura Nader

Introduction

With all that has been written about imperialism and colonialism it is remarkable how little has been said about the uses made of law in that process. The omissions are significant. While theoreticians of imperialism recognize the uses of culture in the imperial project, it was and is specifically the rule of law discourse and practice that were and are keystones of the continuing Euro-American civilizing project. How the recent rule of law and democracy discourse – the law from above – works in the service of political, military and economic power in Iraq is a primary example in this chapter. It is addressed to and about social science colleagues, as well as powerful actors who use 'culture' as a terrain for expanding American legal universalism along with ideas of private property and neoliberal economics.

Although history indicates that colonial law is inextricably implicated with illegalities and organized violence, nevertheless it is habitual for Anglo-Americans to idealize their law or the rule of law. This idealization is especially noticeable when scholars engage in comparison. The idealized aspects of Western rule of law are compared, for example, with the practices of law in a Muslim setting, resulting in the derogation of law in one or the other. Similarly, when legal scholars or practicing lawyers speak of the law, they commonly refer to the purposeful functions of the law as continuity and doctrinal consistency, as a process for facilitating and protecting voluntary arrangements or as a process for resolving acute social conflict as in labour law (Berman 1958) in a static and, strangely, a historical manner. Not included in such standard listings are extralegal or illegal practices. Law and legitimacy, legalities and illegalities are all intertwined in any transparent study of law practices set in the grand scheme of geopolitics. How illegalities are changed into legalities without rule of law ideology also changing is part of what Giorgio Agamben describes (2005: 58, 86) as 'confusion between the exception and the rule', 'two somewhat antagonistic yet functionally connected elements'.

Academics have called attention to examples where law is used to compete for social status, for political and economic dominance, to feed systems of ethnic brokerage, as a mechanism of harassment and more, although social science writing has for the most part been anecdotal (see Nader 1965). In an essay written jointly with Barbara Yngvesson, we wrote about the extralegal, and illegal, workings of law:

> [T]he law does not function solely to control. It educates, it punishes, it harasses, it protects private and public interests, it provides entertainment, it serves as fund-raising institution, it distributes scarce resources, it maintains the status quo, it maintains class systems, it integrates and disintegrates – all these things in different places, at different times, with different weightings. It may be a cause of crime; it plays, by virtue of its discretions, the important role of definer of crime. It may encourage respect or disrespect for the law, and so forth ... We have concentrated in the main on law as a system of social control and have not even opened up the possibility that the law might at times function *as a system of discontrol*. (Emphasis added, Nader and Yngvesson 1974: 909)

That was 1974.

In 1979 Michel Foucault published *Discipline and Punish – the Birth of the Prison*. In it he draws a distinction between systems of legalities and systems of illegalities (Foucault 1979: 82). He notes that while systems of legalities are rather easily identified by discourse and specialized institutions, systems of illegalities are not so easily identified because they are illicit and punishable by the state. Foucault saw that creating the legal also means creating criminals, and that the legal and the illegal are part of one system (see Nader 2001).

Expanding on Foucault's work, Mindie Lazarus-Black (in a 1994 volume co-edited with S.F. Hirsch) writes, from a historical perspective of three hundred years of social life on the Caribbean islands of Antigua and Barbuda, about the transformations resulting from the rather unexpected observation that the same laws used by ruling classes as tools for punishment served the powerless as both instruments of defense and resistance under colonialism and slavery, and in the post-emancipatory era. In a chapter on 'Legalities, Illegalities, and Creole Families' Lazarus-Black makes clear that legalities refer to 'codes for conduct, prescriptions for ideal behavior, rules to maintain order, and sanctions for those who depart from the law', as contrasted with illegalities: 'the non-application of the rule, the non-observance of the innumerable edicts or ordinances' (Lazarus-Black and Hirsch 1994: 73). What if, under conditions of rapid change or rupture (like the war in Iraq), illegalities from above become the law? What if systems of legalities and systems of illegalities are not two domains but one? Such questions are inspired by the colonial present, in which lawlessness and plunder appear in blatant forms, often supported by 'rule of law' and democracy discourse both nationally and internationally, about the United States and the Arab world particularly after the invasion of Iraq in 2003 (Gregory 2004). This chapter reflects decades of anthropological work and, though perhaps not novel, is intended for academics, the military, the Congress and Executive Branch, corporate interests and the believing public because we are all complicit, partners in the colonial present that is anything but democratic.

Awareness of law as prone to create illegalities was adumbrated in the research on European colonialism, as in the work on legal orientalism inspired by Edward Said's *Orientalism* (1979), in the work on law and development by James Gardner in *Legal Imperialism* (1980), and in the current work on plunder and empire by Mattei and Nader (2006). Said focused on the orientalist lens through which the other may be viewed as both irrational and inferior. Gardner saw firsthand on the ground the frontiers of illegalities and observed that an instrumental imported law can result in the concentration of the power of law in the state or in large multinational corporations. Mattei and Nader examine work on empire that is justified through imperial law, while activists analyse the law constructed by means of the WTO Agreement on Trade Related Aspects of Intellectual Property Rights (TRIPS) (Nader 2002: 213–30) as law that also justifies looting. At issue in these works and the work of others is the law operating in the context of colonialism and imperialism, where law practices become oppression. While this is not the place to review the contributions of law and society, scholars (e.g. Fitzpatrick 1980; F. von Benda-Beckmann 1981; Snyder 1981) it is important that anthropology and colonialism are not thought things of the past – there are continuities.

Patterns of law have historically been exported by colonial or imperial powers within a variety of models (Mattei and Nader 2006). The first is the imposition of legal patterns like the civil reorganization accompanying military intervention, as in the example of MacArthur's reforms in post–World War II in Japan, or present-day Iraq. A second model can be described as imposition by bargaining, in the sense that targeted countries are persuaded to change the law according to Western standards in order to get access to the international economic market. This is the way in which the World Bank, IMF, WTO, and many Western development agencies operated throughout the developing and former socialist bloc. A third model, constructed as voluntary or consensual, has been presented as diffusion by prestige or persuasion, focusing on a deliberate process of institutional admiration that leads to the reception of law partly in search of predictable outcomes. The prime example, in addition to specific democracy promotion, is the process of universalizing American law in recent years (Nader 1999), and under the Bush administration the struggle to supersede international law. Whether law is imposed or part of a bargaining process or openly received does not diminish the dance between systems of legalities and legal justification of illegalities. Under colonialism and empire of the American sort, dominant legal systems operate predominantly to subvert local law rather than working within arrangements of co-existence and legal pluralisms.

What is central to this chapter is the large-scale expansion of a dominant Euro-American system, and how such expansion today is facilitated by the American ideology of 'rule of law' and 'democracy'. Although conditions of imposition are of concern to some, colonizers commonly argue that regardless of methods used both in imposing law and in creating law ad hoc, in the long run importance should not be attached to the means (violence, looting, war, genocide), but to the result – the rule of law as a legacy of the 'civilized' world. Property rights are secured, good governance, predictability and so forth are positive results (Ferguson 2003). Today, law practice is constructed internationally within the inequalities of the contemporary international economic system, thereby marking continuities between colonial and present international systems of law that contradict any sweeping ideas about *post*coloniality (Nader 1999). In a cutting critique, William Alford of Harvard Law School notes that such promoters 'fail to appreciate how much of what they present as universal, upon closer scrutiny, mirrors our own quite distinctive legal and political institutions' (2000: 64).

Colonialism and Empire Today: The Case of Iraq

> We're an empire now, and when we act, we create our own reality. And while you are studying that reality – judiciously, as you will – will act again, creating other new realities, which you can study too, and that's how things will sort out. (Suskind 2004: 44)

An illustration of the law as a frontier of illegality is the case of Iraq and the contemporary occupation of Iraq by American and British forces. Circumstances in Iraq are a reminder for any student of earlier colonial violence. A non-elected Paul Bremer and the Committee of the Iraqi Governing Council passed edicts, closed newspapers under 'the rule of law', ordered curfews, and wrote and spoke about sovereignty, or what one political journalist calls 'Phantom Sovereignty' (Schell 2004: 8). Paul

Bremer used military force, not law, to back these moves, and a military force allowed for the disorganization of competing legal controls in Iraq. As Jonathan Schell correctly notes, the interim Constitution – a series of temporary regulations – is misdescribed as a Constitution, if a Constitution is the fundamental enduring law of a country that proceeds from the will of the people, given that it is to be a democracy. The tendency in Iraq and elsewhere is to treat situations fraught with complex political and cultural considerations as if they were amenable to formulaic solutions, a universalizing strategy. Such grand strategies impact donor societies as well.

In the United States, Executive Orders increasingly pass for law seemingly independent of the other two branches of government, unless challenged.[1] War in the United States is supposed to be declared by Congress under the U.S. Constitution, but we have not had such a declaration since the Second World War. This is to say that the Executive branch of the United States government has been fighting wars that were not legally declared by the U.S. Congress. The Italian political theorist Giorgio Agamben (2005) argues that such extension of power or state of exception is a powerful strategy with a potential to transform democracies into totalitarian states. Weapons of mass destruction were the justification George W. Bush used for a war of exception in Iraq. When weapons of mass destruction were not found in Iraq, the justification for war also changed. The drum beat became Rule of Law (see Mattei and Nader 2008). Henceforth, the occupation in Iraq was about bringing the Rule of Law to Iraq as part of democracy promotion measures. Headlines in U.S. media reflected the change in White House strategy. The following selected newspaper excerpts of the numerous eye-catching headlines that appeared in U.S. newspapers and magazines indicate how systems of legalities and illegalities come together with journalists, legal specialists, the military at all levels and special-interest groups, all participating, all complicit in the contemporary daily propaganda processes that are barely remembered in so-called post-colonial critical writings.

There is little context in the reports that follow. One might call it liminal reporting – between places, between historical times, between differences – no context with which to map the colonial present and the long experiences of British and American interventions in the Middle East. Iraq's current legal system derives from the nation's 1924 constitution, which created a parliamentary monarchy similar to the one that rules Jordan today, and it contained certain basic guarantees of human rights indicative of influence from France's Napoleonic code. In the 1960s, Iraq adopted a new set of codes; a 1968 Baath Party established a council that circumvented existing laws by means of courts, their version of the Patriot Act, allowing people to be tortured or killed.

Today, the occupation argues, there is need to strip the Iraqi system of the laws and special courts established by the revolutionary command council. Modifying the existing system means not changing the substantive law but changing the procedures to ensure that they are fair and efficient. Once again we 'approach legal reform in other societies as if the past were little more than an encumbrance, that the clear-minded should be only too ready to discard for a future remarkably akin to ours' (Alford 2000:64). (See also T. Mitchell 2002.) As in other locales, the rapid funding of such philosophies of legal development by USAID makes the attempts in Iraq anything but unique. Imperial hubris rarely challenges basic development assumptions, and questions are not likely to be answered by sound bite reporting: what Western ideals, whose model of democracy, why democracy? In whose interest? Does not the experience of trying to shape others inevitably shape us as well as them? And what about the Fourth Geneva Convention of 1949, which contains the principles of a legal occupation law?

IRAQ'S JUDICIAL SYSTEM LACKS PRACTITIONERS, SCHOLARS SAY by Reynold Holding, *San Francisco Chronicle,* 11 April 2003: '[T]he transition from the rule of a dictator to the rule of law could be easier and faster in Iraq than, for example in the recently liberated nations of Eastern Europe ... But whether the Bush administration will preserve a modified version of the current legal system or create something different is still unclear.'

U.S. SEEKS SOLID CORE TO FIX IRAQ'S BROKEN LEGAL SYSTEM by Bernard Weinraub, *New York Times,* 27 April 2003: 'Maj. Charlotte Herring, an army lawyer, sat at the corner of a conference table on Thursday facing a nervous Iraqi lawyer ... A translator sat between them ... The Americans want both to help rebuild the nation's shattered legal system and to understand the basic structure of a court and prison system ... to find a core group of individuals to initiate this new judicial system. Maj. Herring said the meeting had been personally satisfying – comparing herself with the Iraqi lawyer of the same age she said, "It really makes me proud to be here and really makes me proud to be an American."'

TEAM TO REBUILD IRAQ'S COURTS INCLUDES THREE FEDERAL JUDGES, *Wall Street Journal,* 29 April 2003: '[M]embers of the team, which includes federal prosecutors, public defenders, court administrators, and a state judge have signed on ... to assess the condition of Iraq's judicial system ... to develop an independent judiciary so that Iraqi people will have confidence in their courts. Khaled Abou El Fadl warned they are not writing on a clean slate ... "watch mucking around with the tribal courts and customary law"'.

ISLAMIC JUSTICE TAKING HOLD IN BAGHDAD by Anthony Shadid, *Washington Post,* 9 May 2003. 'Clerics Fill Void … While Moving Against Western Influences': 'The biggest disaster will be a lack of morality and immoral behavior in the name of freedom and democracy – alcohol, pornography, restore order on the streets – underground Islamic courts under Hussein, now they deal with alimony, looting, marriage license.'

Washington Post, 4 May 2003: 'Noah Feldman, professor of law at NYU with a doctorate in Islamic law, named advisor on efforts to draft a new Iraqi constitution … believes that Islam is compatible with Western ideals as there are varieties of democracy in the Muslim world.'

AMERICAN WILL ADVISE IRAQIS ON WRITING NEW CONSTITU-TION by Jennifer Lee, *New York Times,* 11 May 2003: 'Noah Feldman … will try to blend American ideas of democracy with Islamic traditions … Looking for common ground between Islam and American democracy'.

AD-LIBBING IRAQ'S INFRASTRUCTURE by William Booth, *New York Times,* 21 May 2003. 'U.S. troops face daily scramble in "Bringing Order to Chaos": Chicago policeman has been assigned to train police officers': 'Rachael Roe swept through Najaf, entered the main courthouse where all the records criminal and civil had been burned. Roe's mission was to reestablish the courts, but to do this necessitated a judiciary. But who? Before the war, there were 41 judges.'

IN IRAQ, A JUSTICE SYSTEM WORTH SAVING by Richard Coughlin, *New York Times,* 26 July 2003: 'Help the judges who withstood Saddam Hussein … a foundation built on respect for the rule of law and human rights'.

IN NAJAF, JUSTICE CAN BE BLIND BUT NOT FEMALE by Neil Mac-Fafquhar, *New York Times,* 31 July 2003: 'The U.S. Marine colonel supervising the reconstruction of the Shiite holy city's government indefinitely postponed the swearing in of this first-ever female judge today after her appointment provoked a wave of resentment, including fatwas from senior Islamic clerics and heated protests by the city's lawyers … the sudden firestorm was emblematic of the tension between the American desire to leave an imprint on the levers of government in Iraq versus a conservative religious establishment determined to fight what it sees as a military invasion dragging Western cultural norms in behind the tanks.'

WITH IRAQI COURTS GONE, YOUNG CLERICS JUDGE, *New York Times,* 4 August 2003.

OCCUPIERS AND THE LAW by William Greider, *The Nation,* 1 November 2003: 'Under international law, the U.S. is prohibited from simply seizing Iraqi oil revenues and spending the money however it chooses. Indeed, the U.S. occupying force cannot remove the country's judges and suspend Iraq's domestic laws … In fact; international law is designed to prevent an occupying nation from transforming a defeated society into its own likeness.'

NEXT STEPS: OPEN FAIR TRIAL BEST FOR IRAQI PEOPLE – AND THE WORLD by William Beeman, *San Francisco Chronicle*, 13 December 2003: 'Having Hussein talking may implicate his captors in an uncomfortable manner.'

WOMEN IN IRAQ DECRY DECISION TO CURB RIGHTS by Pamela Constable, *Washington Post*, 16 January 2004. 'Council Backs Islamic Law on Families': 'For the past four decades, Iraqi women have enjoyed some of the most modern legal protections in the Muslim world, under a civil code that prohibits marriage below the age of 18, arbitrary divorce, and male favoritism in child custody and property inheritance disputes … But the U.S. backed Iraqi Governing Council has voted to wipe them out, ordering in late December that family laws shall be "cancelled" and such issues placed under the jurisdiction of strict Islamic legal doctrine known as sharia … and opposed by women's groups.'

Early on after the invasion of Iraq, the distinguished Islamic scholar Khaled Abou El Fadl, a law professor at UCLA, wrote an opinion piece for the *Wall Street Journal* (21 April 2003) titled 'Rebuilding the Law'. In this piece Abou El Fadl maintains that Iraq had a rich and venerable jurisprudential tradition long before Saddam Hussein came to power. He notes that, '[b]eing geographically at the intersection of Arab, Persian, Kurdish, and Turkish cultures, the country has been home to both Shi'ite and Sunni centers of religious study'. He also notes that after gaining independence from Britain in 1930, Iraq, like most Arab countries, adopted civil and criminal law codes from the French and Germanic legal systems. Iraq's personal law, however, continued to be based primarily on Islamic law. As he put it,

> The Iraqi Civil Code of 1953 was one of the most innovative and meticulously systematic codes of the Middle East. Iraqi jurists, working with the assistance of the famous Egyptian jurist Abd Al-Razzaq Al-Sanhuri, drafted a code that balanced and merged elements of Islamic and French law in one of the most successful attempts to preserve the best of both legal systems. In 1959 Iraq promulgated the Code of Personal Status, which on issues of family and testamentary law was at the time the most progressive Muslim code of law. Importantly, for our purposes now, this code merged elements of Sunni and Shi'ite law to grant women greater rights in marriage, divorce, and inheritance.

According to Abou El Fadl this was changed when the Baath Party came to power in 1968. Saddam involved Iraq in a series of wars that enabled him to declare a constant state of national emergency and to rule mostly by executive order. Iraq became one of the few countries that legally sanctioned the use of torture in pre-trial investigations as a punitive measure, and the death sentence was prescribed for a large variety of offenses. Law became contingent on the will of the party and the president. After the Gulf War of 1991 Saddam announced that he would implement Islamic law in Iraq, a theatrical move the point of which was public spectacle. Abou El Fadl concludes his opinion piece by recommending that the Iraqis reclaim the creative legacy that was there before the Baathists imposed rule of fear rather than the rule of law: 'American policy makers must understand that Iraq's legal and ethical history did not start with the overthrow of Saddam.'

His comments make the informed reader uneasy. There are uncomfortable parallels. If we fast forward to and Paul Krugman's column 'Just Trust Us' in the *New York Times* on 11 May 2004, the underground picture begins to gel.

> Just trust us, John Ashcroft said, as he demanded that Congress pass the Patriot Act ... After two and a half years, during which he arrested and secretly detained more than a thousand people, Mr. Ashcroft has yet to convict any actual terrorists. Just trust us. George Bush said, as he insisted that Iraq, which had not attacked us and posed no obvious threat, was the place to go in the war on terror ... "Just trust us", Paul Bremer said, as he took over in Iraq. What is the legal basis for Mr. Bremer's authority? You may imagine that the Coalition Provisional Authority is an arm of government subject to U.S. law. But it turns out that no law or presidential directive has ever established the authority's status. Mr. Bremer, as far as we can tell, answers to nobody except Mr. Bush, which makes Iraq a sort of personal fief. In that fief, there has been nothing that Americans would recognize as the rule of law ... And finally: 'Just trust us', Donald Rumsfeld said early in 2002, when he declared that 'enemy combatants' ... don't have rights under the Geneva Convention.[2]

Is it any surprise that the Princeton professor, who observes the liminal status of the fiefdom, asks that something like the prison scandals at Abu Ghraib in Baghdad would eventually come to light?

Let us look back now to Max Weber and Euro-American legal Orientalists to see how scholarship is implicated in contemporary U.S. foreign policy in the Islamic world. The attitudes towards Islam and Islamic law do not come newly sprung in the twenty-first century.

Max Weber, the Father of Legal Orientalism

Legal orientalism has been receiving a good deal of attention of late. Teemu Ruskola, in an article that appeared in the *Michigan Law Review,* observes that 'by considering Legal Orientalism as an ongoing cultural tradition we can understand better why, even today, claims about the status of Chinese law are so relentlessly normative ... because ... they support an overly idealized self-image of the American legal subject and an unduly negative view of the Chinese (non)legal (non)subject: Chinese are ruled by morality, Americans by law; Chinese are lemmings, Americans individuals; Chinese are despotic, Americans democratic; China is changeless, America dynamic'. In his essay, Ruskola wishes to challenge the historic claim made by many Western observers that China lacks an indigenous tradition of 'law', while doing more to understand how the West 'has come to understand itself through law'. After all, China boasts dynastic legal codes going back to the Tang dynasty. Yet the West has constructed its cultural legal identity against China, and despite vigorous efforts to debunk the view of China as lacking in law we still have scholars such as Thomas Stephens (1992) arguing that Chinese law is not even worthy of the term 'jurisprudence'. The task, Ruskola argues, may be to 'provincialize Europe' and by doing so explore, as some scholars like Dipesh Chakrabarty are doing, a renewal of European traditions 'from and for the margins'.

A comparable condition of legal orientalism exists in relation to Islam and its law. Jedidiah Kroncke's article on 'The Flexible Orientalism of Islamic Law' (2005) takes up John Strawson's thesis in *Islamic Law and English Texts*: 'English texts do not merely present Islamic law, they construct it.' (1995: 21–38). Kroncke's section titled 'Weber's Taxonomy and Islamic Law' illustrates the pervasive power of these constructs by quoting not Weber but Supreme Court Justice Felix Frankfurter, who had undoubtedly read Max Weber: '[The Supreme Court] is not a tribunal unbounded by rules. We do not sit like a kadi under a tree dispensing justice according to considerations of individual expediency.'

Kroncke, who specializes in Chinese law, summarizes ideas of Max Weber as published in his book, *Economy and Society* (Weber 1968), in order to understand why Weberian legal orientalism remains entrenched. Weber focuses on several historical legal traditions, including Islam. He uses the term 'kadi' to describe a system of justice that is not focused on a formally rational law but on the ethical, religious postulates of a substantively rational law.[3] The term 'substantively rational' is part of a fourfold taxonomy of legal systems with two dimensions, formal/substantive and rational/irrational, thereby generating four categories. For Weber, Western continental law fits into the ideal type of 'formal rationality'. In contrast, Islamic law is one of 'substantive rationality' concerned with the implications of Islam's religious norms: 'The dominance of law that has been stereotyped by religion constitutes one of the most significant limitations to the rationalisation of the legal order.' (1968: 657). Weber defines the groundwork of subsequent legal orientalism in making the distinction between the substantive rationality of

Islamic law and its substantively irrational administration of justice. As he puts it, 'a typical feature of the patrimonial state ... is the juxtaposition of traditional prescription and arbitrary decision-making, the latter serving as a substitute for a regime of rational rules.' (1968: 1041).

Weber rejects the possibility of an Islamic jurisprudence. Kadi opinions may be authoritative, but they vary from person to person and are given without any statement of rational reasons. While Weber's analysis has been called into question by a number of scholars, that is not Kroncke's point. Rather, he is concerned with the relatively undisturbed aspect of Weber's characterization of Islamic law. Kroncke finds that people like Bryan Turner (1978: 87) continue the stereotype with essentialized comments such as 'Islamic Law provided society with a tight, normative structure which ... cannot change rationally to meet new contingencies.' Another Islamic scholar, Wolfgang Schluchter (1999: 108, co-edited with T. Huff), writes that Islamic 'legal development was paralyzed'. Patricia Crone (1999) reiterates the impossibility of Islamic law as an effective legal system because of its substantive grounding. Kroncke does mention the work of critics, Moosa (1999) and Hanif (1999), who take a more historical perspective, but indicates that their work does not make a dent in the pejorative representation of Islamic law. He then goes further to examine the major work on Islamic law by the influential scholar Joseph Schacht (1950) and by American anthropologist Lawrence Rosen (1989, 2000).

For Schacht (1950, 1964), Islamic legal theory is rote and mechanical, and he succeeds in stigmatizing even the ideal type that Weber argued for Islam. After all, Islam is 'only arbitrary opinion', presenting 'a formidable obstacle to every innovation, and in order to discredit anything it was, and still is, enough to call it an innovation' (1950: 129). For Schacht, Islamic law is only a 'jurist's law', concerned with its own internal logic and having nothing to do with social reality, while suffering from 'an inherent rigidity ... disinterested in any notion of justice', the 'letter rather than the spirit of the law' (1950: 72), a concern with appearances. Irrationality and unreality are the common themes. While there may be a growing mistrust of Schacht's assumptions (see Haim Gerber's *Islamic Law and Culture*), his continuing stereotyping of Islamic law is orientalist and gives full expression to the negative implications of Weber's work for representing 'the anarchy of the Arab way of life' (1964: 23).

When Kroncke (2005) moves to the work of Lawrence Rosen, things don't get much better, even though Rosen is an anthropologist. Rosen revives Weber's characterization of the capricious kadi, thereby reaffirming the basic structure of Islamic legal orientalism. In his books,

The Anthropology of Justice (1989) and *The Justice of Islam* (2000), Rosen uses the concept of totalizing subjectivity as well as the metaphor of the bazaar to describe an essentialized Muslim society, a world of premonitory chaos, one in which Arabs lack an appreciation for regularity and tangibility of space and of time. In his neo-Weberian view of kadi justice, Rosen explains that part of the trauma of colonialism for Muslims was the fact that European powers tried to introduce specific legal codes, especially troubling in a world where truth and veracity are not motivating concerns!

Both authors flesh out Islam's place in Weber's taxonomy, with 'Rosen exploring the injustice born out of total whimsical substantive irrationality and Schacht exploring the injustice born of a totally mercilessly formal and inflexible substantive rationality' (Kroncke 2005: 63). Weber, not merely an originator of social science paradigms but himself a product of a particular time and place, represents a process still noted today. Kroncke concludes: 'Rosen and Schacht both exhibit the same inability to make reference to Western law in anything but the most idealized representations. Western law becomes the evaluative standard and both are oblivious to peoples who have been radically impacted by colonialism ... The legacy of colonialism continues and expands to include those who self-colonize thereby reaffirming Weber's caricatures and uncritical idealisations of Westernisation and law or even to idealisations of Islamic law.'

Rule of Law or Misrule?

Idealizations have been of concern to ethnographers because of the use of idealizations in shaping hegemonies or counter-hegemonies (Nader and Ou 1998). But anthropologists are not the only professionals who worry about idealizations as an impediment to understanding how law works, or indeed, what law is. Legal scholars such as Judith Shklar (1964: 31) observe the tendency among legal scholars caught by 'the ideal purposes of law to govern one's thinking about law in general. It means thinking of law only as it ought to be – as legalism wants it to be, not as it actually is.' For Shklar, this means a legal system that meets the formal qualifications of being 'self-regulating, immune from the unpredictable pressures of politicians and moralists, manned by a judiciary that at least tries to maintain justice's celebrated blindness' (Shklar 1964: 31). We are all limited by the belief systems and thought structures of our own cultures and disciplinary paradigms. And different versions of this problematic of an internalist perspective dominating the investigatory capacities and theorists of law appear in the work of legal theorists such as H.L. Hart (1961), although not apparently in the work of Max Weber and his heirs. Nowhere are such issues more salient than under colonial or imperialist conditions where such legal ideologies are normalized.

When Marc Galanter (1972: 54) wrote about '"Indigenous" Law in India' he noted:

> The dichotomy between the official law and popular legality has been the theme of a continuing stream of criticism from administrators, nationalists and students of Indian society, who have emphasized the unsuitability of British-style law in India. As a scholarly British District Officer plaintively concluded in 1945: '… we proceeded with the best of intentions to clamp down upon India a vast system of law and administration which was for the most part quite unsuited to the people … In Indian conditions the whole elaborate machinery of English Law which Englishmen tended to think so perfect, simply didn't work and has been completely perverted.'

Galanter continues: 'Administrators and observers have blamed the legal system for promoting a flood of interminable and wasteful litigation, for encouraging perjury and corruption, and generally exacerbating disputes.' He quotes an observer:

'The course of justice, civil as well as criminal, is utterly confounded in a maze of artifice and fraud.' Is this rule of law, or misrule?

In another part of the world, James Holston (1991) writes about 'The Misrule of Law: Land and Usurpation in Brazil', the title of which, once again, suggests that there is an ideal 'rule of law'. In this piece on the legalization of usurpation, Holston argues that

> Brazilian law regularly produces unresolvable procedural and substantive complexity in land conflicts … this jural-bureaucratic irresolution … initiates extrajudicial solutions; and these political impositions inevitably legalize usurpations of one sort or another. In short, land law in Brazil … sets the terms through which encroachments are reliably legalized. It is thus an instrument of calculated disorder by means of which illegal practices produce law, and extralegal solutions are smuggled into the judicial process … distinctions between legal and illegal are temporary and their relations unstable. (1991: 695)

What Holston referred to as law's dystopias indeed do not seem to be external to the system. But the headlines are found less frequently in scholarly work than in stories written by journalists.[4]

If Holston's argument may be generalized, that is that 'legal landholdings are at base usurpations legalized thereby perpetuating or facilitating stratagem and fraud'. If indeed using the law legally also creates malpractice or devious practice of law, then what we sometimes call 'extrajudicial' means that such solutions are a way to redefine the legal arena. In this sense, systems of legalities and systems of illegalities are part of one and the same complex. If we take this further to the colonial foundations of Euro-American law we see the law influenced, albeit unevenly at times, by the need to legalize usurped rights. From the beginning of European expansion there was a need to establish a legal foundation for the empire's policy of owning and redistributing conquered land for the purposes of economic exploitation and Christian religious expansion. Asserting higher status ('positional superiority', in legal orientalism) was part of this plan, as was 'the rule of law' as ideology, a strategy that continues to this day, whether it be in Iraq or in areas of intellectual property issues. Co-existence was never the point. Holston refers to this as 'usurpation through the legalisation of illegal acts'. Although Holston is speaking about Brazil and land seizures, his conclusion is more widely applicable to illegalities by those structurally enjoying positional superiority: 'Illegal practices produce law, extra-legal solutions are incorporated into the judicial process, and law is confirmed as a channel of strategic disorder.' (1991: 722). Perhaps it is time to fight law with law. Even Kofi Annan (McCarthy 2004: 1) noted that the occupation of Iraq was illegal and supported by no United Nations Security Council resolution.

Discussion

Order and disorder, stabilities and instabilities, legalities and illegalities, a republic or an empire – all are enmeshed with law, and it is messy. 'Rule of law' and legitimacy are at stake. Without legitimacy we have a 'runaway world' (Leach 1968) in which might makes right. For such reasons legal philosophers such as Locke and Vattel went to great lengths to justify the take in the early expansion of Europe by recourse to law. Early European colonial plunder was followed by 'the rule of law', immediacy operating with an idea of civilization as the opposite of chaos and irrationality, where rules precede actual disputes. Is history repeating itself in Iraq, or is something new happening?

Even a cursory examination of Bremer's edicts suggests that privatization today is a new word for looting and plunder, just as democracy is increasingly interchanged with neoliberalism. Iraq's occupation not only by the military but also by American corporations is justified as a state of exception, a working paradigm of state power and law. The Bush administration has been open about wanting to make an Iraq that 'favors market systems' and encourages moves to privatize state-owned enterprises. Iraqis, accustomed to a state-run economy, may hold preferences and plans that run counter to such neoliberal visions as 100 percent private ownership of Iraqi businesses, unrestricted tax-free remittance of all profits, forty-year ownership licenses and more (Juhasz 2004). (See also Chandrasekaran and Pincus 2004.)

The law and the constitutional structure that is the keystone of the U.S. republic are in competition with the empire. In an early U.S. Supreme Court brief on the detentions in Guantánamo, former federal officials argued that if no constitutional rights applied to offshore detainees, the government would be creating a parallel system of extraterritorial courts and extraterritorial prisons to punish extraterritorial crimes without legal oversight or constraint: 'The republic requires a single standard, to which all are subject – the law. But the empire requires one set of regulations for others, and another set, or none for the ruler. Other countries must obey the Geneva Conventions, but the U.S. is exempt. Other countries must wage war only defensively; the United States may do so preemptively.' (Schell 2004: 7).[5]

The rest of the world is not blind to double standards, nor to the history of colonialism. An article in the Egyptian weekly *Al-Ahram* (Bishara: 2004) reports: 'America, a country that boasts about democracy and the rule of law, issues an arrest warrant for the young cleric in connection with a murder case but than uses the warrant as a bargaining chip to make him alter his political stand … The occupying authority is now above the law … The foreign army arrives accompanied by another army of fortune-seeking civilians, individuals who the locals are bound to identify with the occupiers' – the modern-day carpetbaggers.

In the end, something more than social justice is at stake. Law must contrast with violence by its very definition. The hegemonic distinction between the 'civilized world' and the rest may collapse under recent revelations about American-run prison facilities in Iraq.

> *The Wall Street Journal* (5-21-04) had the following headlines: BEHIND BARS: FINDING U.S. ABUSE LEFT RED CROSS TEAM IN A QUANDRY; NOT USED TO SEEING SUCH ACTS BY A DEVELOPED COUNTRY, SOME DEBATED EXPOSING IT: AN INSPECTION OF CELLBLOCK 1A, by Farnaz Fassihi and Steve Stecklow: 'Accustomed to documenting human-rights violations in dictatorships and developing nations, the Red Cross was suddenly confronting evidence of harsh treatment by the world's leading power, a country that prided itself on its humanitarian record.'

The sensational photos told the story that will only lastly appear in courts of law, whether they be international, Iraqi, military or domestic

American courts. Yet the invocation of law generates a manipulation of institutions, ideologies and other parameters of power that blur differences between legal and illegal.

The separation of law from politics, a law above politics, economics or personal values, is idealized, especially in the U.S., which has a political system distrustful of the exercise of personal decision-making. Practices belie the ideal or ideological. The legal realists were aware of this, and more recently the critical legal studies scholars realized this and at least implicitly recognized the political, economic, racist and sexist components of law (Kairys 1998). That the rule of law is not quite a law of rules (Kairys 1998: 15) was also well recognized by those involved in the law and development movement in the United States (Trubek and Galanter 1974).

To focus on practice need not entail repudiating ideals, but it does entail repudiating ideology and legal hegemonies for what they are in order to take seriously the law as a terrain of political struggle with the intermingling of 'us and them', 'civilized and barbaric'. In Iraq, positional superiority based on democracy as posture and law as sham will backfire on any presumed ideas of 'bringing democracy and freedom to the Middle East'. In the United States executive orders, the USA PATRIOT Act and other strategies of fearmongering put democracy itself at risk, as Agamben (2005) would have predicted. There is here a serious undertaking required for understanding how law in the colonial present really works in the service of power and empire, and whether Bush administration practice is fundamentally changing what U.S. law means. This is the time to examine the extensions of state power or 'state of exception' and the role of contradictions in the formation and implementation of law (Chambliss 1989) to understand how it is that state legitimacy remains virtually unchallenged in the United States and elsewhere (Klein 2004). How far can the frontiers of illegality be pushed before we understand the threat of such ruptures to the very definitions of legality and rule of law?

Acknowledgements

Franz von Benda-Beckmann, Martha Mundy, James Holston, Carol Greenhouse, Laura Carrier, Monica Eppinger and Mayssoun Soukariah commented on earlier versions of this paper. I benefited greatly from their comments although full consideration of their suggestions will await an extended publication.

Notes

1. 'The limiting factor, of course, is that only certain parties have the legal right – standing – to raise such challenges. The Bush administration is undertaking a targeted expansion of executive power. Not every frontier is being pushed. One could say previous administrations or generations pushed different frontiers, e.g. some forms of discrimination in housing or employment were made illegal. The current administration is choosing its own frontiers for targeted expansion.'

2. Other examples besides standing support the contention that those in power in the U.S. are conducting expansion, i.e. transformation of illegalities into legalities, by carefully targeting liminal areas in order to expand executive power. Examples of targeted liminality are the exploitation of 1) liminal status of persons (torture and disregard of international treaty obligations in regard to non-state or uniformed combatants, like al Qaeda or Taliban prisoners of war; detention without charge or trial of visitor-visa or green-card holders, or transit passengers); 2) liminal places (torture or other disregard of treaty obligations in Guantanamo or creation of new liminal places for violations of U.S. laws of war via rendition of detainees who remain in U.S. custody although suffering treatment outsourced interrogation); 3) liminal times (the emergence of a new post 9/11 security apparatus; the first few months of U.S. occupation); 4) liminal status of territories (Iraq fiefdom).

3. Today we call this 'formally rational' or 'procedurally rational'.

4. Note the headline from *The Nation* (in an article by Ashley Shelby, 5 April 2004): EXXON HAS USED THE LEGAL SYSTEM TO AVOID PAYING DAMAGES FOR THE VALDEZ SPILL, or an article about resistance by Elaine Scarry (reprinted in *Harper's Magazine* [2004]: 15) in which she speaks about the resistance to the USA PATRIOT Act:

   The fact that the Patriot Act has engendered such resistance may at first seem puzzling. True, its legislative history is sordid: It was rushed through Congress in several days; no hearings were held; it went largely unread; only a few of its many egregious provisions were modified. But at least it *was* passed by Congress: many other blows to civil liberties have been delivered as unmodified executive edicts, such as the formation of military tribunals and the nullification of attorney-client privilege ... the Patriot Act has degraded the legal stature of the United States by permitting the executive branch to bypass constitutional law, but our legal degradation has gone even further: Evidence indicates that the Bush Administration has created offshore torture centers ...

   Scarry goes further to point out that the Patriot Act inverts constitutional requirements that people's lives be private and the work of government be public.

5. Mark Danner's (2005: 5) observations about the Bush administration are pertinent: 'What is interesting (is that) ... the wrongdoing is right out in front of us ... What we don't have is any clear admission – or adjudication of – guilt, such as a serious congressional or judicial investigation would give us.'

References

Abou El Fadl, K. 2003. 'Rebuilding the Law', *Wall Street Journal,* 21 April, section A, p. 12, column 3.

Agamben, G. 2005. *State of Exception.* Chicago: University of Chicago Press.

Alford, W. 2000. 'Law, Law, What Law?', in K.G. Turner, J.V. Feinerman and R.K. Guy (eds), *The Limits of the Rule of Law in China.* Seattle: University of Washington Press, 45–64.

Beeman, W. 2003. 'Next Steps: Open, Fair Trial Best for Iraqi People – and World', *San Francisco Chronicle,* 13 December, pp. A-29.

Benda-Beckmann, F. von. 1981. 'Some Comments on the Problems of Comparing the Relationship between Traditional and State Systems of Administration of Justice in Africa and Indonesia', *Journal of Legal Pluralism* 19: 165–75.

Berman, H.J. 1958. *The Nature and Functions of Law.* 3rd edition, 1972. Brooklyn, NY: Foundation Press.

Bishara, A. 2004. 'The Dynamic of Occupation', *Al Ahram Weekly,* 22–28 April, issue No. 681, also available at http://weekly.ahram.org.eq/print/204/681/op62.htm (last accessed 19 October 2008).

Booth, W. 2003. 'Ad-libbing Iraq's Infrastructure', *Washington Post,* 21 May, A01.

Chambliss, W. 1989. 'State Organized Crime', *Criminology* 27(2): 183–208.

Chandrasekaran, R. and W. Pincus. 2004. 'U.S. Edicts Curb Power of Iraq's Leadership', *Washington Post,* Foreign Service Sunday, 27 June, A01.

Constable, P. 2004. 'Women in Iraq Decry Decision to Curb Rights', *Washington Post,* 16 January, A12.

Coughlin, R. 2003. 'In Iraq, a Justice System worth Saving', *New York Times,* 26 July, section A, col. 1, p. 13.

Crone, P. 1999. 'Weber, Islamic Law and the Rise of Capitalism', in W. Schluchter and T. Huff (eds), *Max Weber & Islam.* New Brunswick: Transaction Press, 247–72.

Danner, M. 2005. 'What Are You Going to Do with That?' *New York Review of Books* 52(11): 5. See http://www.nybooks.com/articles/18094.

Fassihi, F. and S. Stecklow. 2004. 'Behind Bars – Finding U.S. Abuse in Iraq Left Red Cross Team in a Quandary', *Wall Street Journal,* 21 May, A 21.

Ferguson, N. 2003. *Empire: How Britain Made the Modern World.* London: Allen Lane, Penguin Press.

Fitzpatrick, P. 1980. *Law and State in Papua New Guinea.* New York: Academic Press.

Foucault, M. 1979. *Discipline and Punish – The Birth of the Prison.* New York: Vintage Books.

Galanter, M. 1972. 'The Aborted Restoration of "Indigenous" Law in India', *Comparative Studies in Society and History* 14(1): 53–70.

Gardner, J. 1980. *Legal Imperialism: American Lawyers and Foreign Aid in Latin America.* Madison: University of Wisconsin Press.

Gerber, H. 1999. *Islamic Law and Culture, 1600–1840.* Boston: Brill.

Greider, W. 2003. 'Occupiers and the Law', *The Nation,* 17 November, vol. 277, issue 16, pp. 5–6.

Gregory, D. 2004. *The Colonial Present*. Oxford: Blackwell Publishing.

Hanif, N. 1999. *Islamic Concept of Crime and Justice*. New Delhi: Sarup.

Hart, H.L. 1961. *The Concept of Law*. Oxford: Clarendon Press.

Holding, R. 2003. 'Iraq's Judicial System Lacks Practitioners, Scholars Say', *San Francisco Chronicle*, 4 November, A 21.

Holston, J. 1991. 'The Misrule of Law: Land and Usurpation in Brazil', *Comparative Studies in Society and History* 3(4): 695–725.

Juhasz, A. 2004. 'Foreign Policy in Focus', Foreign Policy in Focus Policy Report.

Kairys, D. (ed.). 1998. *The Politics of Law – a Progressive Critique*. New York: Basic Books.

Klein, N. 2004. 'Kerry and the Gift of Impunity', *The Nation*, 13 December, 14.

Kroncke, J. 2005. 'Substantive Irrationalities and Irrational Substantivities: The Flexible Orientalism of Islamic Law', *UCLA Journal of Islamic and Near Eastern Law* 4(1): 41–73.

Krugman, P. 2004. 'Just Trust Us', *New York Times*, 11 May, A 23.

Lazarus-Black, M. and S.F. Hirsch (eds). 1994. *Contested States: Law, Hegemony and Resistance*. New York: Routledge.

Leach, E. 1968. *A Runaway World?* New York: Oxford University Press.

Lee, J. 2003. 'Americans Will Advise Iraqis on Writing New Constitution', *New York Times*, 11 May, section 1, col. 1, Foreign Desk, p. 14

MacFafquhar, N. 2003. 'In Najaf, Justice Can Be Blind but Not Female', *New York Times*, 31 July, A1.

Mattei, U. and L. Nader. 2008. *Plunder: When the Rule of Law is Illegal*. Malden, MA: Blackwell Publishing.

McCarthy, S. 2004. 'Annan and Bush Clash at UN over Iraq War', *The Globe and Mail*, Toronto (Vancouver edition), 22 September, 1.

Mitchell, T. 2002. *Rule of Experts: Egypt, Techno-Politics, Modernity*. Berkeley: University of California Press.

Moosa, E. 1999. 'Languages of Change in Islamic Law: Redefining Death in Modernity', in R.S. Khare (ed.), *Perspectives on Islamic Law, Justice, and Society*. Lanham, MD, Boulder, CO, New York, Oxford: Rowman & Littlefield Publishers, Inc., 161–97.

Nader, L. 1965. 'The Anthropological Study of Law', *American Anthropologist*, Special Issue: *The Ethnography of Law* 67(6): 3–32.

———. 1999. 'The Globalization of Law: ADR as 'Soft' Technology', *American Society of International Law Proceedings* 93: 304–11.

———. 2001. 'Crime as a Category', *Windsor Yearbook of Access to Justice* 19: 326–40. Special Issue.

———. 2002. *The Life of the Law*. Berkeley: University of California Press.

———. 2003. 'Iraq and Democracy', *Anthropological Quarterly* 76(3): 479–83.

Nader, L. and B. Yngvesson. 1974. 'On Studying the Ethnography of Law and Its Consequences', in J. Honigmann (ed.), *Handbook of Social and Cultural Anthropology*. New York: Rand McNally, 883–921.

Nader, L. and J. Ou. 1998. 'Idealization and Power: Legality and Tradition', *New Directions in Native American Law*. Special Issue of *Oklahoma City University Law Review* 23(82): 13–42.

Rosen, L. 1989. *The Anthropology of Justice*. Cambridge: Cambridge University Press.

———. 2000. *The Justice of Islam*. Oxford: Oxford University Press.

Ruskola, T. 2002. 'Legal Orientalism', *Michigan Law Review* 101(October): 179.

Said, E. 1979. *Orientalism*. Hardmondsworth: Penguin Books.

Scarry, E. 2004. 'Acts of Resistance', *Harper's Magazine*, February/March: 15.

Schacht, J. 1950. *Origins of Muhammadan Jurisprudence*. New York: Oxford University Press.

———. 1964. *An Introduction to Islamic Law*. Oxford: Oxford University Press.

Schell, J. 2004. 'Letter from Ground Zero: Empire without Law', *The Nation*, 31 May, vol. 278, issue 21, p. 7.

Schluchter, W. and T. Huff (eds). 1999. *Max Weber and Islam*. New Brunswick: Transaction Publishers.

Shadid, A. 2003. 'Islamic Justice Taking Hold in Baghdad', *Washington Post*, 28 May, A 01.

Shelby, A. 2004. 'Exxon Has Used the Legal System to Avoid Paying Damages for the Valdez Spill', *The Nation*, 5 April. vol. 218, issue 13, pp. (16, 18, 19, 22, 23), 16–23.

Shklar, J. 1964. *Legalism: Law, Morals and Political Trials*. Cambridge, MA: Harvard University Press.

Snyder, F. 1981. 'Colonialism and Legal Form: The Creation of "Customary Law" in Senegal', *Journal of Legal Pluralism* 19: 49–90.

Stephens, T. 1992. *Order and Discipline in China*. Seattle: University of Washington Press.

Strawson, J. 1995. 'Islamic Law and English Texts', *Law and Critique* 6(1): 21–38.

Suskind, R. 2004. 'Without a Doubt', *New York Times*, 17 October, Sec.6, Col. 1, Magazine Desk.

Trubek, D. and M. Galanter. 1974. 'Scholars in Self-Estrangement: Some Reflections on the Crises in Law and Development Studies in the United States', *Wisconsin Law Review* 1974: 1062–101.

Turner, B. 1978. *Marx and the End of Orientalism*. London: Allen and Unwin.

Weber, M. 1968. *Economy and Society: an Outline of Interpretive Sociology*, vols. 1–3. New York: Bedminister Press.

Weinraub, B. 2003. 'U.S. Seeks Solid Core to Fix Iraq's Broken Legal System', *New York Times*, 27 April, N. 24.

3

SELECTIVE SCRUTINY
Supranational Engagement with Minority Protection
and Rights in Europe

Jane K. Cowan

Remember those heady early days of globalization theory, its prophets confidently predicting the demise, the irrelevance, even – shades of Marx – the withering away of the state? Like Vladimir and Estragon for Godot, we are still waiting. The meanings and powers of statehood are nevertheless changing. Nowhere is this clearer than in Europe, where the nation state form historically emerged. Under the federalizing tenets of a Europeanization process launched soon after the Second World War, all member states have had to cede certain traditional prerogatives of state sovereignty and to submit to European institutions. Yet the degree of accountability to 'Europe' (the shorthand for this array of institutions) has been heightened for the applicant states responding to the project of European enlargement. Ten countries were admitted to the European Union in 2004, and two in 2007; seven remain candidates or potential candidates. Of these nineteen countries, all but two (Cyprus and Malta) are former socialist states.[1] The more stringent conditions for membership that these countries have faced reflect not merely the growing penchant in the international sphere to discipline through 'conditionality'; they also respond to the intervening years' tumultuous transformations in Eastern Europe. Sobered by the Yugoslav violence, largely interpreted as the bursting forth of ancient ethnic hatreds once the repressive socialist lid was lifted, and worried by other legacies of socialist rule, European institutions have approached the accession process with something of the spirit of a civilizing mission. Among other requirements, applicant states have had to demonstrate efforts toward democratization, the development of civil society and respect for human and minority rights. Such requirements evoke for many citizens of these states a sense of déjà vu.

In this article, I draw attention to striking parallels in the ways relations between supranational bodies, some European states and their minorities were reconfigured in two post-imperial moments: the de-

cade following the First World War when, with the demise of the multinational Ottoman, Habsburg, Romanov and Hohenzollern empires,
nationally defined states were founded or expanded and began to consolidate; and the present period of transformation of former socialist
polities upon the collapse, after 1989, of what is often dubbed the Soviet empire. In both of these periods, supranational bodies developed
regimes of supervision whose rationale and focus were minority rights
and the state's governance of 'difference'. These regimes have not im-
pinged equally upon all states, however. Delineating a figure I call 'the
supervised state', I highlight *asymmetrical* aspects of the two regimes of
supranational governance.[2] At the same time, 'the supervised state' offers an especially clearly drawn example of broader processes of supranational scrutiny that nowadays affect all European states. I therefore
endeavour to bring this material into engagement with recent anthropological debates around audit and accountability processes within
Europe. I conclude by addressing the indeterminacies of supervision.

Supranational Scrutiny: Parallels

The year 1919 can be seen as a definitive moment in the shift from empire to nation state in Europe, marking its emergence as the hegemonic
political form of modernity (Giddens 1985). The nationality principle
had animated many of the struggles that culminated in the First World
War; the grand words emerging from the Paris Peace Conference at
Versailles seemed to vindicate it. But the diplomats and statesmen's
redrawing of the European map both honoured and violated this principle. This was not simply a matter of the unavoidable compromises
of realpolitik. With particular intensity in certain regions of Europe,
such as the Balkans and parts of the Habsburg territories, populations
among which many (but by no means all) had by the early twentieth
century come to think of themselves as distinct 'nationalities', lived in-
termingled in towns and countryside. According to one definitive reference work of interwar scholarship, the new political order 'detached
almost one hundred million people of the three great, pre-war empires of
Central and Eastern Europe, of which twenty to twenty-five million
became minorities' (Robinson et al. 1943: 35); Mazower (1998: 41) reck-
ons that Versailles 'gave sixty million people a state of their own' while
turning another twenty-five million into minorities.

Conveying the vast scale of the transformations, such statistics imply
that the new Europe already divided neatly into majorities and minorities. In fact, apart from the happy nationals who found themselves in

'their own' state, the remaining inhabitants formed a decidedly mixed category. Notwithstanding intense local identifications, many remained indifferent about nationality. Others felt themselves distinct but either sought no territory, as was true of the Gagauz or the various lineages of European Roma (Gypsies), or had no national state to champion their claims, like the Ruthenians or the Kurds. In practice if not in law, and with the significant exception of the Jews and Muslims, only those who identified with a highly developed national project –and preferably an already existing state – that is, persons normally referred to as '*les nationalités*', were likely to become categorized as 'minorities' with respect to the peace treaties.[3]

Having mapped out a new Europe that so poorly corresponded to the neat, homogeneous units beloved of national ideologues, and responding to pressures from many quarters, the Committee on New States at the Versailles negotiations inserted minority treaties or agreements within certain peace treaties. In other words, rather than making minority protection a *universal* treaty obligation for all states implicated in the Versailles arrangements, including Britain with its 'Irish problem', France with its Bretons and Basques, and Italy with its multinational Tyrol, the Allied and Associated Powers imposed such treaties only upon particular states, largely in Eastern and Southeast Europe.[4] 'Treaty-bound states', or as they are tellingly called by some analysts, 'minority states' (Claude 1955; Fink 1995), were compelled to accept the minorities treaties as the price of their international recognition.[5] In signing treaties or agreements concerned with 'protection of minorities', states promised equality before the law and full civil and political rights to all nationals without distinction as to race, language or religion. They also recognized rights of persons belonging to racial, linguistic or religious minorities to free exercise of their language and religion, and to the establishment, at their own expense, of charitable, religious and social institutions, schools and other educational institutions. The state agreed to provide facilities (e.g. translators) enabling minorities to use their own language before the courts. Where numbers warranted, minorities would be entitled to a share in public resources for educational, religious or charitable purposes. The covenant drafted at Versailles dictated the founding of a League of Nations, whose obligation to 'guarantee' these minorities treaties had the character of a 'sacred trust'. Whereas in the past, particular powerful states (such as Russia, Great Britain, France) had acted as patrons and protectors of specific *nationalities*, for the first time in history minorities as a category and a set of populations became a matter of *international* concern (Jackson Preece 1998: 72). The responsibility of the League to oversee treaty-bound states' fulfilment of their treaty obligations was unambiguous, even though the actual mechanisms of supervision were not spelled out.

When the Paris Peace Conference established the League of Nations, as well as sister institutions like the International Labour Office, or ILO, in 1919, it was authorizing the creation of structures to oversee the implementation of the treaties, as well as to facilitate future agreements and shared projects among member states. Among the groundbreaking elements of the covenant was the agreement to create an international administrative structure (the League Secretariat) and a new class of international civil servants. State bureaucracies had become well entrenched by the early twentieth century, but an international administration was an entirely new creature. Inasmuch as details on exactly *how* the League was to 'oversee' treaty implementation were left hazy, and since no precedents existed, League civil servants, particularly at higher levels, had unusual latitude to define their roles as well as their practices (see Azcárate 1945; Ranshofen-Wertheimer 1945; Monnet 1978). My own tracing of the everyday activities of one group within the League Secretariat, that concerned with minorities, confirms that civil servants (known, irrespective of rank, as 'officials') not only administratively supported, but indeed often designed and guided the implementation of diplomatically determined, international agreements. Officials of the Minorities and Administrative Commissions Section (normally referred to as the 'Minorities Section') of the League Secretariat, for instance, quickly became resident experts on minority situations in particular treaty-bound states. Overstretched states' delegates, who sat on the 'minority committees' ('Committees of Three', i.e. three League member states) set up to investigate when a state was accused of violating its minority obligations, relied upon them for advice and even recommendations of courses of action.

Better known as an important founder of the idea of an integrated Europe, Jean Monnet honed his supranational skills as one of the architects of the League of Nations Secretariat. He played a key role in forging 'the international', envisaging this as a space for a new spirit of cooperation and pragmatic action (Monnet 1978). The close working relationship he encouraged between state delegates and the secretariat is nowhere more evident than in the invention and development of supervisory mechanisms pertaining to the governance of persons and places that stymied neat national logics. The primary mechanism of minority supervision became known as the 'minority petition procedure' (see Mair 1928; League of Nations 1929; Azcárate 1945; Jackson Preece 1998; Cowan 2003a). Its rudiments were worked out by a committee of the League of Nations Council, led by the Italian delegate, Mr Tittoni, and presented to the council as 'The Tittoni Report' in October 1920. It entitled anyone to submit a letter – in League parlance, a *petition* – to the secretary general, bringing alleged infractions of a minorities treaty to the League's attention.

Treated as 'information' rather than a political or legal claim within a quasi-judicial process, each petition was examined by Minorities Section officials for its 'receivability' according to five specific criteria.[6] If deemed receivable, it was normally passed on to the accused government for comment; the accused government was required, within two months, to submit its response to the council's 'Committee of Three' set up to examine each receivable petition. Should that response be deemed unsatisfactory by the committee, its three state members, along with the Minorities Section director, would first meet with a state's delegate and, using discussion and diplomatic pressure, try to persuade the state to put its house in order. For petitions whose alleged 'infractions' were deemed serious and could not be resolved through such closed-door negotiations, there existed an option to place the allegations on the agenda of the council, whereupon the state representative faced fellow delegates' enquiries and possibly a collective reprimand. Though seldom used, the prospect of a public interrogation was generally enough to compel reflection in even the most intransigent minority states. By the same token, minority states bitterly resented the threat of such disciplinary spectacles. Even the more discreet modes of supervision evoked enduring protest – and not only from minority states but also from many humanitarian and internationalist organizations – not merely because they constituted a violation of these states' hard-won sovereignty, but because they were not universally applied.

With its fraught politics of sovereignty, the minority petition procedure became the focus of states' attention, a focus replicated in the scholarship of the League's scheme of minority protection. Supervision entailed, however, a much more polymorphous and dispersed set of practices. Apart from the petition procedures, along with the liaising, information-gathering and informal negotiating that accompanied them, the Minorities Section coordinated the supervision of other bodies to which the League had delegated responsibilities pertaining to minorities. For instance, the Greek and Bulgarian governments had concluded a bilateral agreement (as opposed to the minority obligations that the Allied and Associated Powers had imposed upon individual states) to encourage the emigration of their respective minority populations. Phrased as the Convention Concerning Reciprocal and Voluntary Emigration, a 'protocol' attached to the 1919 Treaty of Neuilly, it enabled 'Bulgarians' with Greek citizenship to emigrate to Bulgaria and become

Bulgarian citizens, and 'Greeks' with Bulgarian citizenship to emigrate in the other direction, with the same entitlements. The Voluntary Emigration, as it was known, included provisions for the migrants' fixed property to be valued and compensation awarded. Although this was a bilateral agreement between states, its inclusion in the Treaty of Neuilly warranted the League of Nations' assumption of a supervisory role. The operation of the Voluntary Emigration was carried out via a structure of 'mixed commissions', always including one representative each from Bulgaria and Greece, plus two 'neutral' members. Based in Sofia and Athens, these mixed commissions regularly sent in reports of the emigration programme's progress to the Minorities Section (see Ladas 1932). Several years later, the Minorities Section similarly supervised the compulsory population exchanges between Greece and Turkey set out in the Lausanne Convention agreed in January 1923.

Finally, the Minorities Section dealt with questions relating to territories whose political affiliation the Peace Conference could not resolve within the new system of national states or that had been granted special status: the Saar, the Aaland Islands, Memel, the Free City of Danzig (present-day Gdansk), and Upper Silesia. Jean Monnet insists that it was not statesmen but 'the Secretariat' who should be credited with devising imaginative solutions to the governance of these usually contested regions. A key example is Upper Silesia, an industrialized region with a mixed population of Germans and Poles, claimed by both countries. A plebiscite had been held in 1921 under the auspices of the Allied Powers; although an absolute majority favoured Germany, the plebiscite was held on a municipal basis, with a more mixed result. As the municipal districts were assigned to Germany or Poland according to the municipality's voting outcome, an interior frontier divided the territory, creating obstacles to the movement of goods and peoples. The task of finding a workable solution was assigned to the representatives of Belgium, Brazil, China and Spain, all members of the League Council (Azcárate 1945: 138); Monnet claims that the 'real work was done by the Secretariat' (in this case, himself and a colleague, Pierre Denis). It 'had to take account of the wishes of the population, but also geography and the economic situations of the areas concerned' (Monnet 1978: 89). Within three weeks, they devised a scheme that recommended a partitioned territory that nonetheless permitted free movement of persons and goods across the frontier, and the holding of a special conference between Germany and Poland – 'under the presidency' of a third, neutral country – to reach agreement on a range of matters. These included economic measures, nationality, domicile and the protection of minorities, the mixed commission and the arbitral court (the voluminous document that resulted was known as the 'Geneva Convention', Azcárate 1945: 139). The Geneva Convention mandated a transnational regime (with a tenure of fifteen years) governed by a mixed commission consisting of a German and a Polish national and a president from a neutral country – Switzerland, in this case (Azcárate 1945: 154).

Even this cursory sketch of League activities in relation to persons and places perceived as 'matter out of place' within the categorical logic of national states, and to sites that could not be squeezed into the new, nationally configured map of post-war Europe, gives a sense of their multiple resonances in more recent international interventions in the contemporary Balkans and Eastern Europe. The upheavals after 1989 in the former Soviet Union, as well as in Eastern and Southeast European polities and societies, some of them violent and protracted, have led to a vastly increased degree of supranational and international involvement in this broad and diverse region. That involvement has taken various forms. Most dramatically, entirely new state entities are being designed, constructed, audited and governed by authorities beyond the state. Intriguingly, in ways that suggest a certain amnesia concerning an earlier era's projects, these entities are often described using a discourse of *empire*. The 1995 Dayton Accords dictated for post-conflict Bosnia-Herzegovina a 'federation': a formidably complicated interlocking structure of legal and political bodies, with an Office of the High Representative (OHR) established to oversee implication of the agreement's 'civilian aspects' (Bose 2002). Michael Ignatieff (2003: 36) describes the OHR as 'an international official who functions as a kind of viceroy' (see also Cohen 1998). Certainly, incumbents of the OHR did not hesitate to use their powers, and several were willing, figuratively speaking, vigorously to knock together Bosnian, Croat and Serb heads when those citizens resisted reforms that the international community deemed essential. Not surprisingly, pundits are divided on the wisdom of the alleged 'new imperialism' in the Balkans. Knaus and Martin (2003) excoriate the governing arrangements in Bosnia and Kosovo as the unacceptable 'indirect rule' of a new liberal imperialism. In the spirit of Sebastian Mallaby's (2002) famous – or infamous, depending on one's perspective – argument for 'the reluctant imperialist', Ignatieff (2003) defends 'empire lite' as a necessary, and temporary, protection against the anarchy of warring factions. Such loose talk of empire is unhelpful. For all its evocative power, empire is an imperfect and misleading metaphor with which to describe the nature, objectives and parameters, geopolitical and economic, of these particular interventions.[7]

Kosovo offers another example of international administration. Following the Yugoslav conflict, in 1995 it was placed under the jurisdiction of the United Nations Mission Interim Administration (UNMIK). Until its declaration of independence in February 2008, a status recognised as this book goes to press by only some states in the international community, Kosovo (or officially, Kosovo Under UN Security Council Resolution 1244) functioned as a peculiar hybrid. It was described by Ignatieff (2003: 71) as 'a protectorate, an international legal entity in which nominal sovereignty is being exercised by a phantom state, actual sovereignty is being exercised by a UN viceroy, and day-to-day administration is increasingly exercised by locally elected officials'. Elsewhere in the region, international intervention has had a preventative and sometimes a mutually agreed character. Thus, in the mid 1990s, the government of the Republic of Macedonia invited *United Nations Protection Force* (*UNPROFOR*) to enter its territory with the express aim of preventing the Yugoslav violence from 'spilling over' into that country (Ackerman 2000).

While the two sites of Bosnia-Herzegovina and Kosovo reveal the most direct involvement by 'internationals' within Europe, virtually all states now installed in former socialist territories are currently subjected to scrutiny by supranational organizations and often, too, by NGOs closely tied to them (Hayden 2002; Coles 2004). Typically, this is being done in the name of rights – human rights, and quite frequently minority rights. The high commissioner for minorities of the Organization for Security and Cooperation in Europe (OSCE) is an active presence in the region, quietly trouble-shooting and arranging dialogues between minority organizations and state officials. Amnesty International and Human Rights Watch, which have set up branches throughout Eastern and Southeast Europe, closely monitor minority/state tensions and report incidents widely. A plethora of NGO-type organizations have sprung up: some are local in origin, some are international operations, and many others are a combination of both. Initiating projects on 'strengthening civil society', 'building links between divided communities' and 'promoting minority rights', they are kept alive by funds from foundations like USAID and the European Union, as well as Soros, Ford, MacArthur, and Fulbright.

Perhaps the closest and most uncanny parallel with the interwar minority supervision is the pronounced emphasis, in the EU enlargement process, on minority protection within states. As part of a broader human rights project, minority rights had risen in the international agenda since the 1980s and were being articulated in a range of international instruments and regional agreements. These included the OSCE, the United Nations Declaration on the Rights of Persons Belonging to National or Ethnic, Religious and Linguistic Minorities (UNDP), the European Framework Agreement for the Protection of National Minorities and the European Charter for Regional and Minority Languages (Rozakis 2000). However, European law and policy on minorities remained piecemeal, not least because of several EU member states' resistance to developing something more comprehensive and coherent. The 1993 'Copenhagen criteria' set a number of conditions, but these pertained only to prospective EU members; among them, as Hughes and Sasse (2003: 5) remark, 'the principle or "norm" of minority protection was rhetorically prominent'.

In the fields of politics and international relations, as well as within a 'grey' literature produced by European regional institutions, think tanks and NGOs concerned with democratization, ethnic minorities and human rights, EU conditionalities in the accession process have become a focus of considerable attention. At the same time, scholars and practitioners have examined conditionalities in terms of theories, principles, functions, practicalities and problems, sometimes even in respect to specific cases, in a way that almost always seems to gloss over the actual practices and mechanisms through which an individual country's attempt to meet the conditions – say, around minority rights – would occur, and would be scrutinized and judged. The anthropologist Gregory Feldman's presentation of material on Estonia is one of the only published empirical cases so far (see Feldman 2005a, 2005b). As communications officer of the Integration Foundation and later as an independent consultant for UNDP, Feldman was able to observe Estonian state bureaucrats interacting with minority leaders, European, Russian and Nordic diplomats and organizations like UNDP and the OSCE, as well as various international NGOs, over the course of several years. By Feldman's account, the task of scrutinizing Estonia's minority rights policy fell to the OSCE, which had a local office, deep familiarity with the Estonian specificities and very considerable experience with minority issues. OSCE took its task seriously and raised certain objections to Estonian policies. But Estonian state officials were extremely savvy in presenting minorities as a 'security threat' to the Estonian nation, in ways that responded to European concerns with security and commitments to the nation state system. They were thus able to persuade the European Union to approve Estonia's State Programme: Integration in Estonian Society, 2000–2007, in which support of minority programmes was subordinated to national 'integration', despite the OSCE's clearly expressed reservations. Even this brief account hints at the conflicting priorities of two different European agencies, and the far from foregone conclusions in conditionality decisions.

In sum, states applying for membership as part of the enlargement process were asked to meet a much higher standard of compliance on minority rights than existing member states had ever been able to agree upon. This remains a fact, even though the Estonian example demonstrates how an applicant state might negotiate this requirement by appealing to other 'European' values and concerns. Although the worsening conditions for minorities in the past two decades in many post-socialist societies, including a number of the applicant states, seemed to justify these more stringent standards, the glaring discrepancy generated numerous complaints about 'hypocrisy' and 'double standards'. Echoing the call for *universal* obligations (a demand championed by internationalist organizations in the interwar years, too), human and minority rights activists nonetheless also stressed the importance of applying this leverage to states for minorities' benefit. Although there has been no public recanting, it looks as if the moral argument against special obligations for newly joining members could not forever be resisted. By the time of the 1997 Treaty of Amsterdam, the EU had quietly dropped the minority provision for *future* candidates, now defining the 'common values' of member states as 'liberty, democracy, respect for human rights and fundamental freedoms and the rule of law' (Article 6[1]), and expressly excluding the phrase 'respect for and protection of minorities'. Yet because many European bureaucrats and policy makers explicitly saw minority protection as central to a transmission of European democratic norms and values, it retained its rhetorical prominence throughout the enlargement process (Hughes and Sasse 2003: 11).

Audit and Accountability in Europe

At least two wider frameworks of narratives and processes suggest themselves for making sense of the kinds of supranational involvement that I have outlined. The first is the framework of *empire*. Currently, this framework is dominant, but its capacity to illuminate depends greatly on how the concept 'empire' is defined and used. As readers will have grasped from my earlier comments, I am sceptical of the easy recourse to this concept: the 're-emergence of empire' is too often presented as simply self-evident, distracting us from the important task of grasping the *specificity* of changing legal, political and economic relations between 'the international', states and various categories of subjects in particular historical moments and contexts. Of course, the imperial metaphor is not always ill-chosen; as a description of America's global ambitions and strategies in recent years, I find it relatively persuasive. As a framework for understanding extra-state intervention in minority rights and protections within Europe, however, 'empire' is misleading.

The second framework I will call, for want of a better term, *the new internationality*. It is a framework my current research compels me to try to develop, in order to make more penetrating theoretical sense of League of Nations processes around states and minorities. Foucaldian understandings of modern modalities of power – which are, in part, Weberian formulations read through a Foucaldian lens – are my theoretical starting point, and like others inspired by this work, I am concerned with bureaucratic practices and their effects on both categories and subject formation. However, whereas most analysts have retained Foucault's own preoccupation, in his studies of bio power, with the circulation of power between a state and its populations, I ask how practices and relations *beyond* the state are also implicated in the creation of populations. Taking some cues from my study of interwar international institutions as well as certain interventions in the debates on globalization (e.g. Sassen 2000) and critical theories of international law and practice (e.g. Brubaker 1992, 1996; Berman 1993), I am interested in the reformulation of relations between states, subjects and 'the international' in early, key moments. In particular, my concern is with the impact of this post-imperial reformulation on subjectivities and conceptions of citizenship, citizens' and other subjects' understandings of 'rights' and their senses of 'entitlement'. Thus, the present article explores parallels between two historical moments initiated by imperial collapse, the establishing of a 'new world order' and the emergence of new forms and practices of internationality. I emphasize the contested quality of the emerging reconfigurations, and the productive dimensions of the new international practices, with their profound implications for the construction and consolidation of both political/legal categories – 'minority', 'majority', 'state', among others – and the ratification or denial of particular instantiations.

In the space left to me, I wish to bring my discussion of the supervised state into (brief) engagement with a third – I believe, complementary – framework. Recent work on audit and accountability within European institutions – that is, both of European nation states and of 'Europe' as a supranational entity – has been similarly focused on questions of governmentality and subjectification (e.g. Rose 1992, 1999; Power 1994, 1997; Law 1999). While the introduction of audit mechanisms into higher education provided a key impetus, anthropologists are increasingly engaged, along with sociologists, political theorists and management theorists, in the investigation of 'audit cultures' in a wide array of institutions (see especially Shore and Wright 1997, 1999; Strathern 2000). Apparent parallels between the supervision processes I have highlighted and ever-proliferating audit processes are worth examining a little more closely. The conditionalities that the European Union has imposed on applicant countries are, to a large extent, dictated by the project of 'harmonization' of the laws and institutions of European member states, although the *additional* requirements for these countries to demonstrate their commitment to democracy, respect for human rights and minority rights betray convictions about their inadequate 'Europeanness'. In fact, it is the *methods* used that would seem to place European enlargement within the broader framework of the contemporary drive for accountability: I include here both the European Union's monitoring of applicant states' efforts to fulfil those conditions, and the task enthusiastically embraced by European NGOs, notably by the Open Society Institute in Budapest, to 'monitor the monitors' (Open Society Institute 2002; Hughes and Sasse 2003).

One could argue, as I do, for a *genealogical* relationship between the monitoring of EU conditionalities and the League's interwar minorities treaties supervision, in Foucault's sense of a historically prior institution or set of practices that made present institutions and practices thinkable and thus possible. At the same time, the rationales and logics of the two accountabilities are not identical. The audit and accountability literature stresses the origins of auditing fever in the turn to neoliberalism, at global as well as national levels, since the 1970s (Shore and Wright 2000: 58). Manifesting a conceptual migration from the domain of finance, audit reflects a concern with 'value for money'. More potently, it links concerns about economic efficiency with those about ethical practice; in Marilyn Strathern's crisp phrasing, audit is 'where the financial and the moral meet' (Strathern 2000: 1). Although the League's minorities treaties supervision took shape in an economic environment dominated by capitalism, the rationale for supervision was not financial. More, even, than the protection of minorities, the ultimate rationale was security: the prevention of interstate conflict. Having said this, the preoccupation with potential conflicts between states, and the conceptualization of minorities as a security 'risk' or 'problem' for the nation state that Feldman (2005a, 2005b) has similarly observed in contemporary accession negotiations, seems to represent a continuity between the interwar and post-1989 regimes. Minorities regimes have focused on security rather than economic efficiency. These two distinct concerns have nonetheless prompted a common response: institutional practices of accountability. Although predating the wave of audit processes set in motion by financial imperatives, supranational scrutiny of laws and policies pertaining to minorities has evolved over the century, and current monitoring practices form part of the wider network of accountability practices within European institutions.

Indeterminacies of Supervision

A tone of moral reproach runs through much of the literature upon which this article draws, and to some extent, in my article, too, around the *selective*, rather than *universal*, nature of the scrutiny that supranational regimes have undertaken on behalf of minorities. However this selectivity has been rationalized, one cannot get round the double standard that it manifests, nor the fact that the more privileged, more powerful states have always been the ones able to avoid scrutiny. The League of Nations' minorities regime arguably foundered on this inequality of treatment of putatively equal states; the European Union, in some respects repeating the same mistake, was forced ultimately to back down on the minority rights element of the Copenhagen criteria when inconsistency within its own house was revealed. The case of minorities serves as well as any in demonstrating the pragmatic – and not simply the moral – justifications for a principle of equality between states at the level of international relations.

Asymmetry of treatment has not, though, been the only grounds of resistance. The argument of state *sovereignty* is also ubiquitous. Historically, the two arguments have been inextricable: states compelled to sign minorities treaties after the First World War resented such infringements on their newly won sovereignty; that other states were not so bound made them even more difficult to bear. Selective enforcement remains a key complaint today whenever some supranational entity ('the international community', NATO, 'The Allies') decides to violate a state's sovereignty, as in, for instance, the bombing of Serbia or the invasion of Iraq. Understandably so; rarely is the state singled out for the designated offence uniquely guilty. "Why us?" they protest. "Why not them? Why not yourselves?" Advocates of intervention do not necessarily deny that international pressure is applied selectively, even if the justifications offered by a Michael Ignatieff (2004) overlap only partially with those of a George W. Bush. And while unequal treatment of states by larger supranational entities is unavoidable, inasmuch as it expresses a highly unequal world in which complaints of double standards will inevitably continue to muddy the moral waters, state sovereignty itself – its nature, scope, limits – is also at issue. Apart from what is occurring in the explicitly political sphere of interstate relations and international collective action – in UN meeting rooms in Geneva and New York, in EU forums in Brussels and Strasbourg, and at the alternative globalization movements' annual European Social Forum in Florence, Paris, London, Athens – economic, political, technological, even environmental dimensions of globalization are forcing a reconsideration of the nature and limits of state sovereignty.

Examining responses from *beyond* the state to minority situations *within* a state necessarily involves us in debates about the ethics and politics of state sovereignty, sovereign equality and humanitarian intervention. It is right that arguments for and against supranational engagement (ranging from supervision to military intervention) be explored rigorously at the level of moral principle as well as of political efficacy (see, e.g. International Commission on Intervention and State Sovereignty 2001; Wilson 2005). I want to close my discussion, however, by taking a different tack, reflecting in a more open-ended way on the complicated politics of supranational supervision. I am mindful here of insights developed during previous projects concerning the immensely variable purposes for which rights and culture claims can be mobilized, the uncertain outcomes and the potential unintended consequences (Cowan, Dembour and Wilson 2001; Cowan 2001, 2003b; Povinelli 2002). Supranational or international supervision involves, moreover, an array of actors, and any analysis needs to acknowledge their varying positions, interests, identifications and indeed, fantasies.

As an argument (whether legal, moral or pragmatic), 'state sovereignty' leads us quite directly into supervision's indeterminacies. One important source of indeterminacy is the paradox of the state's position, from the perspective of its subjects. Simply put, in contexts of supranational supervision the state is both subordinate and superordinate. At this point, we cannot avoid entering a symbolic terrain of the *political imaginary*, where we encounter processes of fantasy, including identification, projection and mirroring.[8] One way that these processes operate is through the ubiquitous anthropomorphizing of states (or similarly, countries and nations) within Western political discourse, evident in the common practice, among lay persons as much as diplomats, of speaking of 'England' or 'France' or 'Greece' as sentient, acting persons, and moreover, as gendered persons: with 'her' borders, 'her' citizens. Conceiving the state as an *individual* writ large has a long pedigree; it was the naturalized, taken-for-granted personhood projected onto territorial and political unities that Richard Handler (1988) rightly flagged and urged anthropologists to examine and deconstruct. And certainly, the public representation, no less than the diplomatic discourse, of interstate relations throughout the twentieth century has retained this anthropomorphic aspect, observable in the preoccupation with a cluster of concepts that delineate and locate persons vis-à-vis others: 'honour', 'status' and 'respect', as well as their transgressive opposites: 'insult' and 'humiliation' (Cowan 2003a).

'Double standards', in respect to the minority standards required of states, index an inequality at the level of interstate relations that may be easily represented as relations between gendered human beings; political cartoons employ this grammar on a daily basis. Representations of states as persons have an obvious ideological dimension: in Althusser's terms, they interpellate national subjects/citizens, calling upon them to identify *with* – perhaps even *as* – the figure of the state.[9] To the extent that subjects/citizens recognize themselves in the state, or at least in the community that the state figure *embodies*, they are likely also to recognize, in another sense, the state's lesser position – its literal *subordination* – vis-à-vis 'stronger' states, and even to identify with the state's 'experience' of weakness, humiliation and injustice. Indeed, this is an enduring theme of nationalist cultural production. For instance, Greek vernacular political discourse has long employed an imagery of interstate relations that is, perhaps surprisingly, both conspiratorial and comic: of gigantic Great Powers pulling the strings of tiny but pugnacious Balkan nations. This imagery, in turn, builds on an earlier Greek nationalist appropriation of the peripatetic Ottoman popular theatre that, with Rabelaisian humour, performed tales of the downtrodden wielding proverbial 'weapons of the weak' against their masters.[10] In colonialism, neocolonialism and military occupation, too, nothing rallies a divided population like a more powerful enemy; when 'he' or 'they' threaten 'us', such battle is infused with the character of David facing Goliath. When Turkish, Serbian, Greek or Romanian politicians, left-wing as much as right-wing, protest EU regulation by describing it as 'imperialism', they reinscribe current struggles in terms of familiar political imaginaries, continuously revitalizing them.

State citizens/subjects are themselves differentiated, however, in ways that affect and potentially disrupt political identification. Those whom the state identifies as 'minorities' or somehow as internal 'others' may, even so, identify with the state, and with the state's own predicament in the interstate realm. Alternatively, or – in a more complex way – *simultaneously*, they may resist or reject this identification. That repudiation may be a response by certain citizens/subjects to actions by 'the state', including their own mistreatment, misrepresentation and exclusion. In such cases, international supervision is perceived very differently. For those who face state authoritarianism and violence, or those who speak on their behalf (such as local, national and international

NGOs, lawyers, political activists and other concerned individuals), international supervision is frequently welcomed as a means to compel accountability from a state that would otherwise act with impunity.

The fact that in supranational supervision in this region, these two unequally structured interactions – between a supranational body and minority states, on the one hand, and on the other, between minority states and their own minorities – are concurrent and interlocking, with the state simultaneously subordinate and superordinate, makes for a complicated politics at the local level while also facilitating new opportunities for minorities. Thus, Turkish citizens campaigning for prison reform, for measures addressing violence against women and for Kurdish political rights chose, in some cases, to intensify their efforts precisely in light of EU scrutiny of Turkey's human rights policies in the lead-up to decisions about Turkey's EU membership. Similarly, Roma activists in Hungary and Slovakia have used the accession requirements around minority rights to render visible their fight against discrimination, as well as to put pressure on their national governments.

Such strategies have not infrequently been effective, but there is always a possibility of backlash against such organizations and the categories and groups for whom they speak. While this may originate with the state, it does not always. Retaliation may come from groups – often deeply though mysteriously linked to the state apparatus, yet in other cases beyond its control – which take it upon themselves to 'defend the fatherland' (or motherland) against those they deem 'internal enemies' or 'national traitors' who provoke the state's 'humiliation' by calling upon the international community to discipline it. Such hostile reactions were no less a problem in the past. Officials in the League of Nations' Minorities Section were acutely conscious that an overzealous approach on their part could backfire precisely on the minorities they were charged to protect. In his account of his many years working in, and ultimately directing, the Minorities Section, the Spaniard Pablo de Azcárate responded to criticisms that the League had failed in its minority protection work because it was too conciliatory toward governments, at the expense of minorities:

> Readers of the story of Don Quixote will remember that as soon as the latter had been dubbed a knight by the innkeeper, he set off for his native village for a supply of money, clean shirts, and a squire to attend him. Passing by a thicket, he heard the sound of doleful cries and hastened forward to 'redress the wrong', in accordance with the laws of the order of knighthood which he had just entered. The cries proceeded from a young boy of fifteen named Andrew, who John Haldudo, his master, had tied to an oak tree and was beating mercilessly because the lad had claimed

certain wages which were owing to him. Don Quixote, as a champion of justice, forced Haldudo at the point of the lance to untie the boy and to promise him his just dues. But no sooner had Don Quixote left them than Haldudo, far from fulfilling his promise, tied the boy up to the oak tree again, and gave him twice as many lashes as he had originally intended. This was recounted to Don Quixote by Andrew himself when the two met again later. 'And now I may thank you for this, for had you rid on your journey, and neither meddled nor made, seeing nobody sent for you, and it was none of your business, my master, perhaps, had been satisfied with giving me ten or twenty lashes, and after that would have paid me what he owed me; but you was [sic] so huffy, and called him so many names, that it made him mad, and so he vented all his spite against you upon my poor back, as soon as yours was turned, insomuch that I fear I shall never be my own man again.' (Azcárate 1945: 134–35)

Azcárate meant this as a cautionary tale to those 'called upon to assist in the process by which the world will pass from nationalism to supernationalism' (Azcárate 1945: 135). It was not a call to do nothing, but rather, to acknowledge the delicacy and complexity of the project, as well as the potential for unintended consequences of even the most righteous efforts.

Acknowledgements

This article has benefited greatly from the comments of Keith Brown, Marie-Bénédicte Dembour, Greg Feldman, Anne Griffiths, Laurie Kain Hart, Elizabeth Kirtsoglou, Yael Navaro-Yashin and Richard Wilson. I am grateful also to panel audiences and fellow speakers at the American Anthropological Association meetings in Chicago (November 2003), the workshop on 'Developing Anthropology of Law in a Transnational World: Governmentality, the State and Transnational Processes of Law' in Edinburgh (June 2004) and the European Association of Social Anthropologists meetings in Vienna (September 2004).

Notes

1. The countries admitted in 2004 were Cyprus, the Czech Republic, Estonia, Hungary, Latvia, Lithuania, Malta, Poland, the Slovak Republic and Slovenia. Bulgaria and Romania were admitted in 2007; Turkey, Croatia and the Republic of Macedonia are Candidate Countries, while Albania, Bosnia and Herzegovina, Serbia and Montenegro, and Kosovo under UN Security Council Resolution 1244 are named as Potential Candidate Countries.

2. I develop the analysis of the supervised state, and the critique of some aspects of the anthropology of the state literature, in a related paper entitled 'The Supervised State' (Cowan 2007). Some portions of the first section of the present article first appeared in published form in that 2007 article.

3. In respect to the Polish Minorities Treaty, the first to be negotiated and approved at Versailles and the prototype of all the rest, the Polish government objected to the proposed treaty on the grounds that it seemed to sanction 'a state within the state' and thus a threat to Polish sovereignty. The object of these anxieties appears to have been the Jews, despite the fact that the territorial ambitions of the Jewish Zionists who were already active did not concern Poland. As a result of these negotiations, the category term '*les nationalités*' ('*nationalities*') was abandoned in favour of the term '*les minorités*' ('*minorities*') in the treaties' formal wording. With this simple decision, the term 'minority' took on a new, subtly different nuance: an internationally sanctioned and politically consolidated category whose primary reference was to the nation state in which the minority held citizenship, rather than the one to whom he/she 'racially' belonged (in the traditional terms, the new meaning emphasized affiliation to the 'host', rather than the 'home', nation state).

4. By 1924, fifteen states had accepted minority obligations: Albania, Austria, Bulgaria, Czechoslovakia, Estonia, Finland (in respect to the Aaland Islands), Greece, Hungary, Latvia, Lithuania, Poland, Romania, Turkey, Yugoslavia and Germany (in respect to Upper Silesia).

5. I adopt this evocative phrase in the present essay. Additional key works in the prolific literature on the League of Nations include Mair (1928); Macartney (1934); Azcárate (1945); Bagley (1950); Mazower (1997); Jackson Preece (1998).

6. According to the agreed conditions of receivability (Mair 1928: 69), petitions:
   1. must have in view the protection of minorities in accordance with the treaties;
   2. in particular, they must not be submitted in the form of a request for a severance of political relations between the minority in question and the state of which it forms a part;
   3. must not emanate from an anonymous or unauthenticated source;
   4. must abstain from violent language;
   5. must contain information or refer to facts that have not recently been the subject of a petition submitted to the ordinary procedure.

   These were conceived by the architects of the procedure and are described by most scholars as 'merely formal' rather than substantive conditions. My article exploring the use of the fourth condition (Cowan 2003a) demonstrates that, in actual practice, this was not always the case.

7. For critical discussions of the 'empire' debate, see e.g. Kelly (2003); Purdy (2003); Nederveen Pieterse (2004) and Kalb (2005).

8. I draw attention here to the groundbreaking work of Yael Navaro-Yashin (2002) and Begoña Aretxaga (2003, 2005) in their focus on the dimension of 'fantasy' in the anthropological study of politics and the state. The theme is

further developed in a special issue of *Anthropological Theory* dedicated to Aretxaga's legacy (Navaro-Yashin and Cowan 2007).

9. As many scholars of European nationalisms have noticed, national ideologies often use kinship imagery, not infrequently representing the nation and/or the state as 'mother' or 'father'. Among many examples, see Anthias and Yuval-Davis (1989); Yuval-Davis (1997); Navaro-Yashin (2002).

10. In the tradition of Turkish shadow puppetry, the hunchbacked, 'simple' but cunning anti-hero, Karagöz, challenges the authorities through hilariously inept but occasionally successful tricks and subversion. By the eighteenth century, the form began to be Hellenized. Greek nationalists transformed Karagöz into Karaghiozis and made him a specifically Greek anti-hero (and in some cases, a proper hero), anarchically resisting the plans of the Turkish deputy (Myrsiades 1986). In essence, the characters were recast to personify Greece and the Ottoman Empire and tell a nationalist story.

References

Ackerman, A. 2000. *Making Peace Prevail: Preventing Violent Conflict in Macedonia*. Syracuse, NY: Syracuse University Press.

Anthias, F. and N. Yuval-Davis. 1989. *Woman-Nation State*. London: Palgrave Macmillan.

Aretxaga, B. 2003. 'Maddening States', *Annual Review of Anthropology* 32: 393–410.

———. 2005. *States of Terror: Begoña Aretxaga's Essays*. Ed. Joseba Zulaika. Reno: Center for Basque Studies, University of Nevada Press.

Azcárate, P. de. 1945. *League of Nations and National Minorities: An Experiment*. Washington, D.C.: Carnegie Endowment for International Peace.

Bagley, T.H. 1950. *General Principles and Problems in the International Protection of Minorities*. Geneva: Imprimeries Populaires.

Berman, N. 1993. '"But the Alternative Is Despair": Nationalism and the Modernist Renewal of International Law', *Harvard Law Review* 106(8): 1792–903.

Bose, S. 2002. *Bosnia after Dayton: Nationalist Partition and International Intervention*. London: Hurst and Co.

Brubaker, R. 1992. *Citizenship and Nationhood in France and Germany*. Cambridge, MA, and London: Harvard University Press.

———. 1996. *Nationalism Reframed: Nationhood and the National Question in the New Europe*. Cambridge: Cambridge University Press.

Claude, I. 1955. *National Minorities: An International Problem*. Cambridge, MA: Harvard University Press.

Cohen, L.J. 1998. 'Whose Bosnia? The Politics of Nation Building', *Current History* 97(617): 103–12.

Coles, K. 2004. 'Election Day: The Construction of Democracy through Technique', *Cultural Anthropology* 19(4): 551–80.

Cowan, J.K. 2001. 'Ambiguities of an Emancipatory Discourse: The Making of a Macedonian Minority in Greece', in J.K. Cowan, M.-B. Dembour and R.A.

Wilson (eds), *Culture and Rights: Anthropological Perspectives*. Cambridge: Cambridge University Press, 152–76.

———. 2003a. 'Who's Afraid of Violent Language? Honour, Sovereignty and Claims-making in the League of Nations'. Special Issue on 'Violence and Language', *Anthropological Theory* 3(3): 271–91.

———. 2003b. 'The Uncertain Political Limits of Cultural Claims: Minority Rights Politics in Southeast Europe', in R.A. Wilson and J.P. Mitchell (eds), *Human Rights in Global Perspective: Anthropological Studies of Rights, Claims and Entitlements*. London and New York: Routledge, 140–62.

———. 2007. 'The Supervised State', *Identities: Global Studies in Culture and Power* 14(5): 545–78.

Cowan, J.K., M.-B. Dembour and R.A. Wilson. 2001. 'Introduction', in J.K. Cowan, M.-B. Dembour and R.A. Wilson (eds), *Culture and Rights: Anthropological Perspectives*. Cambridge: Cambridge University Press, 1–26.

Feldman, G. 2005a. 'Estranged States: Diplomacy and Containment of National Minorities in Europe', *Anthropological Theory* 5(3), 219–46.

———. 2005b. 'Essential Crises: A Performative Approach to Migrants, Minorities and the European State-System', *Anthropological Quarterly* 78(1): 213–46.

Fink, C. 1995. 'The League of Nations and the Minorities Question', *World Affairs* 157(4): 197–205.

Giddens, A. 1985. *The Nation State and Violence*. Cambridge: Polity Press.

Handler, R. 1988. *Nationalism and the Politics of Culture in Quebec*. Madison: University of Wisconsin Press.

Hayden, R. 2002. 'Dictatorships of Virtue? States, NGOs and the Imposition of Democratic Values', *Harvard International Review* 24(2): 56–62.

Hughes, J. and Sasse, G. 2003. 'Monitoring the Monitors: EU Enlargement Conditionality and Minority Protection in the CEECs', *Journal on Ethnopolitics and Minority Issues in Europe* 1: 1–38.

Ignatieff, M. 2003. *Empire Lite: Nation-Building in Bosnia, Kosovo and Afghanistan*. London: Vintage.

———. 2004. *The Lesser Evil: Political Ethics in an Age of Terror*. Princeton, NJ: Princeton University Press.

International Commission on Intervention and State Sovereignty. 2001. *The Responsibility to Protect*. Ottawa: International Development Research Centre.

Jackson Preece, J. 1998. *National Minorities and the European Nation States System*. Oxford: Oxford University Press.

Kalb, D. 2005. 'From Flows to Violence: Politics and Knowledge in the Debates on Globalization and Empire', *Anthropological Theory* 5(2): 176–204.

Kelly, J.D. 2003. 'U.S. Power, after 9/11 and before It: If Not an Empire, Then What?' *Public Culture* 15(2): 347–69.

Knaus, G. and F. Martin. 2003. 'Travails of the European Raj', *Journal of Democracy* 14(3): 60–74.

Ladas, S. 1932. *The Exchanges of Minorities: Bulgaria, Greece and Turkey*. New York: Macmillan.

Law, J. (ed.). 1999. *Actor Network Theory and After*. Oxford: Blackwell.

League of Nations. 1929. *Protection of Linguistic, Racial or Religious Minorities by the League of Nations: Resolutions and Extracts from the Minutes of the Council,*

Resolutions and Reports Adopted by the Assembly, Relating to the Procedure to be Followed in Questions Concerning the Protection of Minorities (Document C.24. M.18.1929.1). Geneva: Series of League of Nations Publications.

Macartney, C.A. 1934. *National States and National Minorities.* London: Oxford University Press.

Mair, L. 1928. *The Protection of Minorities: The Working and Scope of the Minorities Treaties under the League of Nations.* London: Christopher's.

Mallaby, S. 2002. 'The Reluctant Imperialist: Terrorism, Failed States and the Case for American Empire', *Foreign Affairs* (March/April).

Mazower, M. 1997. 'Minorities and the League of Nations in Interwar Europe', *Daedalus* 126(2): 47–63.

———. 1998. *Dark Continent: Europe's Twentieth Century.* London: Penguin.

Monnet, J. 1978. *Memoirs.* London: Collins.

Myrsiades, L. 1986. 'Adaptation and Change: The Origins of Karaghiozis in Greece', *Turcica* 18: 119–36.

Navaro-Yashin, Y. 2002. *Faces of the State: Secularism and Public Life in Turkey.* Princeton, NJ: Princeton University Press.

Navaro-Yashin, Y. and J.K. Cowan (eds). 2007. 'Phantasmatic Realities, Passionate States', Special Issue in Memory of Begoña Aretxaga, *Anthropological Theory* 7(1).

Nederveen Pieterse, J. 2004. *Globalization or Empire?* New York: Routledge.

Open Society Institute (OSI). 2002. *Monitoring the EU Accession Process: Minority Protection (2002).* EU Accession Monitoring Program, Open Society Institute: Budapest.

Povinelli, E. 2002. *The Cunning of Recognition: Indigenous Alterities and the Making of Australian Multiculturalism.* Durham, NC: Duke University Press.

Power, M. 1994. *The Audit Explosion.* London: Demos.

———. 1997. *The Audit Society: Rituals of Verification.* Oxford: Oxford University Press.

Purdy, J. 2003. 'Liberal Empire: Assessing the Arguments', *Ethics and International Affairs* 17(2): 35–48.

Ranshofen-Wertheimer, E.F. 1945. *The International Secretariat: A Great Experiment in International Administration.* Washington, D.C.: Carnegie Endowment for International Peace.

Robinson, J., O. Karbach, M.M. Laserson, N. Robinson and M. Vichniak. 1943. *Were the Minorities Treaties a Failure?* New York: Institute of Jewish Affairs of the American Jewish Congress and the World Jewish Congress.

Rose, N. 1992. 'Governing the Enterprising Self', in P. Heelas and P. Morris (eds), *The Values of the Enterprise Culture: The Moral Debate.* London: Routledge, 141–64.

———. 1999. *Powers of Freedom: Reframing Political Thought.* Cambridge: Cambridge University Press.

Rozakis, C. 2000. 'The Protection of Human Rights in Europe: Evolving Trends and Prospects', Discussion Paper No. 1. The European Institute: The Hellenic Observatory. London: The London School of Economics and Political Science.

Sassen, S. 2000. 'Spatialities and Temporalities of the Global: Elements for a Theorization', *Public Culture* 12(1): 215–32.

Shore, C. and S. Wright. 1999. 'Audit Culture and Anthropology: Neoliberalism in British Higher Education', *Journal of the Royal Anthropological Institute* 5(4): 557–75.

———. 2000. 'Coercive Accountability: The Rise of Audit Culture in Higher Education', in M. Strathern (ed.), *Audit Cultures: Anthropological Studies in Accountability, Ethics and the Academy.* London: Routledge, 57–89.

——— (eds). 1997. *Anthropology of Policy: Critical Perspectives on Governance and Power.* London: Routledge.

Strathern, M. (ed.). 2000. *Audit Cultures: Anthropological Studies in Accountability, Ethics and the Academy.* London: Routledge.

Wilson, R.A. (ed.). 2005. *Human Rights in the 'War on Terror'.* Cambridge: Cambridge University Press.

Yuval-Davis, N. 1997. *Gender and Nation.* London: Sage.

4

THE GLOBALIZATION OF FATWAS AMIDST THE TERROR WARS AGAINST PLURALISM

Upendra Baxi

Preparatory Remarks

This essay aspires to explore a difficult terrain, namely the place and future of legal pluralism amidst the current ongoing global wars of, and on, 'terror'.[1] It raises a whole range of discrete and desperate questions: How may pluralist readings go beyond the understanding that terrorism 'is not a single causally coherent phenomenon?' (C. Tilly 2004: 12). In what directions may deft legal pluralist moves comprehend 'terror' outside the state-centralist perspectives? In what ways may these further enable us to grasp the multifarious constitutions of violent subjectivities and the new forms of institutionalization of biopolitics that these wars now proliferate? Further, how may we construct the futures of legal pluralism in the contexts of these two wars? How does the ongoing destruction of *jus cosmopoliticum* endanger 'substantive international law as a source of legal pluralism' (K. von Benda-Beckmann 2001: 34–36)? How may we speak to the discrepant discourse that celebrates in the very first years of this century the Golden Jubilee of the Universal Declaration of Human Rights and at the same moment, also ushers in an era of its recessional futures? How may legal pluralist traditions of learning and research begin to ethnographically engage the consequentialist claims that justify feats of state terrorism as jurisgenrative?[2] How may pluralist traditions of knowing grasp, in turn, the global subaltern justifications for the texts of 'terror'?

As if these questions were not enough, both the 'terror' wars thrive on multiple ambiguities of the term 'war'. The 'war *on* terror' mobilizes the imagery of wars waged on a host of other social evils, such as 'war' on poverty, drug trafficking, AIDS, and cyberporn; it also presents an agenda of international cooperation concerning counterterrorism measures (aimed at such problems as illicit arms traffic, provision of mercenaries to promote regime change, hostage-taking, and money laundering for mercenary 'terrorist' purposes). But as hostile counterresponse to 'war *of* terror' it also signifies much more by way of consolidating the New Empire (see Hardt and Negri 2000, 2004). It harnesses the enormous military power of a solitary superpower and, in concert with the coalition of willing states, proceeds to use vast quotients of unsanctioned force to promote regime change (in effect, into free market democracies). In the process, it blatantly recomposes international law and even the standards of international humanitarian law. All this is said to be necessary and justified to combat the 'war *of* terror', now understood as 'the deliberate killing of randomly selected non-combatants for political ends' so as 'to promote a political outcome by spreading terror and demoralisation throughout a population' (Jordan 2002). This war is, in the oft-quoted words of M. Cherif Bassiouni, 'a strategy of violence designed to achieve a power-outcome, propagandize a cause, or inflict harm for vengeful political purposes' (2002: 83, 84; see also Tiefenbrun 2003). Any endorsement by legal pluralists of this description must necessarily acknowledge that it would extend in fullness also to feats of 'war *on terrorism*', as waged in Afghanistan and currently in Iraq. Deep legal pluralism challenges any hegemonic enterprise at 'defining' terrorism.

Messianic politics inflects both the terror wars. Both lend themselves to description in terms of the millenarian jehadi global politics. No reader of President Bush's Second Inaugural Address[3] can fail to sense this quasi-religious flavour and fervour that matches the militant Islamic 'jehadi' insurgent politics. Pluralist approaches would not present the 'war *of* terror' as a species of premodern quasi-religious political violence contrasting with the 'war *on* terror' as an action providing a platform for postmodern global secularizing politics (Philpott 2002). Nor would these authorize the presentation of the 'war *on* terror' in crude hegemonizing terms such as the 'clash of civilizations' (cf. An-Naim 2002: 162; Alamdari 2003; Mamdani 2004). Further, legal pluralist modes of reading texts on both the terror wars undermine any ethical defence of American exceptionalism as constituting a singular ethical burden of 'American power in a violent world' (Elshtain 2003: 169–70). Likewise, Shariah pluralism interrogates, and even condemns, the moral logics of acts of mass terrorism. Pluralist perspectives thus lift us beyond the Manichaean discourse. Even so, in these troubled times, any construction of discursive equal 'level playing field' for reading the texts, and critical events, authored by some salient perpetrators and exponents of 'war *of* terror'[4] remains a hazardous enterprise. In offering an ethnographic understanding of terror wars, descriptive relativism remains a troubled virtue.

Likewise, the very notion of anthropology as 'intervention' remains also an agonizing open question, given the fact that some practices of doing anthropology were deeply implicated in the performances of the old 'Cold War'. The reinvention since then of jural and social pluralisms may, one hopes, prevent a similar emergence in these halcyon days of new 'terror' wars. But how may this task ever be fully accomplished unless anthropologists and pluralists more reflexively address their vocation in the new moments of 'terror' already thus constituted?

Understanding 'Terror'

A threshold problem concerns choice of narrative strategies. The binary distinction between insurgent as opposed to state 'terror' misleads (Badiou 2003: 144). Badiou, referring to the Jacobins during the French Revolution who 'had no problem in declaring themselves "terrorists"', thinks it remarkable that 'the word "terrorism", which clearly qualified a particular figure of state power, has come, little by little, to signify exactly the contrary' (see also C. Tilly 2004: 8–9). But the constitutive ambiguities of 'terror/terrorism' invite further close attention to other sites of terror, if only because political practices of terror do not exhaust all varieties of 'terrorisms' and are not the only practices of terror in the life in society.

For example, Claudia Card (2003: 179) insists that we ought to recognize multiple terrorisms of familial and marital spaces, manifest in 'rape, both stranger and acquaintance rape, with which women and girls are left to cope routinely, even in many states that are considered relatively secure from external attack'. Likewise, deep ecology activism speaks of 'eco-terrorism', of the contemporary forms of global capitalism and of the militant animal rights movements retaliating against forms of technoscience 'terrorism' that impose mindless cruelty on sentient experimental animals. The violated of Bhopal, Ogoniland and other catastrophes speak of the planned productions by 'terrorist' multinational corporations. New human rights constituencies such as the indigenous peoples, lesbigay transgender communities and people living with disabilities have yet to christen their violent stigmatization as a structural instance of state/civil terror. Multiple terrorisms that go beyond the manifestly political form operate at an everyday level in the family and the marketplace as well as the domains of faith and worship, learning and education, profession and avocation, technoscience regimes, and governance of sexuality and of 'technologies of self'.[5] Studies in legal pluralism have yet to find their epistemic niche in these discourses.[6]

Studies in legal pluralism have so far have, some notable exceptions apart, insufficiently addressed ethnographies of 'terror'.[7] No doubt, pluralist anthropological studies of 'authority and ambiguity' (Harris 1996), legal pluralism (Griffiths 2002), anthropology of colonial law (Baxi 2003 and the literature cited therein), the emergent fields of anthropology of contemporary globalization (see Coombe 1998; Gessner and Budak 1998; Burawoy et al. 2000; Nader 2002), sociology of ethnic conflicts (Horowitz 1985, 2001; Chua 2003; Mamdani 2004), and feminist and critical race-theory approaches deal with varieties of violence and some contemporary forms of production of human rightlessness. We learn from these that behind every system of sanctioned violence lie congeries of unsanctioned violence, and that the distinction between violence sanctioned by the law and violence beyond the law (Derrida 2002; Tuitt 2004) is often illusory. The situation concerning people's law formations is no different.[8] The mission of 'terror', state or nonstate, is to construct 'communities of danger' and of fear (Mehta and Chatterji 2001). Persons become marked subjects of the practices of political terror by the fact of what Heidegger named as the 'thrownness of being into this world'. Yet active agency operates even within these reconstructions of thrownness (cf. Walter 1969: 335–44; Guha 1983; Baxi 1985: 125–30). Talk of legal pluralism and human rights, in the main, presents narratives of varieties of thrownness and agency, the ways of violent subjection and resistance (cf. Asad 1997).

Justifiable concerns, I note at the outset, attend the discursive introduction of the term 'terror' in describing social and political violence. The terms 'terror', 'terrorist' and 'terrorism', as Alain Badiou suggests in the aftermath of 9/11 (a phenomenon that he describes as the 'crime of New York'), remain 'intrinsically propagandist'. They offer 'no neutral readability'. Even worse, this language 'dispenses with all reasoned examination of political situations, their causes and their consequences' (Badiou 2003: 7). And writing prior to 9/11, Cynthia Mahmood insightfully suggests that 'anthropology as intervention' ought to put into question the epistemic violence of 'terror' narratives.[9] 'Ethnographers of conscience', she suggests, should develop 'reasonable ethnographic assessment' of the perpetrators of 'terror' by developing 'face-to-face knowledge' and 'grassroots perspective'. Ethnography of 'terror' then invites rather different and distinct tasks compared with the description of combinatory violence of state and peoples' law formations in their culturally specific habitats. I say this, following Badiou, because languages of terrorism determine the 'subjects' and 'their supporting predicates' and determine 'the sequence of response'.[10] Understanding 'terror' as a circuit of violent nihilisms (cf. Badiou 2003: 38–53) further imperils our understandings of legal pluralisms. Meanwhile, 'reasonable ethnographic assessment' also enables us to pursue the tasks of anthropological exploration of what John Rawls (1999) names as the 'foreign policy of liberal' and 'well-ordered' peoples directed against 'outlaw' peoples and societies. The central question then concerns not so much our preferred ways of understanding legal pluralisms but rather how these leave intact the structures of global violence and the carriers of costs of legal pluralism.

The Phenomenon of Globalization of Fatwas

The events of 9/11, with their equally cruel aftermaths and aftershocks, pose the narrative risk of constructions of 'terror' as if it lacked any prior histories. The risk is grave indeed when the 'war on terror' stands perceived as a response to a 'war against pluralism' (Phillips 2003: 101–13). We need to recall that both these 'wars' present human histories with a specific date. I do not revisit in this presentation the many histories of 'terror' (see Laquer 1977, 1999; Baxi 2005). Instead, I focus here on a moment in which the war *of,* and *on,* terror assumes a particular form in which public statements justify use of terror as a necessary, if not sufficient, condition for the pursuit of the just cause, the latter howsoever conceived. These statements may or may not present any doctrinal argument, but they are presented in a 'command mode legal pronouncement' and 'refuse to acknowledge multiple normative orders ('legal pluralism')'. Further, these enjoin acts of war *of* and *on* terror that ignore most, if not all, ethical constraints on means, methods and targets of violence. In 'wars *of* terror', typically waged by nonstate actors, such violence is often waged in the name of a 'quasi-religious imperative against a category of persons rather than a state'; the wars *on* terror, typically waged by coalitions of willing states, are animated by similar imperatives expressed, say, in terms of 'defence' of human civilization or 'freedom', and likewise are aimed primarily against nomadic insurgent multitudes in ways that identify regimes and even states worthy of both destruction and eventual violent reconstruction.[11] I here designate the apparent authority that these statements come to command in terms of the globalization of fatwa cultures.

In so doing, I do not intend (and this does need saying in the current hegemonic cultures of Islamophobia) by any means to trivialize the venerable hermeneutic feats of a legitimately proud world religious tradition, in which fatwas command a hoary Shariah history. Rather, I refer variously to the ways in which the practices of construction of political Islam formations seek to impart legitimacy to the exigent and even expedient reconstruction in aid of the ongoing wars *of* terror. I further wish to suggest that the various pronouncements leading to the war *on* terror (against Afghanistan and against Iraq) assimilate elements of a fatwa culture in the construction of a counter-terror-type global militaristic response.

A mimesis is here fully and cruelly at work in an analogous decretal culture now fostered by the agents and managers of the edicts of the New Empire that enact Afghanistan and Iraq invasions. The White House and Whitehall unilaterally decide the meanings of international law, defining at will its aspirations and objectives, from which stem the notions, for example, of a pre-emptive war justified under an innovative doctrine of regime change and the unusual notion of 'unreasonable veto' in the Security Council; they decide what is reasonable and proportional force and put forth the associated notion of 'collateral damage' to 'justify' hitherto unlawful bombings of civilian targets beyond manifest military necessity; they decide to rewrite both the normative regimes of military occupation and international humanitarian law. In thus describing these performances (because evaluation remains a necessary task that I undertake elsewhere) I wish here to make a limited point concerning the 'foreign policy of liberal peoples' that constructs the notions of 'outlaw' peoples and states: namely, that a fatwa-type hermeneutic also inflects the prose of imperial power. 'Globalization of fatwas' indicates the processes by which an ancient tradition secularizes itself and by which secular public cultures of modern democracies seek to fashion a new global civic religion.[12] The globalization of fatwas moves along the axis of the violence of a secularizing religious tradition and metamorphosis of civic religion into a spiritual faith. I further suggest that this production of contemporary globalization of fatwa cultures adds an explosive new chapter in our understanding of legal pluralism, and its costs.

The Shariah Tradition

A preliminary understanding of fatwa cultures[13] surely reveals that fatwas represent pious acts of hermeneutic jurisprudence.[14] They constitute authoritative understandings both of the meaning of Islam and the Shariah. Only the learned and pious epistemic communities may thus bear these hermeneutic burdens.[15]

A fatwa, in any of the best interpretative usages of that notion, is a written response by a mufti to the interlocutor who seeks authoritative interpretation 'to regulate the individual's personal affairs, or with litigation or some other form of settlement in mind', where always the interlocutors 'appear as individuals, not in adversarial pairs' (Messick 1993: 136). Yet, '[m]uftis who were so inclined ... could be important actors in "the world"' (1993: 145, and here Messick invokes 'in this century the notorious example of the mufti of Jerusalem'). Islamic jurisprudence throughout its history, and across the globe, has evolved through authoritative fatwas that in their original forms only obligate the interpreters but in the long run also claim to bind the global faith community as a whole.[16]

The authority to issue fatwas has been appropriated variously. Collectivities such as committees or councils of the leading ulama now also supersede, in certain contexts, the role of individual interpreters, the muftis. The sites of enunciation, never predetermined by the revealed Islamic texts and corpus, have yielded themselves to the new communication and information technology; Messick instances the radio talks in Yemen known as 'fatwa shows'; more recent appropriations include Al-Jazeera–type global television pronouncements. They also cover an enormous range of subject matter, which remains hard to classify. Fatwas provide a remarkable discourse (in the words of the nineteenth-century C.E. jurist Rudolf Stammler) of 'natural law with changing content'.[17] Moreover, politicization of fatwas (that is, regime-sponsored or compatible acts of interpretation) has a longer history than is suggested by those who hold Ayatollah Khomeini's fatwa against Salman Rushdie to have been inaugural.[18] Because Islam does not in principle recognize territorial national boundaries as constituting also the frontiers of faith, fatwas carry always a global potential binding the dispersed communities of belief. In this sense, at the very least, studies of politics of interpretation in legal pluralism have so far neglected the fatwa cultures and their histories. We need to recall at the very outset that this tradition was never wholly militant or jehadi.

Yet it remains true that interpreters of Islam have often to choose among interpretations of the sacred text, and corpus, that oscillate between harmony and peace on the one hand and on the other incite 'the passion of death'[19] that defines as well as deifies recourse to acts and performances of the currently ongoing wars of 'terror'. In this respect the hermeneutic power is indeed awesome but scarcely unique to Islamic traditions.

The Passion for Death

In this section, I focus upon a specific form of fatwa culture that celebrates 'the passion for death'. I examine, in the main, the militarization of fatwa culture, an expression that gets awfully complicated by a specific view of politics most eloquently expressed by Muhammad Husayn Shykh Fadlallah:

> As Moslems, we consider politics to be a part of our whole life, because the Koran emphasizes the establishment of Justice as a divine mission … In this sense, the politics of the faithful is a kind of prayer.[20]

But the 'politics of the faithful' varies a great deal because 'the establishment of justice' can be constructed in various modes, both pacific and militant. The justice of recourse to 'terror', even *in extremis*, remains heavily problematized in both the classical and the contemporary Shariah discursive tradition. Further, as Charles Kurzman (2003) insightfully demonstrates, most 'influential' Islamic thinkers have condemned the 9/11 attacks as a 'grave sin', urging deterrence via due process of criminal enforcement against the guilty. In this genre, the exalted authority of the 'Prophet (Peace Be on Him)' is constantly invoked in ways that remain quite compatible with cosmopolitan theories that now urge the fashioning of 'a global rule of law'.[21]

The constitutive ambivalences manifest fully, for example, in the discourse of Aziz Bin Baz, chair of the Supreme Council of Ulama of Saudi Arabia. Charles Kurzman (2003: 155–58; see also Esposito 1995 and Porter 2003) shows how Baz, on the one hand, issues fatwas that caution against *Bitnah* (friendship, counsel, help, protection, and counsel) from the infidels 'since they will not fail do their best to corrupt you' because only the 'brotherhood in true faith is the true brotherhood', and on the other hand unhesitatingly issues a fatwa in the wake of Iraqi occupation of Kuwait in 1990. He there speaks in a remarkably contemporary idiom of preparation of a collective anticipatory self-defence, invoking, through the doctrine of 'necessity', collaboration with the first President Bush. Faced with 'a painful necessity', he now says that a '[m]an in charge of the affairs of Muslims should seek the assistance of one who has the ability to attain the necessary aim'. Indeed, he considers this as an aspect of a 'legitimate jihad' against 'Saddam, the enemy of God', and those assisting him, because he 'has wrongly transgressed and committed aggression against and invaded a peaceful country'. On this register, one may even say that Bin Baz's edict re-enacts the values, standards and norms of the United Nations Charter! His fatwa summons dedication of all pious Muslim worldwide praxes to the restoration of post-Westphalian world orderings.[22]

Osama bin Laden enacts global militarization of the fatwa cultures in ways that deeply confront 'liberal' Islamic culture (Kurzman 1998). I am not competent to adjudge the question of his 'authority' to issue any fatwa because *prima facie* he does not quite measure up to a figuration of keeper of a sacred tradition signified by hallowed descriptions of a Mufti, Alim or Ayatollah. Bin Laden historically emerges no doubt (in Weberian terms) as a 'charismatic law-giver' for communities of faith that repose trust in him, even to the point of jehadi martyrdom. His invocation of a charismatic tradition suggests the 'plasticity' of a Shariah juristic heritage that radically decentralizes the power to name the law: a global code of binding/authoritative obligation. It seems, nevertheless, that he has acquired that status among his followers and even a wider community of faith[23] that goes so far as to justify a war on global pluralisms. And in the process he marshals traditions of interpretation of martyrdom and suicide in Islamic jurisprudence. Most of Osama bin Laden's post-9/11 'fatwas' articulate some new forms of militant globalizing Islam. I here focus on his co-authorship of the 1998 World Islamic Front's fatwa that urges as an

> individual duty of every pious Muslim who can do it in every country in which it is possible to do so ... to kill the Americans and their allies – civilians and military – ... in order to liberate the al-Asqua Mosque [in Jerusalem], the Holy Mosque [in Mecca], from their grip and in order to move out of all the lands of Islam, defeated and unable to threaten any Muslim ... We – with God's help – call on every Muslim who believes in God and wishes to be rewarded to comply with God's order to kill Americans and plunder their money wherever, and whenever, they find it. We also call on Muslim Ulema, youths, and soldiers to launch the raid on Satan's U.S. troops and the devil's supporters siding with them, and to displace those who are behind them so that they may learn a lesson.

The entire language is unfamiliar to the more conventional jurisprudence of fatwa culture, and even its conventional prose. I suspect that many legal pluralists may receive with a sense of shock Bernard Lewis's description of this fatwa as 'a magnificent piece of eloquent, at times poetic, Arabic prose'.[24] Regardless, the question remains: how may studies of legal pluralism usefully contribute to some understanding of this form of juridicalization of 'terror'? Of course, even the raising of this question invites a one-way ticket to Guantanamo or Belmarsh! I believe that some narrative risks have to be borne in the pursuit of 'anthropology as intervention'.

The fatwa warrants anxious textual analysis, if only because it constitutes an aspect of war on pluralisms viewed in terms of Ayatollah Khomeini's notion of 'Westoxification' (see Baxi 2002: 112–13). 'Liberation' is the key term of this distinctly political but also pervasively religious/spiritual rhetoric. Going beyond the restoration of the Holy Land as a core aspect of the violent struggle, 'liberation' also features in this text (and related texts) as a historically concrete construction of a post-colonialist time and space for Islamic peoples. Because the belligerent occupation of Islamic societies and peoples is seen as constituting not just a universal *misfortune* but also a globally sponsored form of *injustice*, the fatwa summons the community of the faithful to combat the community of the infidels. This latter community is an ever expanding category, which initially articulates in terms of 'Americans and their allies', a term that expands it by manifold referents through association with other allies in the war against the Taliban in Afghanistan, and now in Iraq, also perceived to be generally in the unfolding 'war on terror'.[25] This 'ruling' at the same moment centralizes and decentralizes violence and 'terror'. The 'individual duty' of every pious Muslim, while uniquely performed in each instance, stands everywhere dictated by some claimed or assumed charismatic/revelatory authority figuration. The performance of a pious jehadi obligation thus imposed is singular and unique for each actant; however, it makes collective present 'sense' only within the grid of centralization of direction, strategies, the hardware (armaments) and the cultural software (proselytization/propaganda) of wielding worldwide the passion *of* and *for* death. It is this 'passion' that creates a new episteme.

Complexity and Contradiction in the Emergent Global Culture of Fatwas

My notion of globalization of the fatwa cultures provides one way of reading the texts and events of the two terror wars. It thus far relies on a globally militant reconstruction of political Islam and the coequal emergence of 'divine violence' (as Walter Benjamin named it in related contexts) in the performances by which global ideologies and strategies of counterterrorism are produced. Both invite the suspension of ethics and law; and both demonstrate the imagery of Bataille, wherein 'violence and its phantasmic reversal of slaughter into "glory" go beyond the order of homogeneity'. To be sure,

> the two orders of 'terrorist violence and the violence of the state share the symbolic register of sovereignty. They are both examples of heterogeneous excess and spectacle that exceed the logic of a carefully ordered and administered homogeneous society'; violence that is characterized by a dimension that exceeds the paradigms of power and law; that is excessive, heterogeneous and spectacular; that involves the sacrifice of life and the symbolism of death, and the terrifying nihilism of 'pure means' (Newman 2004: 27, 30).

However, the current and ongoing forms of the Islamic reconstitution of suicide and martyrdom, while singular, are not unique. Legal pluralists need also to attend to prior varied cultural histories of martyrdom as shaping people's law formations, inclusive of self-immolation by the Buddhist monks protesting the Vietnam War, as well as the practices of suicide bombing outside Islam, as, for example, in Sri Lanka.[26] In these and kindred practices, the human body itself becomes a weapon of mass destruction directed towards the violent installation of insurgent truths of a peoples' law formation.[27] How, then, may pluralists read the texts of 'war *of* terror'? As entirely devoid of 'carefully measured strategic or political goals' that instrumentalized violence as 'a means to what Benjamin would call 'natural ends' or 'in Foucaldian terms, as an act of resistance, as a form of counter-power', or in the alternative as violence that 'is no longer intelligible in this dialectic' and can 'no longer be measured by the operation of power it contests'? Is it 'a nihilism at whose heart there is nothing but emptiness, the terror of pure form, and the death-drive that approaches the edges of the abyss', this 'nihilistic void' (Newman 2004: 29)? This Badiou-type narrative both fascinates and compels, but it may also obscure other ways of reading the texts, and events, of 'terror'.

What other readings of the globalization of fatwa cultures remain possible? Ulrich Beck (2003) invites, I think, a striking mode of legal pluralist engagement with this materiality when he describes 9/11 as 'the Chernobyl of globalization', which 'puts to rest' the 'neoliberal promise of salvation' (2003: 262) in ways that present the 'suicide attacker' as the 'most radical counter-image of the *homo economicus*' (2003: 260). In this sense, the 'war *of* terror' may even be perceived (if I may thus trespass upon the authorial intent) as 'an attempt to outline and test *other modernities*' (2003: 259). How may a legal pluralist reading offer a freestanding grasp of global technopolitics and techno-resistance? In what ways might the 'war *on* terrorism' irreversibly foster globalizing secular fatwa cultures, 'justifying' some Star Wars–type massive retaliation couched in the languages of the defence of civilization, liberty and freedom, the rule of law, human rights and similar forms of gigantomachy? Do these ominous genres, accompanied by awesome practices of the rather instantly justifiable forms of politics of global cruelty and massacre, portend the very end of pluralisms, social and juridical, as also specifically legal? Further, does my notion of globalization of the fatwa cultures mitigate some persistent difficulties arising from 'orientalism' (both legal and cultural) that, at the end of the day, frame both the 'terror' wars in terms merely of the politics of cultural, even civilizational, hatred of the 'West' by 'Muslims'?[28]

Finally (without being exhaustive), the global 'war *on* terror' (see Badiou 2003; Baxi 2003a and the literature cited therein; Fitzpatrick 2003) seems to the authors of 'terror' fatwas to be only different in degree, not in kind. Put another way, the unilateral recourse to use of force by the even unstable coalitions of willing states stands perceived as an exercise of 'dominance without hegemony', as Ranajit Guha (1997) describes it, which then viciously justifies further 'terrorist' performances and enactments. We ought to pause here at least to note that even cosmopolitan liberals also find the doctrine of 'pre-emptive war', directed at violent regime change, unacceptable at the bar of contemporary international law and unconscionable even as a serial exercise of realpolitik (see generally Sterba 2003).

What May 'Reasonable Pluralism' Thus Entail?

Do legal pluralists need to further aggravate their agenda by any acceleration of some theory-oriented reengagement with John Rawls? The practitioners of legal ethnography may well celebrate his insistence concerning 'the fact of pluralism', a fact that 'is not merely a historic condition that will soon pass away' but rather signifies a 'permanent feature of the public culture of modern democracies'. I wonder, however, whether these epistemic communities will endorse his further claim that the task of construction of reasonable pluralism emerges only with the 'public culture of modern democracies'. Rawls makes an empirical and a normative claim. The empirical claim is that the fact of pluralism remains linked to its fate in democratic rather than in 'nondemocratic' regimes. The latter decree bodes ill for the fact of pluralism because 'oppressive use of state power' will lead to reduction of 'the diversity of views'[29] concerning conflicting conceptions of 'good' life. The normative claim is that only a 'public culture of democracies', which repudiates imposition of a 'general and comprehensive doctrine', remains capable of generating the very 'ideal' notion of 'free public reason'. It is 'free' in the sense of being uncoerced by oppressive use of state power, and its nature as 'public reason' stands constituted by the doctrine of 'overlapping consensus'. In other words, free public reason only occurs in societies of well-ordered liberal peoples.

Serious students of legal pluralism may claim (or presume) to know otherwise. They know full well that the diversity of views constituting notions of good life escalate almost equally in public cultures of all human societies, whether or not they are regarded as 'democratic'. They also know that while some state orderings even when not manifestly subscribing to any comprehensive conceptions of good life do in fact variously reduce the sway of free public reason within national political communities and more crucially in their international relations with other states. The difference that matters thus is, I here perforce cryptically say, a difference of degree, rather than a difference of kind. All the same, the tasks of a post-Rawlsian pluralist sociology of law still await us all in a very violent world ushered in by globalization of fatwas, whether they be issued by Osama bin Laden or of the Bush-Blair genre. This distinction is not wholly devoid of difference. But this poses at the very least a whole new agenda for practising legal pluralism. How may we achieve understandings of 'reasonable pluralism' in a world made infinitely violent by pre-, and post-, histories of 9/11? How, indeed, may we innovate the 'theory of practice', to deploy a difficult conception of Pierre Bourdieu?

Notes

1. The difficult distinctions between the two forms of 'war' are discussed elsewhere: see Baxi (2005).
2. I here invoke Robert Cover's notion (Cover 1983). See also Baxi (2005).
3. See the White House (2005) news release, "President Sworn-In to Second Term" (20 January), online: The White House http:/www.whitehouse/.gov/nes/rleases/2005//01/20050120-1-html
   Laura Nader insightfully demonstrated in her Edinburgh Conference presentation how American mass media amplified this form of messianic and millenarian practices in the not-so-secular presentation of the 'war *on* terror'.
4. Pluralist approaches may not escape acute moral and ethical anxiety in relation, for example, to globally televised hostage executions, or to forms of some extortionate bargaining for the hostage release, or even further, to the war *of* terror–type effects on the political life of a nation, as was recently revealed in the complex fallout of regime change in Spain resulting from the Madrid catastrophe.
5. The foregoing are described by Louis Althusser, following Antonio Gramsci, via 'ideological state apparatus', Felix Guttari and George Deleuze in terms of 'microfacism' of desire of power, and Michel Foucault, memorably, in terms of both the regimes of 'disciplinary' and 'sovereign' power. I desist here from voluminous citations.
6. Achieving this entails close attention to the 'costs' of legal pluralism arising as a function of both social necessity and individual choice. By costs of legal pluralism, I refer to, in rolled-up ways, the imposition of preventable and unjustifiable human suffering and loss inflicted on individuals and communities by hegemonic actors and performances. Each one of these operative terms – 'preventable', 'unjustified' and 'suffering'– constitutes a conceptual minefield (see Herzfeld 2001: 217–39; Ophir 2005). Further,

'costs' are often willingly borne and at times are even not experienced as such, being legitimated until the advent of 'the external point of view' (Hart 1961). Ethnography of law often crucially attests to these costs in manifold and multifarious ways, offering understanding of the constitution of violent subjection.

7. E.V. Walter (1969), in a magisterial study of terrorist governance and resistance in some 'primitive African communities', shows how absolute power and authority may be based on consent and tradition. It is time to revisit this rich narrative.

8. By this term I have sought to finally resolve for myself the politics of naming law beyond and before the state, otherwise variously referred to as 'customary' law or 'informal', 'folk', 'non-state' law in all their symbiotic co-presences and their hybrid cross-relations. This has enabled me to trace the dialectic between 'state' law and peoples' law formations. See Upendra Baxi (1982).

9. See Cynthia Keepley Mahmood (2001: 524), who suggests that 'the adrenaline-charged milieu in which the concept of terrorism flourishes is itself an indicator of the term's mythic power' and urges that 'deconstruction of this myth in favour of reasonable anthropological assessment is the first step in actually working toward curbing such violence in the future'.

10. Badiou (2003: 142–43) suggests that the discourse of 'terrorism' determines the subject 'who is targeted by the terrorist act, who is struck, who is plunged into mourning, and who must lead a vengeful riposte' into metalanguages of 'Our Societies', 'Democracies' or even 'America'. The supporting predicates frame 'terrorism' as Islamic. And the sequences of response stand determined by the opaque languages of 'war against terrorism', a 'long war', even an 'entire epoch'.

11. I owe some of the above formulations above, in single quotes, to a personal communication by Martha Mundy and Laura Nader, who remained heavily critical of the very idea of 'fatwa culture' at the initial presentation of this paper at the Edinburgh legal anthropology seminar but subsequently, and thankfully, remained more hospitable to the enunciation.

12. See the interesting analysis by Daniel Philpott (2002).

13. Muhammad Khalid Masud, B. Messick and D.S. Powers (1996) provide a most comprehensive recent collection tracing the origins, history and social function of the fatwa. See also M. Cherif Bassiouni and Gamal M. Badr (2002); Sayyid Mohsen Sa'idzadeh (2002). For a wider conspectus see also N.J. Coulson (1964). The diversity of Islamic traditions is indeed astounding; see for a recent affirmation Francis Robinson (2001).

14. Among the contemporary living traditions, Islam, along with rabbinic law, remains probably the only notable survivor of the genre of authoritative jurist-based legality and justice.

15. See the interesting entry in Al-Manhaj.com by Shaikh 'Alee Hasan-Al-Halabee, Conditions of Being Muftee' (visited 10 August 2004).

16. I am unable to specify, for want of competence in the Shariah tradition, the 'community'-binding arc of fatwas having multiple sources of origin. My colleague Professor Shaheen Sardar Ali, in her comments on the draft of

this paper, suggests that we ought to relate fatwa (as a mere opinion) to 'ijtihad, or independent judicial reasoning exerting one faculty of thought and mind (using Rahim's expression), and taqlid (duty to follow/stare decisis in the common law tradition), where the individual does not feel competent or adequate to make that autonomous, intellectual 'exertion'.

17. For example, when a former professor of surgery and chairman of a hospital in Riyadh encountered religion-based resistance to an 'analgesic ladder' [use of opium and other analgesics] in cancer treatment, he successfully persuaded the Mufti General and President of the Committee of the Leading Ulam'a to issue a fatwa justifying this therapy on the ground of 'necessity'. See Isbister (2002).

18. See Lisa Appignanesi and Sara Maitland (1989).

19. I here invoke this phrase of Jean Baudrillard (1993: 172). Islamic interpreters furnish yet another illustration of the oft-quoted insight of Robert Cover that interpretation occurs 'on the plane of pain and death'.

20. Quoted in John L. Esposito (1995: 149).

21. See Daniele Archibugi and Iris Marion Young (2003), who seek persuasively to distinguish state-centric reading of 9/11 as an 'act of war against America' from a cosmopolitan reading that characterizes it in terms that replenish affirmations of an emergent 'global rule of law'.

22. It is rather unfortunate that Kurzman describes this performance in the idiom of 'pro-US fatwas' rather than in the prose of inherent Islamic interpretive pluralism.

23. How this comes about may indeed furnish an important narrative in future studies of legal pluralism, and not just in Islamic tradition. As to the 'authority' somehow acquired by bin Laden, see Yossef Bodansky (2001).

24. As quoted in Bodansky (2001: 226–27); see also Porter (2003). Note also the very last phrase in the fatwa that suggests a kind of pedagogic role for 'terrorism'. This form of theocratic commandment at once is heavily secularized and invokes divine wrath for noncompliance. At the same time, it remains mindful of the Koranic injunction that Allah does not command the 'impossible' from his followers; this must surely explain the caveat in the fatwa that relativizes the individual obligation in terms of what every Muslim may do 'in any country in which it is possible to do it'.

25. This also includes 'apostates' like Saddam Hussein and his cohorts, at least prior to the invasion of Iraq; see Bodansky (2001: 227–30).

26. Keebet von Benda-Beckman also invites my attention to Japanese suicide bombers in the Second World War as a further instance.

27. Mohandas Gandhi deployed his body (in pacific modes) as a site of resistance to imperialism/colonization; he thus inaugurally forged a series of transformative praxes that Gramsci described as the originary mode of 'passive revolution' (see Baxi 1993: 177–81). Further, understanding various ways of constitution of violent subjectivity invites attention to new 'technologies of self' (to use a Foucaldian expression) that develop capabilities for surrendering one's own life for a wider (here spiritual) cause. At stake here are new renditions of 'this-worldly' and 'other-worldly' forms of imagining here-and-now, and forever, as it were, oscillations between sociological and cosmological notions of time, and one may even add space, because

zannat, (that form of emancipatory other-worldly state of bliss) attained by *shahada* (*lit.* witnessing of self-annihilation as authentic fulfilment; cf. Freamon 2003) reconstructs the space for emancipatory praxes. The term 'terror' thus fully carries an inherent potential of forfeiting culturally and intercivilizationally constructed understandings of the constitution of violent subjectivity and agency.

28. The metadiscourse enunciated even by Bernard Lewis (2002) is of no help at all, as Kazem Alamdari (2003) demonstrates, for any sustained reading of the texts, or subtexts, of the two 'terror' wars because it obscures various modes of violent subjectivities of their perpetrators and victims that only deep ethnographies of 'terror' may only converse with. See also Mamdani (2004).

29. All quotes cited here, without the burden of pagination, are from Rawls's essay 'The Idea of Public Reason Revisited', edited by Samuel Freeman (1999: 573–615).

References

Alamdari, K. 2003. 'Terrorism Cuts across the East and the West: Deconstructing Lewis's Orientalism', *Third World Quarterly* 24: 177–86.

Al-Manhaj.com by Shaikh 'Alee Hasan-Al-Halabee, Conditions of Being Muftee' (accessed 10 August 2004).

An-Naim, A. 2002. 'Upholding International Legality against Islamic and American Jihad', in K. Booth and T. Dunne (eds), *Worlds in Collision: Terror and the Future of Global Order*. New York: Palgrave MacMillan, 162–71.

Appiganesi, L. and S. Maitland. 1989. *The Rushdie File*. London: The Fourth Estate.

Archibugi, D. and I.M. Young. 2003. 'Envisioning a Global Rule of Law', in J.P. Sterba (ed.), *Terrorism and International Justice*. New York: Oxford University Press, 158–70.

Asad, T. 1997. 'On Torture, or Cruel, Inhuman, or Degrading Treatment', in A. Kleinman, V. Das and M. Lock (eds), *Social Suffering*. Berkeley: University of California Press, 285–309.

Badiou, A. 2003. *Infinite Thought: Truth and the Return of Philosophy*. London: Continuum International Publishing Group.

Bassiouni, M.C. 2002. 'Legal Control of International Terrorism: A Policy-Oriented Assessment', *Harvard International Law Journal* 43(1): 83–104.

Bassiouni, M.C. and G.M. Badr. 2002. 'The Shari'a: Sources, Interpretation, and Rule Making', *UCLA Journal of Islamic and Near Eastern Law* 1(2): 135–59.

Baudrillard, J. 1993. *Symbolic Exchange and Death*. London: Sage.

Baxi, U. 1982. *The Crisis of the Indian Legal System*. New Delhi: Vikas.

———. 1985. *Towards Sociology of Indian Law*. New Delhi: Satvahan.

———. 1993. *Marx, Law, and Justice*. Bombay: N.M. Tripathi.

———. 2002. *The Future of Human Rights*. Delhi: Oxford University Press.

———. 2003. 'The Colonial Inheritance' in P. Legrand and R. Munday (eds), *Comparative Legal Studies: Traditions and Transitions*. Cambridge: Cambridge University Press, 46–75.

————. 2003a. 'Operation Enduring Freedom: Towards a New International Law and Order?' in A. Anghie, B.S. Chimni, K. Mickelson and O.C. Okafor (eds), *The Third World and International Order: Law, Politics, and Globalization.* Leiden: Martinus Nijhoff, 3–46.

————. 2005. 'The "War *On* Terror" and the "War *Of* Terror"': Nomadic Multitudes, Aggressive Incumbents and the "New" International Law', *Osgoode Hall Law Journal* 43(1–2): 7–43.

Beck, U. 2003. 'The Silence of Words: On Terror and War', *Security Dialogue* 34(3): 255–67.

Benda-Beckmann, K. von. 2001. 'Transnational Dimensions of Legal Pluralism', in W. Fikentscher (ed.), *Begegnung und Konflikt – eine kulturanthropologische Bestandsaufnahme.* Munich: Verlag der Bayerischen Akademie der Wissenschaften, C.H. Beck Verlag, 33–48.

Bodansky, Y. 2001. *Bin Laden: The Man who Declared War on America.* California, CA: Prima Publishing.

Burawoy, M., J.A. Blum, S. George, Z. Gille, T. Gowan, L. Haney, M. Klawiter, S.H. Lopex, S. O Riain and M. Thayer (eds). 2000. *Global Ethnography.* Berkeley: University of California Press.

Card, C. 2003. 'Making War on Terrorism in Response to 9/11', in J.P. Sterba (ed.), *Terrorism and International Justice.* New York: Oxford University Press, 171–85.

Chua, A. 2003. *World on Fire.* London: Random House.

Coombe, R. 1998. *The Intellectual Life of Cultural Property.* Chicago: University of Chicago Press.

Coulson, N.J. 1964. *A History of Islamic Law.* Edinburgh: University of Edinburgh Press.

Cover, R. 1983. 'Foreword: Nomos and Narrative', *Harvard Law Review* 97: 4–68.

Derrida, J. 2002. *Acts of Religion.* London: Routledge.

Elshtain, J.B. 2003. *Just War against Terror: The Burden of American Power in a Violent World.* New York: Basic Books.

Esposito, J.L. 1995. *The Islamic Threat: Myth or Reality?* new, 2nd ed. Oxford: Oxford University Press.

Fitzpatrick, P. 2003. '"Gods Would Be Needed...": American Empire and the Rule of (International) Law', *Leiden Journal of International Law* 16(3): 429–66.

Freamon, B.K. 2003. 'Martyrdom, Suicide, and the Islamic Law of War: A Short Legal History', *Fordham International Law Journal* 27: 299–369.

Freeman, S. (ed.). 1999. *John Rawls: Collected Papers.* Cambridge, MA: Harvard University Press.

Gessner, V. and A.C. Budak. 1998. *Emerging Legal Certainty: Empirical Studies on the Globalization of Law.* Aldershot: Dartmouth.

Griffiths, A. 2002. 'Legal Pluralism', in R. Banakar and M. Travers (eds), *An Introduction to the Law and Social Theory.* Oxford: Hart Publishing, 289–310.

Guha, R. 1983. *The Elementary Aspects of Peasant Insurgency.* Delhi: Oxford University Press.

————. 1997. *Dominance without Hegemony.* Cambridge: Cambridge University Press.

Hardt, M. and A. Negri. 2000. *Empire.* London: Routledge.
————. 2004. *Multitudes: War and Democracy in an Age of Empire.* New York: The Penguin Press.
Harris, O. (ed.). 1996. *Inside and Outside the Law: Anthropological Studies in Authority and Ambiguity.* London: Routledge.
Hart, H.L.A. 1961. *The Concept of Law.* Oxford: Clarendon Press.
Herzfeld, M. 2001. *Anthropology: Theoretical Practice in Culture and Society.* Oxford: Blackwell.
Horowitz, D.L. 1985. *Ethnic Groups in Conflict.* Berkeley: University of California Press.
————. 2001. *The Deadly Ethnic Riot.* Berkeley: University of California Press.
Isbister, W.H. 2002. 'A Good Fatwa', *British Medical Journal* 325(23 November): 1227.
Jordan, M.J. 2002. 'Terrorism's Slippery Definition Eludes UN Diplomats', *Christian Science Monitor,* 4 February [electronic resource].
Kurzman, C. 2003. 'Pro-US Fatwas', *Middle East Policy* 10(3): 155–66.
———— (ed.). 1998. *Liberal Islam: A Sourcebook.* New York: Oxford University Press.
Laquer, W. 1977. *Terrorism.* Boston: Little Brown and Company.
————. 1999. *The New Terrorism: Fanaticism and the Arms of Mass Destruction.* New York: Oxford University Press.
Lewis, B. 2002. *What Went Wrong? Western Impact and Middle East Response.* Oxford: Oxford University Press.
Mahmood, C.K. 2001. 'Terrorism, Myth, and the Power of Ethnographic Praxis', *Journal of Comparative Ethnography* 30: 520–45.
Mamdani, M. 2004. *Good Muslim, Bad Muslim: Islam, the USA, and the Global War against Terror.* New York: Pantheon.
Masud, M.K., B. Messick and D.S. Powers (eds). 1996. *Islamic Legal Interpretation.* Cambridge, MA: Harvard University Press.
Mehta, D. and R. Chatterji. 2001. 'Boundaries, Names, Alterities: A Case Study of "Communal Riots" in Dharavi, Bombay', in V. Das, A. Kleinman, M. Lock, M. Ramphele and P. Reynolds (eds), *Remaking a World: Violence, Social Suffering, and Recovery.* Berkeley: University of California Press, 201–49.
Messick, B. 1993. *The Calligraphic State: Textual Domination and History in a Muslim Society.* Berkeley: University of California Press.
Nader, L. 2002. *The Life of the Law: Anthropological Projects.* Berkeley: University of California Press.
Newman, S. 2004. 'Terror, Sovereignty and Law: On the Politics of Violence', *German Law Journal* 5: 1–30.
Ophir, A. 2005. *The Order of Evils: Towards an Ontology of Morals.* Boston, MA: The MIT Press.
Phillips, R.L. 2003. 'The War against Pluralism', in J.P. Sterba (ed.), *Terrorism and International Justice.* New York: Oxford University Press, 101–13.
Philpott, D. 2002. 'The Challenges of September 11th to Secularism in International Relations', *World Politics* 55(October): 66–95.
Porter, J.M.B. 2003. 'Osama bin Laden, Jihad, and Sources of International Terrorism', *Indiana International & Comparative Law Journal* 13: 871–82.
Rawls, J. 1999. *The Law of Peoples.* Cambridge, MA: Harvard University Press.

Robinson, F. 2001. *The 'Ulama' of Farangi Mahall and Islamic Culture in South Asia.* New Delhi: Permanent Black.

Sa'idzadeh, S.M. 2002. 'Fiquh and Fikkayat', *UCLA Journal of Islamic and Near Eastern Law* 1(2): 239.

Sterba, J.P. (ed.). 2003. *Terrorism and International Justice.* New York: Oxford University Press.

Tiefenbrun, S. 2003. 'A Semiotic Approach to the Definition of Terrorism', *International Law Students Association Journal of International and Comparative Law* 9(2): 357–89.

Tilly, C. 2004. 'Terror, Terrorism, Terrorists', *Sociological Theory* 22: 5–13.

Tuitt, P. 2004. *Race, Law, and Resistance.* London: Glasshouse.

Walter, E.V. 1969. *Terror and Resistance: A Study in Political Violence.* London: Oxford University Press.

The White House. 2005. http:/www.whitehouse/.gov/nes/rleases/2005//01/20050120-1-html (accessed 20 January 2005).

5

HUMAN RIGHTS, CULTURAL RELATIVISM AND LEGAL PLURALISM
Towards a Two-dimensional Debate
Franz von Benda-Beckmann

Human Rights as a Resource of Power and Control

'Representations of knowledge give a life to that knowledge. This life shapes the object of the knowledge' (Fitzpatrick 1984: 20)

In the world of national and international relations, human rights have become an important but also contested political topic. Human rights have been elaborated as international law by international organizations and international legal science, and have successfully become globalized. Most categories of human rights are accepted by most states. Western governments and international organizations especially aim at strengthening human rights on a global scale and support human rights NGOs. Acceptance and implementation of human rights have become a frequent conditionality for financial and technical support. Human rights are used as an instrument of pressure on state governments in other parts of the world in order to implement standards of good governance. International rights institutions, governmental and nongovernmental (such as Amnesty International or Human Rights Watch), have become important agencies monitoring and criticizing human rights violations.

The states being pressured by international organizations and Western democracies have reacted in different ways. Some governments deny the universal validity of human rights, asserting that the 'European' notions of rights do not exist in, and do not fit, their cultural and religious systems. When the defensive shield of sovereignty threatens to become too weak, the incompatibility of human rights with culture becomes another justification for not accepting or not implementing human rights. This is especially the case in China and some Islamic countries.[1] The assertion of cultural relativism has become a weapon against what is alleged to be an imposition of Western human rights. It is made most vociferously by autocratic governments who do not seem to care for the political values of their own populations either. However, anthropologists and nongovernmental organizations have also shown and defended the relativity and variability of social organizations and their cultural values, which often were not in conformity with the ideal notions expressed in many human rights.[2]

On the other hand, the worldwide presence of, and possibility of invoking, human rights has become a 'jurisprudence of insurgency' (Tigar and Levy 1977), a resource that could be mobilized to legitimate political and economic resistance in counter-hegemonic struggles of individuals, organizations and social movements that use international human rights to reach out beyond the boundaries of the powerful institutions of their state apparatus and force state governments to accept human rights at least in principle.[3] While one may be sceptical of the direct impact of such 'juridical genuflections toward human rights' and see that they are often 'only the price which vice pays to virtue, the fact that even vicious regimes feel so obliged means that vice can now be shamed and even controlled in ways that were unavailable before 1945' (Ignatieff 1999: 10). This pertains not only to 'vicious' states. The frequent appeals to the European Court of Human Rights, discussions about the permissibility of torture and, last but not least, developments associated with the war against Iraq and the Guantánamo prison show that it also applies to some Western governments to some degree, when human rights do not match their political agenda.

These tensions between the asserted and demanded universality of human rights and cultural relativist positions have been extensively discussed in social anthropological circles.[4] I argue that the anthropological discussions carry the imprint of the dominant ways in which human rights issues are represented. In the following, I want to discuss three aspects of these representations and argue that we need to revise the dominant way in which the human rights issue is represented in the world of political relations and anthropological debates.

The first aspect is a tendency to justify one's moral and political positions (for universalism or for cultural relativism) by referring to the empirical distribution of human rights over states and cultures.[5] This is a consequence of the failure or unwillingness to distinguish between the empirical (historical and contemporary) evidence of the extent to which human rights can be said to 'exist' universally, and the moral-political discussion of whether human rights *should* exist universally. Universalism and cultural relativism are expressions of both empirical *and* political assertions. At the empirical level, both views are faced with the challenge to present sufficient ethnographic evidence for their assertions. At the normative level, both have to provide a justification for demanding universal validity, or for a tolerance of the idiosyncrasies of 'cultures' (however homogenous or heterogeneous) that do not correspond to human rights standards. Attempts to reduce these two dimensions to one lead to confusion in both dimensions – in the empirical and in the moral-political discourse. There has been a gradual shift in anthropological discussions towards a more supportive position on human rights,[6] and from the opposition of universalism versus cultural relativism towards human rights practices in different contexts and 'analyses of power, discipline and social regulation'.[7] But the tensions between ethnographic research and political and moral evaluation have not disappeared and keep shaping the way in which human rights are perceived.[8]

The second aspect is the presentation of the human rights issue as a predominantly international or intercultural issue rather than an intra–state and society issue. This is not to say that state governments, human rights organizations and anthropologists would not have addressed human rights violations or described how human rights are used by actors in local (intrastate) settings (see Wilson 1997b; Merry 2001). But the universalism-relativism issue and the major political arguments concern international and intercultural struggles or negotiations. This is also maintained by the fact that anthropologists traditionally speak for 'the other' living 'elsewhere'.

The third aspect concerns the fact that the representation of the tension between universalism and relativism is mostly one between 'our' (Western) rights and 'their' culture, or if seen from the other side, 'our culture' versus 'their rights'. I argue that the contemporary struggles that really concern and affect people take place not so much between 'Western human rights' and 'Third World cultures' but between different laws and cultures within *all* states. Together, these representations largely structure the ideas and argumentation, as well as the selection of relevant empirical data, of both the proponents of universal human rights and their critics, and help reproduce the law discourse of international law and relations.

First I will address the empirical level and find out what we are talking about when we talk about the existence and distribution of human rights. I will then discuss how perspectives on human rights are influenced by being perceived as a transnational issue and related to culture and/or other law and legal pluralism. Finally, I will return to the issue of moral and political engagement.

What Are Human Rights, and Where Are They?

What Are Human Rights?

The main answer to the question of what human rights are is a reference to the history of what has become known as different generations of human rights in Europe since the sixteenth century. These notions of freedom from political authority, and of the obligation of political authority to guarantee or provide such rights, were elaborated by Enlightenment thinkers and political activists during and after the revolutions in North America and Europe. After the catastrophe of the Second World War, they were transformed into (positive) international law by the international community organized as the United Nations. This is the background of human rights as a 'Western' development (Panikkar 1984).

It has been questioned on different grounds whether 'human rights' must be confined to these rights. As Baxi has stated in his critique of the 'origin myth' of human rights as the 'gift of the West to the rest': 'there is a need to pluralize the original metanarrative – in which all nations come as equal strangers to the task of protection and promotion of human rights' (2002: 26). The elaboration of human rights in the Universal Declaration of Human Rights (UDHR) and their later developments were strongly influenced by non-European actors (Baxi 2002: 27) and later refined, detailed and concretized in a variety of global transnational contexts. Moreover, it has been noted that while human rights may have developed in Europe, they have come to be accepted by many persons, organizations and governments in other parts of the world; sometimes in a vernacular, sometimes in their 'pure' form.[9] Globalization did not start yesterday. Notions of some human rights, such as political equality, freedom of suppression and democratic ideals, had been 'fetched' already by Third World intellectuals and independence movements, very much against the wishes of 'the West' (F. von Benda-Beckmann and K. von Benda-Beckmann 2005). In the course of the past fifty years, these mid twentieth-century human rights have been further globalized. Most contemporary nation states do subscribe to human rights, and many have ratified the international human rights conventions. Many states incorporated human rights into their constitutions.[10] So when looking back at the history of what has become international human rights law, the 'West versus rest dichotomy' has not been and certainly is no longer convincing.

Another question that has been raised is whether our understanding of 'human rights' should be limited to the mainstream human rights law. A less Eurocentric understanding of 'human rights' could include rival constructions of human rights adapted in different cultural or religious contexts as 'Asian or Islamic human rights'.[11] It could also comprise similar notions of human dignity, political freedom and equality in other societies, even if not called 'human rights'.

This raises the issue of comparability and the objectives one pursues with comparisons. In the literature we find opposing views as to whether such equivalents of human rights are relevant in the search of universality and/or whether a comparison of such notions with (mainstream) human rights makes any sense at all. Renteln (1990) has long proposed that 'homeomorphic equivalents' of human rights be sought in non-European 'traditional' cultures.[12] Wilson (1997a) has argued against such a kind of comparison. He approvingly quotes Donnelly (1989), who 'argues what then is being compared with human rights are notions of human dignity, or limitations on the arbitrary exercise of power. These are no rights in the strict sense since they are obligations constituted between rulers and divine authority, not between rulers and ruled' (1997a: 13, 14).[13] In the same spirit, Dembour (2001: 58) states that speaking of human rights before 1948, when the UDHR was signed, is an anachronism. But this is not really convincing.

The kind of comparison Donnelly, Wilson and Dembour seem to have in mind is one of direct translation, where cultural-legal notions of one society are directly translated into the categories of another. But, rather than looking for identity *or* difference, comparison is about looking for similarity *and* difference. It requires the analytical construction of a comparative frame of reference for observing empirical variations of what theoretically or analytically has been defined as 'the same'.[14] We can look for similarities and differences in constructions of human dignity, of freedom from political organizations and of notions of equality beyond class, caste and gender differences, as well as in the political, religious and philosophical legitimation of such constructions. Far from being a 'verbal legerdemain that may allow us to find human rights in a trivial and uninteresting sense' (Donnelly 1990: 57), such a comparative analysis could be a valuable tool for understanding people's notions of rights and serve as a means to get rid of the often stereotypical opposition between 'Western' human rights (individualism, freedom, pursuit of self-interest) and 'non-Western' culture with its emphasis on family, society and social obligations. Engaging in such comparisons does not mean that we are 'projecting the conceptions of international human rights law onto all other formulations and legal categories', as Wilson (1997a: 14) seems to fear. On the contrary, it invites a search for commonalities and differences of such notions between and within societies. In particular, a comparison would also highlight one aspect that is rarely explicitly discussed – namely, whether existing equivalents of human rights also accord (or propagate) such rights to all humans in all parts of the world, or whether they distinguish between those owning such rights and 'others' (barbarians, slaves, enemies, etc.) who don't.[15]

Such a comparison should also be expanded to European and American history. It shows that 'in the West' there also were (and still are) different understandings and interpretations of human rights by different kinds of social actors. There were important developments before and after 1948 with an ever expanding range of categories of human rights (Flinterman 1990). Freezing human rights in 1948 would exclude the pre-1984 historical developments in philosophical thought and political practice in Europe (and elsewhere). Accepting human rights only since 1948, on the other hand, would ignore the inputs of non-European or U.S. actors into the further developments.

In my view, this unwillingness to engage in a comparison is shaped by the effacing of the difference between normative and empirical statements and the urge to justify normative statements – against or for the universality of human rights – by their empirical distribution. This is what lies behind Renteln's (1990) attempt to find legitimacy for human rights standards across the globe that are not grounded in Western theories of natural rights but in the empirically proven universality of moral principles. It is also what is behind Wilson's (1997a) critique of Renteln's endeavours. I would agree with Wilson that such a comparison would be misdirected if its main objective was to find and prove universals, but this should not prevent us from drawing potentially interesting comparisons.[16]

What and Where Is 'Existence'?

How widespread and shared must existences of human rights be? Is it sufficient that some philosophers think and proclaim these ideas, while state governments do not recognize them and continue to oppress people? Do we have to wait until the majority of the population supports human rights, or until a government legislates human rights even if most citizens do not approve of these ideas?

The answers largely depend on one's criteria for 'existence', and on the relevance of different forms of existence for empirical and normative conclusions. Normative sciences such as legal sciences and political philosophy differ from anthropology in their standards of relevant answers. In legal and philosophical assertions, human rights, like any positive law, 'exist' in the temporal and spatial dimension normatively specified, in legal texts, and in their implementation.[17] But from a legal anthropological point of view, there are more 'existences'. The existence in legal texts and implementation processes through government courts are among them. But human rights may also 'exist' in the knowledge of people, in the programmes and strategies and struggles of social movements and individuals, in political philosophies of the powerful and the oppressed. Some human rights may be rejected by governments or the majority, yet a minority may warmly embrace them. In most states, and not only those of the Third World, we come across a potpourri of such existences that often differ along lines of region, class or gender.

All these existences are relevant for an anthropologist, although they may fail to satisfy the relevance criteria of legal sciences. These different existences must be specified in order to avoid misleading generalizations about 'the existence' of human rights. Ideas about human rights may be part of philosophy while never having found their way into actual law or political practice. We know from European and U.S. history that the acknowledgement of human rights coexisted with race and gender discrimination, slavery and legal suppression of human rights in the colonies right into the twentieth century. In a similar way, there must be, for hundreds of millions of Indians, a dramatic difference between their experience of oppression and exploitation and Gupta's statement that 'under Hinduism each individual is considered as an end in his or herself and is believed to be endowed with the capacities of self-realisation. Thus everyone, irrespective of race, caste, class, or sex, is perceived to possess equal potential to become "Brahmin" and is free to chose their own way of attaining Brahmin status' (Gupta 2003: 92). As Indian history has shown, embracing human rights ideas and framing the Indian constitution with bills of rights were not just strategic moves in the anti-colonial struggle or an unnecessary betrayal of 'Hindu culture if only well understood', but also a desperate reaching out for legal principles that the 'really existing' Hindu culture would not deliver.[18] This was no different in Europe, when ideas of fundamental human rights were developed in the course of the struggle against oppression by feudal or dictatorial power.

Human Rights: Transnational and Intrastate Problems

The simplification of the 'existence of human rights' and their (in)compatibility with social norms and political values in other states is also shaped by a strong emphasis on the transnational/globalization aspect of human rights and by a neglect of legal pluralism. Driven by the universalism-relativism debate, most discussions on human rights issues focus on the transnational dimensions of human rights law. Like the study of other kinds of transnationalized law, this is an important and fascinating field for an anthropological study (Merry 2005). This perception, however, encourages the presentation of the human rights issue as one *between*, rather than *within*, societies or states. The focus and the political argumentation concern international and intercultural struggles, negotiations and dialogues. The fact that anthropologists traditionally speak for 'the others' living 'elsewhere' supports this. The international or intercultural representation underlines and justifies the importance of those political and academic actors who are engaged in creating and maintaining the relations, states and cultural brokers. Generally, globalization debates, including the transnationalization of human rights, prioritize flows and interconnections rather than the historical dynamics of (g)localized forms 'after sedentisation' (F. von Benda-Beckmann and K. von Benda-Beckmann 2005: 113).

Of course, much attention is given to human rights violations within states. Influential organizations such as Amnesty International, Human Rights Watch and the International Commission of Jurists, as well as national human rights NGOs, human rights commissions and anthropologists address the many violations of human rights by state agents within states.[19] But this can also be seen as depending on the prior question of whether there are universal human rights at all, whether these, or their Western interpretations, are binding on the states in question, and whether outsiders can legitimately impose their values – by which the issue of interstate relations is problematized again.

Rights versus/to/as Culture, and the Neglect of Legal Pluralism

The other facet of the representation of the human rights issue is that 'the problem' tends to be phrased as 'rights in relation to culture'. The parties involved in this relationship are the 'West' (with its human rights) and 'the rest' (with its culture), which emphasizes the transnational character of the problematic. The consequence of this opposition is that little attention has been given to the fact that both human rights and culture (however it may be defined) in most parts of the world coexist with a variety of legal forms (legal pluralism). This is an important blind spot in human rights discussions.[20] I do not want to dismiss the political significance of human rights rhetoric between state representatives in international relations and organizations. But the major contemporary struggles that really concern people are not so much between 'Western human rights' and 'Third World cultures' but between different laws and cultures within states.

Many authors have deconstructed the simple dichotomy between 'Western rights' and 'cultures' by pointing to the fact that human rights have been quite alive in many non-European states for decades. The assumption of cultural homogeneity implicit in cultural relativist arguments was of course replaced by a more realistic picture of cultural fragmentation and internal contradictions. But even in its newer refinements, which dissolve the assumptions of culture (both here and there) as homogeneous and which point to the various ways in which globalized human rights have been appropriated and used for social struggles within one society, the focus on the *rights versus/as/to culture* paradigm remains pervasive even after the deconstruction of culture. An introductory essay by Cowan, Dembour and Wilson (2001; see also Cowan 2006), for instance, discusses three approaches – rights versus culture, rights to culture, and human rights as culture – thereby refining but not dissolving the culture-rights opposition. Critical of the concept of culture (in certain usages), they propose an analytical understanding of culture (Cowan, Dembour and Wilson 2001: 13).

This would be an answer to the conceptual problem. But such analytical understanding of culture must be accompanied by an analytical understanding of law and rights, and of the possibility of legal pluralism.[21] This will show that the main conflict may be between a state's own law, the plural laws in states, and a population's 'culture' or cultures, however homogeneous or heterogeneous these may be. International human rights law, constitutional state law and 'culture' often coexist with religious and customary laws, which may or may not share human rights and constitutional legal values. Recent developments among the Minangkabau in West Sumatra may illustrate this.

Legal Pluralism, Culture and Human Rights in Minangkabau

The Minangkabau people perceive their identity and culture (*kebudayaan*) as firmly rooted in the inseparable unity of their matrilineal *adat*, an umbrella term for their customs, law and morality, and their belief in Islam. They are also conscious Indonesian citizens and have been prominent in the national parliament and governments during the early decades of independence, but it is *adat* and Islam that make a Minangkabau a Minangkabau. The motto of '*adat* is based on the Shariah, the Shariah is based on *adat*' has for nearly two centuries, and throughout any political turmoil, expressed the insoluble unity of *adat* and Islam. Given the contradictions between *adat*, with its matrilineal structures of political and social authority, property and inheritance, and the normative construction of property and inheritance in Islamic law, the relationship has always been a problematic one. These legal orders, and their Minangkabau protagonists, have coexisted in a variety of ways. They have competed with each other, or made compromise arrangements. They have hybridized elements originating from both orders, or have sharply distinguished between them and mobilized them against each other in social, economic and political struggles. The struggle was, and still is, primarily about legal issues, inheritance, political membership in villages, construction of kinship-support relations and the different categories of marriageable or nonmarriageable relatives.[22] These legal struggles are carried out within a culture that is regarded as an all-embracing whole by all Minangkabau, but in which very different traditional, religious and modernist elements are emphasized by different actors.[23]

Recently, notions of human rights have entered into this sensitive legal dialogue. A member of the National Committee on Human Rights, a Minangkabau living in Jakarta, has raised the issue of whether the legal organization of matrilineal descent and inheritance is contrary to human rights demands for gender equality, and this has triggered off lively discussions in West Sumatra (Bahar and Tadjoeddin 2004). Looking at the Minangkabau case through the 'human rights versus culture' lens would only show us a small portion of the problems involved. What is at stake here is not, and certainly not mainly, 'Minangkabau culture versus human rights', but different legal orders within one single society, state and (heterogeneous) culture. There can thus exist manifold tensions and contradictions between different kinds of law and different kinds of culture within one state.[24]

Rights and Culture: Depoliticizing the Issue

In the discourse on human rights and culture, inter- and intrastate tensions are presented as an opposition between normative orders of different quality. The dominant state law pushes religious and customary laws into the conceptual background of 'norms and values', and indeed of 'culture only'. Anthropologists explicitly and implicitly accepting such state-defined law as law reproduce this opposition and consider the recent proliferation of 'rights talk' an adaptation or an appropriation of the 'Western' notions of law and rights, sometimes implying that people should better keep to 'culture' rather than essentializing themselves in categories imposed by the West. This overlooks the fact that what is at stake for people is not some sponge-like idea of culture, but demands for their own law and the political and economic rights defined in that law – their property, their forests, their autonomy from external power. Reproducing the dominant conceptual language of law and rights creates the image of local people having no rights other than those recognized by state law or construed with reference to international (human rights) law. Moreover, it forces people into the strategic essentializing that the categories of international law demand from them for 'recognition'. Radical proponents of a people's law therefore refuse to accept such 'recognition' and see it as a mere placebo (see F. von Benda-Beckmann 1997).

This becomes relevant where the relation between human rights, state law and customary law is concerned with respect to rights to natural resources, and where human rights are mobilized in order to overcome the nonrecognition of local customary rights by the state. Human rights have a higher status than both state and local laws, but their scope and what they have to offer may be minimal. In the domain of natural resource management and land and water rights, local people(s) claiming human rights may end up with less than they would have, had they based their economic and social claims on their own law. Recent studies on rights to irrigation water in Nepal have shown irrigation systems to be governed by local legal rules existing alongside with state regulations or with project regulations introduced by development agencies that have enlarged or improved an irrigation system. These customary rights are not always acknowledged and respected by state institutions such as the Department of Irrigation, the state courts or foreign NGOs. A 'human right to water' would reinforce claims by (members of) local communities, giving them an additional resource to assert their rights.[25] Ideally, the state would be obliged to guarantee a human right to water according to its capability. Local people would have a nobler and perhaps stronger claim to water – but this right would pertain only to a minimal access to drinking water, at the expense of losing their fuller customary property right to water. Plural legal conditions thus render tensions between culture, human rights law and other (plural) law much more multifaceted than is usually assumed, and form a problem within all legal systems.[26]

Analytic and Normative Reasoning

In my view, the distinction between empirical and normative assertions about the universality/relativism of human rights is a precondition for systematic empirical and comparative research as well as for moral and political argumentation. Anthropologists (and others) will have to live with the fact that human rights (European mainstream or homeomorphic equivalents) are not universally in existence and accepted, just as they were not in earlier European history. The empirical evidence shows that some rights defined as human rights are shared by many people all over the world and also many governments, but also that they are not shared by all in their generality. However little or widely human rights are distributed globally, the extent of their existence is not a conclusive 'proof' for or against the moral-political claim of a universal validity of human rights. While legal sciences and political philosophy can counter the uneven empirical distribution of human rights by reference to the (national, international, natural) law by which human rights 'exist' universally, anthropology, at least in my view, does not offer a scientific legitimation for taking a particular point of view, for or against the universality of human rights.

Is this a problem? Without the shield of a scientific legitimation, anthropologists who promote human rights become vulnerable to the observation and sometimes to the reproach that they are assuming a partisan moral and political view, albeit one shared by many people all over the world. They cannot hide their value statements behind a scientific legitimation provided by their own science. Ethnocentrism is, of course, regarded as one of the major sins anthropologists can commit. But there is a difference between ethnocentric and/or idiosyncratic moral statements of anthropologists and the analytically distanced description and analysis of anthropology.[27] If this distinction is made clear, there seems to be no problem. Why should anthropologists not be open about their moral and political preference? Anthropologists have their own moral and political convictions and often want to act upon them as committed national, ethnic or world citizens, inspired by humanistic or religious values and ideals. These concerns often guide their research interests towards the study of socially and politically relevant issues such as inequality, oppression, exploitation and insecurity, on smaller and larger political scales. It may impel them to a critically engaged activist research (Speed 2006). Their knowledge may enable anthropologists to critically evaluate policies affecting the populations researched, and this evaluation may lead them to take certain political stands for or against such policies.

I do not think that a scientific legitimation is needed for promoting human rights. The raison d'être of the claims for a universality of human rights is that they are *not* (yet) universal. When human rights emerged, very much against the wishes of the then powerful and against (state) law, there clearly was no 'universality'. Human rights were demanded when they were not enshrined in law – when they were 'nonsense upon stilts' (Bentham, see Waldron 1987) indeed. If those who formulated and/or fought for human rights had waited for their universal existence, they would probably still be waiting. On the other hand, if some legal notion (for instance gender discrimination, the *talion* principle, the death penalty) were in some way or other universal in existence, that in itself would not be a good reason to demand its universal application, or to demand the continued maintenance of its application (see Xiaorong Li 2001).

But anthropologists, due to their discipline, have no superior right to pass moral judgments, nor is their discipline normative in the sense that political value statements can be scientifically grounded.[28] I see anthropology's task in describing, analysing and explaining the variability of social and cultural organizations, and not in a search for morally or legally correct solutions to social problems.[29] Whether or not one is inclined to view conditions of legal pluralism – or local law, or religious law, or state law, or human rights law – as 'good' is an expression of moral and political values. It is not a scientific anthropological statement but belongs to a different 'profession', of legal scholar, judge, lawmaker, development worker (see F. von Benda-Beckmann 1997, 2002).

If anthropologists' moral-political considerations are freed from the need to justify them scientifically, more nuanced attitudes towards the tensions between analytical description and moral evaluation become visible beyond the either-or, good-bad, politically correct dichotomies. A wider range of attitudes and practical consequences becomes 'normal', depending on one's temperament, political convictions and one's expectations of the intended and unintended consequences of practices encouraged by one's own initiative. For other actors in human rights politics a more general legitimation is a great need. In an era in which law (still) is the predominant source of legitimation of exercising power, pushing political and moral values (however honestly or cynically) requires the legitimation of law. This is why the *legal*, and not the political character of human rights is emphasized, and the universal existence of human rights as the underlying legitimation of the international codification. Advocating human rights and pressuring other states to adopt them then is not a partisan political preference, but only a guarding and promoting of a pre-existing and accepted common good. It is this need to legitimate human rights law, when engaging in the persuasive or coercive diffusion of human rights, that is behind the postulated universal existence issue, because otherwise it would just be a political claim. This need to legitimate human rights, through international law, and international law by some essentialistic assumptions about human dignity (which are so noble that one cannot simply speak up against them), is, I would argue, the real 'iron cage' imprisoning lawyers and all those who need to legitimate the diffusion of human rights as more than only morally and politically justified, much more than the one of 'culture' suggested by Riles (2006). Anthropologists should look at this cage rather than inhabit it.

Acknowledgements

I am grateful to Chris Hann, Anne Griffiths and Keebet von Benda-Beckmann for their critical and constructive comments on an earlier version of this paper.

Notes

1. There is no uniform 'Islamic' point of view. For the spectrum of Muslim scholars' views, see An-Na'im (1995); Barin (1996). For Asian and African perspectives see the contributions in Berting et al. (1990); Welch and Leary (1990); Van der Heijden and Tahzib-Lie (1998); Meijer (2001).
2. See Ignatieff's critique (1999: 32). Others have criticized (Hardin 1968: 1246) or defended (Barnett 1988: 25) the idea of universal human rights on utilitarian grounds.
3. See for instance Lubis (1990) on Indonesia; Xiaorong Li (2001) on China.
4. To mention just a few: Waldron (1987); Downing and Kushner (1988); Donnelly (1989); Renteln (1990); Welch and Leary (1990); Messer (1993); An-Na'im (1995); Nanda (1995); Wilson (1997a); Ignatieff (1999); Vachon (2000); Merry (2001, 2005); Baxi (2002); Eberhard (2002); Wilson and Mitchell (2003); Goodale (2006a).
5. See also Baxi (2002) on the way in which the 'empirical' question of human rights in the West informs and justifies attitudes that do not accept a universality of human rights.
6. The change and the ambivalence are apparent from the two statements of the American Anthropological Association (AAA) on human rights in 1947 and 1999 that move from a cultural relativist position towards the endorsement of universalist principles with expressions of 'respect to concrete human differences, both collective and individual' (AAA 1999). See Eriksen (2001) on the ambivalent UNESCO position.
7. See Wilson and Mitchell (2003: 4); Goodale (2006b); Riles (2006).
8. See e.g. Dembour (2001); Eberhard (2002); Hastrup (2003). For an approach trying to balance the imperative of respect for other cultures with feminist strategies, see Bunting (1993); Gupta (2003).
9. See Merry (1997 and 2005) on vernacularization of human rights.
10. On the 1993 conference in Vienna see van Genugten (1996).

11. Eberhard (2002) speaks of a 'pluriverse' of human rights. See Mehrpour (1998: 196) on the similarities 'between religious teachings and what social thinkers came to believe at the ... dawn of the enlightenment'.
12. Baxi (2002) relates notions in legal systems in other parts of the world to human rights. Lubis (1990: 127) refers to legal-political principles of democracy in Indonesian local ethnic legal orders. Hastrup (2003) speaks of '"like" concepts'.
13. Wilson includes parallels to human rights in Islamic legal thought or Chinese traditional law (1997a: 13).
14. See F. von Benda-Beckmann (1997, 2002).
15. India is a good example; see the contrasting positions of Donnelly (1990); Joshi (1990) and Gupta (2003).
16. This of course does not preclude following Wilson's demand that we 'examine how this plurality is related; how differences in institutional practices become systematized, and how moral values traverse contexts' (1997a: 14). In fact, such an examination presupposes a comparative analysis of the plurality of forms.
17. In judgments, in international law and conventions, such as the UDHR and the many subsequent UN conventions, in the Human Rights of the European Community or in state constitutions.
18. For a radically different, and in my view more plausible, view on India, see Donnelly (1990); Joshi (1990). See also Nanda (1995).
19. For an interesting anthropological analysis of how human rights violations are constructed, see Wilson (1997b).
20. There are a few exceptions, e.g. Santos (1995); F. von Benda-Beckmann (1997); K. von Benda-Beckmann (1997); Merry (1997, 2001, 2005); Wilson (1997a); Griffiths (2001); Randeria (2003); F. von Benda-Beckmann, K. von Benda-Beckmann and A. Griffiths (2005); Wiber (2005).
21. Not to problematize the concept of law may be a general characteristic of most recent literature on law and human rights; see Riles (2006: 58).
22. The major field of struggle was property and inheritance (see F. von Benda-Beckmann 1979).
23. See Greenhouse (1998) on the non-congruity between ethnic identity, culture and customary law.
24. For France, see Bowen (2003).
25. See the contributions in Pradhan, F. von Benda-Beckmann and K. von Benda-Beckmann (2000). See Gleick (2003) on the importance of having a human right to water; also F. von Benda-Beckmann and K. von Benda-Beckmann (2003).
26. On the tensions in the relations between international human rights law and other international legal regulations, see K. von Benda-Beckmann (1997).
27. No anthropologists would claim that a completely value-free social science is possible. But it would be just as naïve to maintain that one may not be able to distance oneself from the values dominant in one's own time and society or that one may not be able to analytically frame one's conceptual and theoretical assumptions as culturally neutral as possible. 'Analytic' points of view intending to be politically neutral, however, often become politi-

cally charged as they are 'contextually' interpreted by others in the terms of *their* own system of meaning.

28. So also Gordon (2005: 449) and Roughley (2005) in their comments on Carrithers (2005). See Baumgarten (1973) on Weber; also Hastrup and Elsass (1990).

29. This is contested terrain. See the essays of Hastrup and Elsass (1990) and Carrithers (2005) in *Current Anthropology* and the comments on these papers. See also Dembour (2001); Eberhard (2002) and Goodale (2006a: 5).

References

American Anthropological Association (AAA). 1947. 'Statement on Human Rights. Submitted to the Commission on Human Rights, United Nations, by the Executive Board', *American Anthropologist* 49: 539–43.

———. 1999. *Declaration on Anthropology and Human Rights*. http://www.aaanet .org/stmts/humanrts.htm (last accessed 8 March 2008).

An-Na'im, A.A. (ed.). 1995. *Human Rights in Crosscultural Perspectives: A Quest for Consensus*. Philadelphia: University of Pennsylvania Press.

Bahar, S. and M.Z. Tadjoeddin. 2004. *Masih ada harapan: Posisi sebuah etnik minoritas dalam hidup berbangsa dan bernegara*. Jakarta: Yayasan Sepuluh Agustus.

Barin, B. 1996. 'Islam and Human Rights: The Path towards Universal Human Rights', in P. Morales (ed.), *Towards Global Human Rights*. Tilburg: International Centre for Human and Public Affairs, 129–35.

Barnett, C. 1988. 'Is There a Scientific Basis in Anthropology for the Ethics of Human Rights?', in T.E. Downing and G. Kushner (eds), *Human Rights and Anthropology*. Cambridge, MA: Cultural Survival, 21–26.

Baumgarten, E. 1973. 'Einleitung', in M. Weber (ed.), *Soziologie, Universalgeschichtliche Analysen, Politik*. Stuttgart: A. Kroener, xi–xxxvi.

Baxi, U. 2002. *The Future of Human Rights*. New Delhi: Oxford University Press.

Benda-Beckmann, F. von. 1979. *Property in Social Continuity: Continuity and Change in the Maintenance of Property Relationships through Time in Minangkabau, West Sumatra*. The Hague: M. Nijhoff.

———. 1997. 'Citizens, Strangers and Indigenous Peoples: Conceptual Politics and Legal Pluralism', in F. von Benda-Beckmann, K. von Benda-Beckmann and A. Hoekema (eds), *Natural Resources, Environment and Legal Pluralism*. Yearbook Law and Anthropology 9. The Hague, Boston, London: M. Nijhoff, 1–42.

———. 2002. 'Who's Afraid of Legal Pluralism?' *Journal of Legal Pluralism* 47: 37–82.

Benda-Beckmann, F. von and K. von Benda-Beckmann. 2003. 'Water, Human Rights and Legal Pluralism', *Water, Human Rights and Governance*. Special Issue *Water Nepal* 9/10(1/2): 63–76.

———. 2005. 'Democracy in Flux: Time, Mobility and Sedentarization of Law in Minangkabau, Indonesia', in F. von Benda-Beckmann, K. von Benda-Beckmann and A. Griffiths (eds), *Mobile People, Mobile Law: Expanding Legal Relations in a Contracting World*. Aldershot: Ashgate, 111–30.

Benda-Beckmann, F. von, K. von Benda-Beckmann and A. Griffiths (eds). 2005. *Mobile People, Mobile Law: Expanding Legal Relations in a Contracting World.* Aldershot: Ashgate.

Benda-Beckmann, K. von. 1997. 'The Environmental Protection and Human Rights of Indigenous Peoples: A Tricky Alliance', in F. von Benda-Beckmann, K. von Benda-Beckmann and A. Hoekema (eds), *Natural Resources, Environment and Legal Pluralism. Yearbook Law and Anthropology 9.* The Hague, Boston, London: M. Nijhoff, 302–23.

Berting, J., P.R. Baehr, J.H. Burgers, C. Flinterman, B. de Klerk, R. Kroes, C.A. van Minnen and K. Vanderwal (eds). 1990. *Human Rights in a Pluralist World: Individuals and Collectivities.* Westport, CT, and London: Meckler.

Bowen, J. 2003. 'Two Approaches to Rights and Religion in Contemporary France', in J.K. Cowan, M.-B. Dembour and R.A. Wilson (eds), *Culture and Rights: Anthropological Perspectives.* Cambridge: Cambridge University Press, 54–70.

Bunting, A. 1993. 'Theorizing Women's Cultural Diversity in Feminist International Human Rights Strategies', *Journal of Law and Society* 20: 6–22.

Carrithers, M. 2005. 'Anthropology as a Moral Science', *Current Anthropology* 46(3): 433–46.

Cowan, J.K. 2006. 'Culture and Rights after Culture and Rights', *American Anthropologist* 108(1): 9–24.

Cowan, J.K., M.-B. Dembour and R.A. Wilson. 2001. 'Introduction', in J.K. Cowan, M.-B. Dembour and R.A. Wilson (eds), *Culture and Rights: Anthropological Perspectives.* Cambridge: Cambridge University Press, 1–26.

Dembour, M.-B. 2001. 'Following the Pendulum: Between Universalism and Relativism', in J.K. Cowan, M.-B. Dembour and R.A Wilson (eds), *Culture and Rights: Anthropological Perspectives.* Cambridge: Cambridge University Press, 56–76.

Donnelley, J. 1989. *Human Rights.* Ithaca, NY: Cornell University Press.

———. 1990. 'Traditional Values and Universal Human Rights: Caste in India', in C.E. Welch and V.A. Leary (eds), *Asian Perspectives on Human Rights.* Boulder, CO: Westview, 55–90.

Downing, T.E. and G. Kushner (eds). 1988. *Human Rights and Anthropology.* Cambridge, MA: Cultural Survival.

Eberhard, C. 2002. *Droits de l'Homme et Dialogue Interculturel.* Paris: Editions des Ecrivains.

Eriksen, T.H. 2001. 'Between Universalism and Relativism: A Critique of the UNESCO Concept of Culture', in J.K. Cowan, M.-B. Dembour and R.A. Wilson (eds), *Culture and Rights: Anthropological Perspectives.* Cambridge: Cambridge University Press, 127–51.

Fitzpatrick, P. 1984. 'Traditionalism and Traditional Law', *Journal of African Law* 28: 20–27.

Flinterman, C. 1990. 'Three Generations of Human Rights', in J. Berting, P.R. Baehr, J.H. Burgers, C. Flinterman, B. de Klerk, R. Kroes, C.A. van Minnen and K. VanderWal (eds), *Human Rights in a Pluralist World: Individuals and Collectivities.* Westport, CT, and London: Meckler, 75–81.

Genugten, W. van 1996. 'Universality of Human Rights, as Discussed during the 1993 World Conference on Human Rights; Description and Comments', in P. Morales (ed.), *Towards Global Human Rights*. Tilburg: International Centre for Human and Public Affairs, 41–45.

Gleick, P.H. 2003. 'The Human Right to Water', *Water, Human Rights and Governance*, Special Issue *Water Nepal* 9/10(1/2): 117–25.

Goodale, M. 2006a. 'Introduction to "Anthropology and Human Rights in a New Key"', *American Anthropologist* 108(1): 1–8.

———. 2006b. 'Ethical Theory as Social Practice', *American Anthropologist* 108(1): 25–37.

Gordon, E. 2005. 'Comment on Michael Carrithers, Anthropology as a Moral Science', *Current Anthropology* 46(3): 449–50.

Greenhouse, C.J. 1998. 'Legal Pluralism and Cultural Difference: What Is the Difference? A Response to Professor Woodman', *Journal of Legal Pluralism* 42: 61–72.

Griffiths, A. 2001. 'Gendering Culture: Towards a Plural Perspective of Kwena Women's Rights', in J.K. Cowan, M.-B. Dembour and R.A. Wilson (eds), *Culture and Rights: Anthropological Perspectives*. Cambridge: Cambridge University Press, 102–26.

Gupta, N. 2003. 'Women's Human Rights and the Practice of Dowry in India', *Journal of Legal Pluralism* 48: 123.

Hardin, G. 1968. 'The Tragedy of the Commons', *Science* 162: 1234–48.

Hastrup, K. 2003. 'Representing the Common Good: The Limits of Legal Language', in R.A. Wilson and J.P. Mitchell (eds), *Human Rights in Global Perspective: Anthropological Studies of Rights, Claims and Entitlements*. London, New York: Routledge, 16–32.

Hastrup, K. and P. Elsass. 1990. 'Anthropological Advocacy: A Contradiction in Terms?' *Current Anthropology* 31: 301–8.

Heijden, B. van der and B. Tahzib-Lie (eds). 1998. *Reflections on the Universal Declaration of Human Rights*. The Hague: M. Nijhoff.

Ignatieff, M. 1999. *Whose Universal Values? The Crisis in Human Rights*. The Hague: Praemium Erasmianum Essay.

Joshi, B.R. 1990. 'Human Rights as Dynamic Process: The Case of India's Untouchables', in C.E. Welch and V.A. Leary (eds), *Asian Perspectives on Human Rights*. Boulder, CO: Westview, 162–85.

Lubis, M. 1990. 'Asian Cultures and Human Rights', in J. Berting, P.R. Baehr, J.H. Burgers, C. Flinterman, B. de Klerk, R. Kroes, C.A. van Minnen and K. Vanderwal (eds), *Human Rights in a Pluralist World: Individuals and Collectivities*. Westport, CT, and London: Meckler, 125–32.

Mehrpour, H. 1998. 'Human Rights in the Universal Declaration and the Religious Perspective', in B. van der Heijden and B. Tahzib-Lie (eds), *Reflections on the Universal Declaration of Human Rights*. The Hague: M. Nijhoff, 191–96.

Meijer, M. (ed.). 2001. *Dealing with Human Rights: Asian Values and Western Views on the Value of Human Rights*. Oxford: World View Publishing.

Merry, S.E. 1997. 'Legal Pluralism and Transnational Culture: The Ka Ho'kolokolonui Kanaka Maoli Tribunal, Hawai'i, 1993', in R.A. Wilson (ed.), *Human Rights, Culture and Context: Anthropological Perspectives*. London: Pluto Press, 28–48.

———. 2001. 'Changing Rights, Changing Culture', in J.K. Cowan, M.-B. Dembour and R.A. Wilson (eds), *Culture and Rights: Anthropological Perspectives.* Cambridge: Cambridge University Press, 31–55.

———. 2005. 'Human Rights and Global Legal Pluralism: Reciprocity and Disjuncture', in F. von Benda-Beckmann, K. von Benda-Beckmann and A. Griffiths (eds), *Mobile People, Mobile Law: Expanding Legal Relations in a Contracting World.* Aldershot: Ashgate, 215–32.

Messer, E. 1993. 'Anthropology and Human Rights', *Annual Review of Anthropology* 22: 221–49.

Nanda, V.P. 1995. 'Hinduism and Human Rights', in V.P. Nanda and S.P. Sinha (eds), *Hindu Law and Legal Theory.* Aldershot: Ashgate/Dartmouth, 237–47.

Panikkar, R. 1984. 'Is the Notion of Human Rights a Western Concept?' *Interculture* 17(1): 28–47.

Pradhan, R., F. von Benda-Beckmann and K. von Benda-Beckmann (eds). 2000. *Water, Land and Law: Changing Rights to Land and Water in Nepal.* Kathmandu, Wageningen, Rotterdam: Freedeal, WAU, EUR.

Randeria, S. 2003. 'Glocalization of Law: Environmental Justice, World Bank, NGOs and the Cunning State in India', *Current Sociology* (special issue) 51: 305–28.

Renteln, A.D. 1990. *International Human Rights: Universalism versus Relativism.* London: Sage.

Riles, A. 2006. 'Anthropology, Human Rights and Legal Knowledge: Culture in the Iron Cage', *American Anthropologist* 108(1): 52–65.

Roughley, N. 2005. 'Comment on Carrithers', *Current Anthropology* 46: 451–52.

Santos, B. de Sousa. 1995. *Toward a New Common Sense: Law, Science and Politics in the Paradigmatic Transition.* London, New York: Routledge.

Speed, S. 2006. 'At the Crossroads of Human Rights and Anthropology: Toward a Critically Engaged Activist Research', *American Anthropologist* 108(1): 66–76.

Tigar, M.E. and M.R. Levy. 1977. *Law and the Rise of Capitalism.* New York, London: Monthly Review Press.

Vachon, R. 2000. 'Au-dela de l'Universalisation et de l'Interculturation des Droits de l'Homme, du Droit et de l'Ordre Négocié', *Bulletin de Liaison du Laboratoire d'Anthropologie Juridique de Paris* 25: 9–21.

Waldron, J. (ed.). 1987. *Nonsense upon Stilts: Bentham, Burke and Marx on the Rights of Man.* London, New York: Methuen.

Welch, C.E. and V.A. Leary (eds). 1990. *Asian Perspectives on Human Rights.* Boulder, CO: Westview.

Wiber, M.G. 2005. 'Mobile Law and Globalism: Epistemic Communities versus Community-based Innovation in the Fisheries Sector', in F. von Benda-Beckmann, K. von Benda-Beckmann and A. Griffiths (eds), *Mobile People, Mobile Law: Expanding Legal Relations in a Contracting World.* Aldershot: Ashgate, 131–51.

Wilson, R.A. 1997a. 'Human Rights, Culture and Context: An Introduction', in R.A. Wilson (ed.), *Human Rights, Culture and Context: Anthropological Perspectives.* London, Chicago: Pluto Press, 1–28.

———. 1997b. 'Representing Human Rights Violations: Social Contexts and Subjectivities', in R.A. Wilson (ed.), *Human Rights, Culture and Context: Anthropological Perspectives.* London, Chicago: Pluto Press, 134–60.

Wilson, R.A. and J.P. Mitchell (eds). 2003. *Human Rights in Global Perspective: Anthropological Studies of Rights, Claims and Entitlements.* London, New York: Routledge.

Xiaorong Li 2001. '"Asian Values" and the Universality of Human Rights', in M. Meijer (ed.), *Dealing with Human Rights: Asian Values and Western Views on the Value of Human Rights.* Oxford: World View Publishing, 37–47.

AT THE INTERSECTION OF LEGALITIES

6

LEARNING COMMUNITIES AND LEGAL SPACES

Community-based Fisheries Management
in a Globalizing World

Melanie G. Wiber and John F. Kearney

Introduction

I first stepped off the ferry onto the Island[1] in 1969. The Island was shrouded in dense fog, and shearwaters in the harbour indicated it was sufficiently offshore to attract pelagic avian wanderers. The houses formed a semicircle around the main public wharf, with numerous small private wharves and salt-fish processing sheds encircling the cove. There were no hotels, and the one restaurant in the village was a converted fish processing shed situated out on one of the private wharfs. All of this enhanced my impression of a pristine fishing village, isolated from the rest of the world, with human life oriented to the sea and to fishing.

The next morning I woke to the engines of the fishing boats. These boats, all less than 45 feet in length, were streaming out of the harbour by the dozens to catch cod, pollock and haddock with handlines. All around the Island, within a few miles of shore, I could see these inshore vessels, each one surrounded by a flock of gulls diving for the entrails of the harvested fish being gutted and iced at sea. Later I watched the boats return to the wharves, to unload fish into trucks if they were going to the fresh fish market or into barrels of brine if they were to go to household-based salt fish processing.

This scene would have been familiar to another anthropologist, twenty years earlier, who came to the Island as part of an interdisciplinary team of social scientists studying rapid social change in the region. From outward appearances, not much had changed in the intervening years. True, the multinational fish processing company that had been located on the neighbouring island had left, the fishers' union that had organized in response to their fish buying practices was also defunct, as was the fishers' marketing cooperative. The consumer cooperative still existed but was just barely hanging on against the competition of a general store operated by a fish merchant. The fishing boats were probably a few feet longer than they were in the 1940s, with the main technological addition being the echo sounding fish finders that became available after the Second World War. But the fishing methods were still basically the same, fish were plentiful, fathers fished with their sons or close relatives, and the proceeds from the catch were equally shared among all the crew. Social differentiation was minimal, with the population consisting mainly of fishing households, two or three fish processors/merchants, a couple of preachers, a lighthouse keeper, and one schoolteacher.

However, looking out to sea in the 1960s, I could see one glaring anomaly in this relatively egalitarian picture: the fish dragger. The fish dragger used a different technology, catching very large quantities of fish with nets that were dragged along the sea floor. These were not offshore draggers (or trawlers) owned by vertically integrated, large corporations such as one found along other parts of the Atlantic coast. Island draggers were not much bigger than the inshore boats used by the hook-and-line fishers. Dragger technology had been adopted by a few Island fishers some fifteen years earlier, at the instigation of federal government officials who saw it as an effective way to catch flounder, an otherwise underutilized stock. But dragger captains soon directed their efforts at the traditional groundfish species such as cod, haddock, and pollock. The crews were still largely kin-based, although by the 1960s a larger portion of the catch revenues went towards paying capital and operating costs.

Even at this early stage, there was widespread opposition to draggers from other fishers. They feared that the draggers would transform the landscape of the ocean bottom, destroying the ecology and depleting stocks. The team of mid-century social scientists working in the area also saw the draggers as a destructive force, predicting that they would forever transform the socioeconomic landscape of the region. In the 1960s, this prediction appeared to have been an overreaction.

During the 1970s and 1980s, however, as I continued to visit the Island, the number of draggers increased steadily. The size of vessels also increased, up to 65 feet, the limit allowed for inshore vessels. Because they caught large quantities of fish, the draggers were very profitable. But these large quantities also meant that fish could be processed neither partially at sea, nor at the household level, so that the captains depended instead on selling to processing plants. Increased capitalization followed, as dwindling fish stocks required the use of more sophisticated fish finding equipment, larger gear, and gear innovations for dragging in less hospitable environments. And as their capitalization costs increased, so too did their economic capture by the processing companies, as the captains depended more and more on these companies to finance their enterprises, often to the point of surrendering economic control of the boat to the company in order to maintain their job as a fisher.

By the late 1980s, there was an alarming decline of fish stocks. The traditional hook-and-line fishers were having difficulty finding good catches on the grounds located around the Island and blamed the draggers for fishing to extinction each of the highly localized stocks of groundfish that spawned on the inshore fishing grounds. The only remaining groundfish came from stocks that spawned in offshore, deeper, less accessible areas. The growing crisis led the government to limit the entry of new dragging enterprises and to introduce annual quotas. Meanwhile, in order to compensate for lost income, some of the hook-and-line fishers began whale-watching businesses to attract summer tourists to the region. Food services and accommodation began to appear in response to the influx of such visitors.

By 1991, the crisis in the dragger fleet was such that the federal government forced fishers to accept the introduction of individual transferable quotas (ITQs). Each dragger received an annual allocation of cod, haddock and pollock from the total allowable catch.[2] But these allocations were usually not enough to support a viable fishing enterprise, requiring boat owners to buy or lease additional quota from other fishers. As quota prices increased, it became more difficult for the smaller, independent dragger enterprises to survive. Within a few years, the dragger fleet was drastically reduced in size. Those that did survive were tied financially to or were owned by fish processing companies, such that quota control and ownership became concentrated in the hands of a few.

Despite this 'rationalization' of the dragger fleet, groundfish catches continued to decline, and by 1996 it appeared that the hook-and-line fishers were also to be forced into an ITQ system. But unlike the draggers, the hook-and-liners organized a resistance, and after weeks of protests and occupations of government offices by fishers and their supporters, the federal government agreed to let them develop community-based groundfish management boards as an alternative to ITQs.[3] However, the government was not willing to provide legislative support (enabling legislation) for such boards, and as a result, the boards enforced compliance with their management plans through contract law.[4] Each fisher who joined the management plan signed a contract with the board, setting out the volume of fish they could catch and conditions of fishing. The board also established its own infractions committee;[5] severe infractions of contract rules led to the fisher being evicted from the management plan. From the inception of the management boards, hook-and-line fishers had a choice between fishing under the jurisdiction of these community boards or under a management plan devised by the federal government. Over 98 percent of the fishers chose the community management boards.

In organizing an effective and cooperative management body, the hook-and-line fishers in the region avoided government rationalization and privatization of the right to fish. Nonetheless, the volume of fish allocated to these boards was so small that groundfish became a minor component of income for most members.[6] Today when I visit the Island, I see two or three inshore hook-and-line vessels heading out to the fishing grounds during the course of a morning. During the day a couple of fish draggers come into the wharf to unload fish caught in various coastal and deeper water areas. The vast majority of the dragger fish quota in this particular region is owned by one fish processing company. The inshore hook-and-line fishers from the Island survive only by virtue of the fact that they have a licence to fish lobster, the sole remaining economically viable form of independent, household-based fishing.

Thousands of tourists come to the Island each year for whale-watching, nature adventure tours and nature study. The Island is now fully integrated into a global economy, both selling its fish to and attracting tourists from a world that wishes to partake of what is advertised as pristine nature. To attract visitors to the Island, residents market their tourism services on the Internet and through regional and international tourism agencies. They compete with other tourist regions of the country for the government financial support necessary to upgrade and maintain the marine and land-based infrastructure required to support tourism, including tourist accommodation, roads, ferry services and wharves. But the benefits of tourism are not equitably distributed on the Island,[7] and many families have seen a sharp decline in household economic viability. Out-migration is the only reasonable choice for most Island youth.

It took fifty years for the predictions of the mid-century social scientists to come about, but ultimately the fish dragger did transform the region. The social scientists did not predict, however, that a great natural resource, the fishery, would be destroyed in the process. Nor did they predict that the lion's share of the remainder of this public resource would become the private property of a handful of people. And of course, this transformation did not affect just the Island, or the Canadian Maritimes. This transformation has taken place in very similar

form wherever industrialized fishing and scientific fisheries management regimes have been introduced, which is to say, on all of the major
fishing grounds of the world.

In 2004, I ask myself how to characterize this change. Some say that
the Island residents have shown a remarkable resilience in adopting a
successful niche for themselves in a globalizing world, despite over-
whelming forces of economic rationalization and environmental destruction. But as Arturo Escobar has recently noted (2001: 156), it might
be more useful to think outside the globalism box and to resist viewing
the local as deriving meaning only from juxtaposition to the global. It
might also be useful to think outside the capitalism box and to see the
groundfish boards as intrinsic to a local 'model of the economy' (Escobar 2001: 153), a model based on egalitarian and cooperative values,
and on conservation-based ethics. In what follows, we illustrate how
this different way of thinking about the local can be quite fruitful.

Theorizing Community-based Management

The transformation of local spaces as in the above example of the Island
has generated much debate over how local places and communities
can and should organize themselves to ensure survival. One paradigm
much debated in recent years is community-based natural resource
management (CBNRM).[8] Opinion is divided, as some argue that community-based management will facilitate both conservation practices
and equitable local access, while others are more doubtful,[9] particularly
in more complex politico-legal and economic contexts.[10] Opinion is also
divided on the potential for cooptation of CBNRM by more powerful members of communities as opposed to the potential for the community to collectively prevent the powerful few from colluding with
state agents.[11] Yet other concerns address the fit between community
boundaries and the ecosystem-wide, dynamic demands of natural resource management,[12] with Cole (2003: 97) suggesting that only a global
management regime can sufficiently address the broader ecosystem
interactions that pertain in forestry, river system management or the
fisheries.

Recent policy advice has been to keep the government central to the
planning and enhancement of CBNRM (Lindsay 1998; Foster and Haward 2003). Lindsay (1998) views the law as central here and argues for
government control of seven key areas, including: delimiting the respective powers and responsibilities of state versus community agents;
legally recognizing local community institutions; linking responsibili-

ties and rights to particular sites and resources; granting secure rights based on dependency on the resource or on historic patterns of access; defining the boundaries of the community; sanctioning local law making and enforcing it against interlopers; and helping to tune these regulations to current ecological knowledge. But Lindsay also argues, and our research supports this, that the state must enable communities both in a way that promotes local security of access to the resource, *and* in a way that promotes flexibility and leaves legal space for innovation and adaptation. We argue that promoting flexibility and allowing innovation and adaptation is unlikely where any state-centric approach to building CBNRM is taken. Furthermore, the barriers to effective CBNRM do not always arise so much from what is missing in the state legal environment, but rather from what already exists.

In the Canadian fisheries sector, a major barrier to CBNRM is the established state management practice. Bureaucrats often explain their inability to support CBNRM by reference to their legally constituted responsibility under the federal act that empowers the Department of Fisheries and Oceans (DFO). It is true that such legally constituted responsibilities have served as the basis for grievances against the DFO, as in the case of the Guysborough community crab allocation more fully described elsewhere.[13] Local state bureaucrats first allowed and then rescinded local control over community crab allocations. One problem was that fishers who were not members of the communities involved sued both the community management group and the state bureaucracy on the grounds that their exclusion was not justified under the act. But it is also true that, given the political will, enabling legislation would allow bureaucrats to legally empower community-based managers and to recognize community-based rules of access. In many settings, however, such enabling legislation is largely blocked as a result of the dominant privatization regime.

Under the wide mandate of the DFO and the broad responsibilities of the federal minister, a tendency has developed to micro-manage the fishery on all three Canadian coasts – to prescribe in great detail the structural organization of fisher groups and their geographical access to and patterns of fishing. This has proven fatal to local flexibility (Finlayson and McCay 1998). In this micro-management, Canada has relied on technical epistemic communities (Wiber 2005) to identify problems and specify solutions, thereby generating complex management plans that are alien to a wider diversity of production practices or local community socioeconomic realities. One result of this top-down approach has been a 'silo' mentality within a legal structure that compartmentalizes *both* resources *and* the people that use them, writing these compartments (fishery, forestry, mining, river management, near shore, offshore, coastal, estuarine, native, non-native) into mandates and provincial/federal divisions of power (see also Foster and Haward 2003).

This silo structure has a number of impacts that undercut CBNRM. Within fisheries, for example, the multi-species inshore fisher organizations have struggled for a number of years to have government administrators recognize both their special needs and the ecological complexity of their resource base.[14] But this has proven very difficult in a regime that addresses management on a fish-stock-by-fish-stock basis. Similarly, when the Marshall Decision of the Supreme Court of Canada introduced many new native entrants into the East Coast commercial fishery, non-native fishers were advised not to meet with natives to discuss the implications (Wiber and Kennedy 2001). This task was considered the mandate of the federal government, given the legal standing of 'status Indians'. Local solutions to local problems were not encouraged. Carving up access to important species has also pitted local user against local user, individual against community (Milsom 2003), with very little flexibility built into opening season or geographic fishing spaces to allow for conflict management. Disgruntled local users then pull in state bureaucrats, the courts, or local political actors in order to promote their own interests against those of others, especially when local consensus-based decisions go against them. This pattern of seeking political or legal solutions to local conflict is then used by the state, both to demonstrate local management incompetence and to distract from the state's role in generating the context in which conflict erupts.

The context of fishing in Canada is shaped by the state management model of the individual transferable quota, even for species not yet put under quota regimes. Privatization under the ITQ has created individual legal rights that effectively block collective or group management objectives (see also Wingard 2000), creating what has been termed 'the tyranny of small decisions' (Foster and Haward 2003: 550). It has facilitated the outward transfer and concentration of fishing rights and privileges, leaving most members of coastal communities (especially those of the next generation) with no say in the management regime. This in turn has damaged the economic sustainability of communities, as in our Island example.[15] Government bureaucrats deny any responsibility for the consequences, explaining them in two ways, first by reference to broad, naturalizing models and second by reference to property models. In the first case, fisheries bureaucrats view coastal poverty as a natural outcome of 'the tragedy of the commons', given the biological limitation of the fish stocks ('too many fishermen chasing too few fish'). The solution then is to downsize the fishery and encourage surplus harvesters to seek livelihoods elsewhere. Second, bureaucrats argue that just as the state cannot unreasonably interfere with individual private property rights, they cannot unreasonably interfere with choices made by quota holders. Indeed, advice from resource economists is that quota owners must be free to buy and sell quota as they see fit so that quota can be gathered into the hands of the most efficient holders (see Wiber 2000, 2005). But both of these explanations are patently insufficient. It is becoming increasingly evident that 'intrasectoral exclusion mechanisms', propagated under state management regimes that allocate the bulk of fish stock resources to large-scale industrialized harvesters, are the most significant factor influencing present-day coastal poverty (Béné 2003).

Given this fisheries management regime, where CBNRM has begun to emerge it has largely done so in 'the shadow of the law' (Mnookin and Kornhauser 1979).[16] That is to say, most CBNRM institutions have no legal basis, and in many places their shape is determined by an inhospitable legal environment,[17] one framed in turn by the erosion of the relationship between decision-makers and citizens and by the growing irrelevance of the state in regulating internal affairs (Cole 2003: 79). In Canada, for example, recent changes to the Oceans Act allow for devolving more responsibility to communities, but existing policy and practices have not changed, a situation often explained by reference to the need to conform to international management mechanisms. In the fisheries context, these include agreements of the North Atlantic Fisheries Organization, the International Convention on the Law of the Sea (1982), the Agreement on Straddling Fish Stocks and Highly Migratory Fish Stocks (1995) and the UN Food and Agriculture Organization's (FAO's) Code of Conduct for Responsible Fisheries (1995), among others. Communities that set out to find a better balance between the interests of the individual and those of the wider community have had to work within the small legal spaces left in an increasingly tight national and international regime. In non-Western contexts, communities are often dealing with weak enforcement capacity, and thus have more room for maneuver (Lobe and Berkes 2004), but the resulting CBNRM institutions have little legal security and are correspondingly fragile, subject to erosion or destruction when the state begins to pay attention, or when they run up against strong political opposition. In the Canadian context, this fragility is even more marked as there is little legal space for policy innovation in the first place.

Policy Options? State-centric or Community-centered Processes of CBNRM

The recent history of the groundfish management boards of the Canadian Maritimes illustrates that people at the grassroots level who struggle to retain some control over their resources are very innovative in creating alternative models of the economy. The management boards have proven an effective alternative to privatization, in that they have been able to better balance the interests of individual fishers and of coastal communities. But more importantly, since their inception the boards have involved themselves in a process of expanding the boundaries of the relevant community, to include many normally seen to be in conflict with their interests, such as marine scientists, aboriginal peoples and fishers in adjacent U.S. states.

One of the first steps in this direction involved recognizing the importance of broadly based ecological research. At a time when fishers were often in conflict with the scientists of the national fisheries administration, one groundfish board supported the foundation of a non-profit Bay of Fundy Marine Resource Centre. This Marine Resource Centre pursues independent research capacity-building on issues such as tracing ecological interdependencies, geographic information system (GIS) mapping of resources and resource users, and documenting local knowledge. One example of the latter type of research is the recent publication on the historic changes to groundfish spawning grounds in the Bay of Fundy (Graham, Engle and Recchia 2002). This documentation of fisher knowledge about specific bay stocks has influenced the way some marine scientists view groundfish stocks and their complex reproductive and migration patterns, a pattern being repeated elsewhere (Perlman 2003). The groundfish boards and the Marine Resource Centre also collaborated on a region-wide discussion of environmentally sound rules and ethics for the fishing industry (dubbed the Writing the Rules project), which ultimately resulted in a set of best practices that the majority of fishing associations in the region ratified (Bull, Coon and Recchia 2000).

Some groundfish boards took on a greater challenge after the Marshall Decision recognized a right of aboriginal involvement in the commercial fishery. This decision added many new fishers to the industry at a time when the government had been aggressively reducing fishing effort, creating conflict in many coastal communities over access to fishing rights. Along the Nova Scotia Bay of Fundy shore, however, a number of the groundfish boards and fisher organizations welcomed contact with local First Nation communities in their region. Initial meetings encouraged by both sides soon translated into mutual support; for example, the native community aided in organizing against a coastal rock quarry that inshore fishers saw as an environmental threat, while the boards in turn supported the natives in their efforts to initiate an experimental native lobster fishery.

Some boards also set up advisory and research committees, which included community development workers, environmentalists, academics, marine scientists (some of them working for the federal government) and community members, as well as fishers (see Bull 1998: 60). These committees played two roles: first, they assisted with long-term policy development and strategic planning; second, they advised the board on identification, planning and implementation of research. In more recent months, the groundfish management boards have engaged in dialogue across the Canada-U.S. border on transboundary and other policy issues, suggesting and participating in a study tour of corresponding New England fishing communities. This sort of inclusive outreach has not been facilitated under the state management regime, and indeed, some of these activities were actively discouraged by state bureaucrats as they cut across or ignored jurisdictional and administrative boundaries.

Inclusive, Pluralistic Community-based Management: Learning Communities

We agree with Leach, Mearns and Scoones (1999: 226) that the real institutional matrix for management of any natural resource involves significantly undertheorized institutional elements at the micro and the macro levels.[18] Our research illustrates that one undertheorized element is the total legal landscape that affects natural resources and those who rely on them, a landscape that includes significant levels of legal pluralism (including local or customary law as with the Writing the Rules project and private contracts, state management legislation and legal decisions such as the Marshall Decision, and international law and various international agreements, plus the interactions of all three). It also illustrates the need to develop the analytical tools to examine the interconnections and discontinuities in this legal landscape. In our view, the complex elements of this landscape can and have served both as opportunities and as barriers with respect to the process of establishing sustainable CBNRM (see also Pinkerton 1989, 1992).

In this respect, our research differs from other attempts to theoretically conceptualize the local in the global, drawing as it does on the recent experiences of fishermen in the Scotia-Fundy region. We find it significant that some groundfish management boards have consistently viewed sustainable resource management as resting on the foundation of an inclusive notion of community. Their efforts remind us of recent work by Bennell and his colleagues (2000) in theorizing the need for 'learning communities' to assist in education and training for development policy in Africa.[19] Such learning communities, they argue, should include on an equal footing all relevant parties and interrelationships, from bureaucrats to researchers to donor agencies and local practitioners. Further, they should be 'demand driven, focused, high quality, practical and problem-oriented' (2000: 15). They valorize the same 'learning by doing' that has allowed fishermen in Scotia-Fundy to address conflict resolution, the role of science in policy-making and other targeted learning needs.

But evidence from the Scotia-Fundy region suggests that all natural resource management learning communities will need to develop two kinds of cross-scale linkages in order to be inclusive. First, we have observed fishermen struggling to establish vertical linkages that are based on a more equal footing, between their communities and other levels of decision-making and governance. Up until now, the tendency has been for many federal bureaucrats to try to employ such linkages to delegate responsibilities to local actors, without any real transfer of power or enabling resources. Second, horizontal linkages have had to be thrown across geographical community boundaries that could otherwise be quite divisive. In the few cases where other communities have resisted such overtures, these horizontal linkages have proven equally difficult. In our view, overcoming the barriers to both kinds of linkages will be fundamental to building effective learning communities, and we need to learn from those cases where there has been some limited success.

We see a critical difference between such nascent learning communities and other approaches such as the current stakeholder consultation process, which has typically involved state bureaucrats inviting a number of narrowly defined interest groups to the table in order to negotiate protected status for their group interests, while ignoring or dismissing the claims of others.[20] In the Scotia-Fundy region of Canada, we have observed both stakeholder consultation, as in the recent government-sponsored Atlantic Region Policy Review process, *and* the struggle to create inclusive learning communities. We view the latter as having more potential to contribute towards civil society and democratic, transparent processes of governance, as learning communities could effectively challenge not only the decisions taken about access to and harvesting of natural resource stocks (management), but also the mechanisms by which such decisions will be reached (governance).

The struggle to create learning communities is linked to fisher recognition of the complexity of the legal-regulatory landscape affecting them. In a number of instances they have drawn on broadly based and inclusive networks in order to create management processes that affect wider environmental areas, develop common values and manage conflict among wider sets of users. They have worked to build linkages across gear sectors, to create fairer rules of resource access and to define common sets of rules or guidelines for resource extraction. They argue that without this work, and facing a legal environment that encourages individual accumulation at the expense of sustainability, the resource will soon be degraded beyond recovery.[21]

There are continuing roadblocks to the development of learning communities. One example has been the scallop fishery in the Bay of Fundy. While the Canadian government acknowledges both the opportunities in stock enhancement and the need for it, scallop enhancement programmes in the bay have so far been blocked by the different interests of the Full Bay Fleet (with access to both New Brunswick and Nova Scotia waters) and of various regional fishing communities with historic fishing rights in the same waters. Not every scallop fisher is willing to contribute to scallop enhancement, nor will they promise to avoid enhanced beds to allow the seeded spat time to develop. Scallop fishers can be treated as an inherently divisive entity by state bureaucracies, or they can be encouraged and enabled to develop cross-scale linkages and pluralistic and inclusive co-management institutions. Building these cross-scale linkages effectively may create resilient CBNRM management institutions that offer local communities such as our Island some protection from external economic threats and forces, including the effects of international trade agreements (Wiber 1999) and sudden ecological change (Berkes 2003).

Enabling legal contexts are a necessary condition, then, for the sustainable CBNRM; however, they are not a sufficient condition. The state will need to work closely with communities, and be part of the cross-scale linkages established by such communities, in order to achieve the right balance. When communities reach out to build wider coalitions, to elucidate common values and principles that underlie best local practice (as in the Writing the Rules project), it is not enough for governments to acknowledge this work, and then point to the few dissenters to explain why it will not work – governments need to be part of the process of developing common goals and objectives (and not through objectives-based management where the only objectives valued by the state are those created by government scientists and managers). The government role must also include providing important funding or other support for communities that set out to build governance capacity through learning communities.

Fishers' organizations, for example, are currently being asked to carry the cost of stock management, landing assessments and natural science. Any additional costs over and above those for social science research, community capacity building or institutional development must also be born fully by the fishers, but must by necessity come far down the list of organization expenditures, since the other expenditures form a condition of their licences to fish.[22] While many will argue that in the current 'user pays' environment, fishers should fund the cost of the administration of fishing, this does not address the wider question of wise management. We argue that allowing more legal space for local-level governance and management organizations can eventually lead to democratic and participatory decisions (not only for CBNRM but also for broader decisions) that are scaled up into provincial, national and international decision-making frameworks. Working towards the development and secure establishment of vertical and horizontal linkages then, would seem to be a logical and necessary role for government.

Conclusions

In his otherwise excellent article, Escobar neglects the legal dimension of the local political ecology, social movements and networks of alliance he traces among Afro-Columbians. While he examines their efforts to scale up linkages to reach across regions and 'life corridors', he pays little attention to the legal landscape that helps to shape 'the modes of articulation between socio-cultural forms of use and the natural environment' (2001: 161). This is understandable in the space constraints of an article, and yet, too often this important component *is assumed as static background material* in natural resource management studies. Our fisheries research reinforces the need to interrogate this legal landscape, and to expand the legal analysis outward, to trace the wider landscapes of legal interaction that affect those in whom we are interested. This follows in the footsteps of grassroots movements, as when the members of the fixed-gear groundfish boards in the Scotia-Fundy region sequentially involved themselves in wider issues, wider concerns, wider communities of interest. Fishers recognize that they must have more information on *whatever* affects the groundfish fishery and thus their communities, including: the introduction of privatization through the ITQ and possible alternative local arrangements; the legacy of colonialism and the aboriginal claims to the resource on which fishers rely; the transboundary issues and the common cause it is possible to find with similar fishers in adjacent nations. And they are growing increasingly critical of research that fails to adequately explore these interconnections. We too must be prepared to range out into the legal landscape in order to understand the discontinuities and disjunctures that have everyday consequences.

Acknowledgements

This paper was prepared for the *International Conference on Developing the Anthropology of Law in a Transnational World*, 17–19 June 2004, Edinburgh University.

The introduction to this chapter, written by John Kearney, draws on over thirty years of experience working in fishing communities in the Canadian Maritimes. The rest of the essay is coauthored. We wish to thank the Social Sciences and Humanities Research Council of Canada, which funded our collaborative research in the fisheries. We also thank our other collaborators on the project, Fikret Berkes and Anthony Charles.

Notes

1. The 'Island' referred to in this article is located in the Canadian Maritime Provinces. This island was part of a social psychiatry study in the 1940s–1960s that produced a number of well-read publications. Many islanders vigorously object to the image created of their community in these publications, viewing it as derogatory and damaging. Out of respect for their concerns, we identify neither the island nor the citations to the mid-century publications.
2. See Wiber (2000) for an assessment of the economic arguments used in support of the quota regime in Canada and elsewhere.
3. The first board was organized in the Sambro area on the eastern coast of Nova Scotia (Loucks 1998). Within a decade, ten boards had been organized throughout the Canadian Maritimes.
4. For an example contract, see Loucks, Charles and Butler (1998: 62–67).
5. On these infractions committees, see Bull (1998: 60).
6. Between 1984 and 1992, for example, hook-and-line vessels caught less than 17 percent of groundfish landed in Atlantic Canada (Butler 1998: 69).
7. On the politics of place and the distribution of resources under the effects of tourism, see Stokowski (2002).
8. See Brosius, Tsing and Zerner (1998).
9. See Gibson and Koontz (1998); Agrawal and Gibson (1999); Aswani (1999); Pretty and Ward (2001); Li (2002).

10. See Holm, Hersoug and Ranes (2000).
11. See Li (1996); Singleton (2000); Wingard (2000); Potter (2002); Bradshaw (2003) versus Béné (2003).
12. See Leach, Mearns and Scoones (1999: 240).
13. See Wiber (2005) for a description of the community-designed crab lottery allocation process followed for a brief time in Guysborough County, Nova Scotia.
14. Inshore fishermen typically rely on a mix of species, including: groundfish (cod, pollock, haddock, halibut), shellfish (shrimp, crab, lobster, scallop, clams, squid), pelagic species (tuna, herring, mackerel, shark) and others (sea urchin). This creates a logistical nightmare for acquiring licences and negotiating opening and closing seasons.
15. The economic loss when licences and quota are sold outside a community can be estimated by a recent study done in a Nova Scotia county, wherein 250 inshore vessels (fishing under 1,336 licenses), were found to have contributed over 45 million dollars in wharf value of raw product, plus four spin-off jobs for each vessel, to the economic profile of the county (see Boudreau and Boudreau 2003).
16. A huge literature in legal studies has been generated by Mnookin and Kornhauser's (1979) term, originally coined to examine the extent to which legal considerations affect private negotiations. Here, the focus is not so much whether folk norms or the law will be employed in social situations of conflict or negotiation, but rather on the struggle to maintain folk norms in the spaces left by the law.
17. Of course, legal cultures and contexts differ dramatically even within national boundaries. On the unique situation confronting South Pacific fisheries in the context of chieftainships and local authority, for example, see Adams (1998); Graham and Idechong (1998); Johannes (1998); Ruddle (1998); Aswani (1999).
18. However, Leach et al. make two comments that need to be qualified. First, they (1999: 230) argue that community is a 'more or less temporary unity of situation, interest or purpose', which may not always be the case. Some communities have enormous time-depth and share practice-based knowledge, commitment to place and the vulnerability of a resource-dependent livelihood. Second, whereas Leach et al. (1999: 232) note that not all environmental change is degradation, we argue that a great deal of it is, and viewing the environment as contingent, chaotic or dynamic cannot mask the declining productivity [commercial biomass has declined but not necessarily total biomass] and population crashes that have marked the global fisheries.
19. For a grassroots example, see Müller (2003). Here we extend the concept of learning communities to initiatives within fishing communities in the developed world, to show their relevance in any situation of natural resource management and to the enhancement of civil society. On educational initiatives and CBM, see Evans and Birchenough (2001).
20. The resistance to aboriginal claims on natural resources is a longstanding example of this problem. See Pinkerton (1992), for example, on the complexities of the implementation of the Boldt decision in Washington state.

21. Indeed, there is evidence that the dramatic collapse of the Atlantic ground-fish stocks has not been slowed or reversed under the current management policy. The Canada Sentinel project has assessed the groundfish stock levels since the East Coast moratorium on fishing and continues to find little or no recovery of these important commercial stocks (see http://www.osl.gc.ca/pse/en/rapports.html).
22. Such 'conditions of licence' fees are unilaterally set by government and often include significant research costs that are driving some fishers out of business.

References

Adams, T. 1998. 'The Interface between Traditional and Modern Methods of Fishery Management in the Pacific Islands', *Ocean and Coastal Management* 40: 127–42.

Agrawal, A. and C.C. Gibson. 1999. 'Enchantment and Disenchantment: The Role of Community in Natural Resource Management', *World Development* 27(4): 629–46.

Aswani, S. 1999. 'Common Property Models of Sea Tenure: A Case Study from the Roviana and Vonavona Lagoons, New Georgia, Solomon Islands', *Human Ecology* 27(3): 417–53.

Béné, C. 2003. 'When Fishery Rhymes with Poverty: A First Step beyond the Old Paradigm on Poverty in Small-scale Fisheries', *World Development* 31(6): 949–75.

Bennell, P., E. Masunungure, N. Ng'ethe and G. Wilson. 2000. 'Improving Policy Analysis and Management for Poverty Reduction in Sub-Sahara Africa: Creating an Effective Learning Community', Institute of Development Studies, University of Sussex.

Berkes, F. 2003. 'Alternatives to Conventional Management: Lessons from Small-scale Fisheries', *Environments* 31(1): 5–19.

Boudreau, R. and G. Boudreau. 2003. *Socio-economic Snapshot: The Impact of the Inshore Fishery in Guysborough County.* Guyborough County Inshore Fishermen's Association, Canso, Nova Scotia.

Bradshaw, B. 2003. 'Questioning the Credibility and Capacity of Community-based Resource Management', *The Canadian Geographer* 47(2): 137–50.

Brosius, J.P., A. Tsing and C. Zerner. 1998. 'Representing Communities: Histories and Politics of Community-based Natural Resource Management', *Society and Natural Resources* 11(2): 157–69.

Bull, A. 1998. 'The Fundy Fixed Gear Council: Implementing a Community Quota', in L. Loucks, T. Charles and M. Butler (eds), *Managing Our Fisheries, Managing Ourselves.* Halifax: Gorsebrook Research Institute for Atlantic Canada Studies, Saint Mary's University, 59–61.

Bull, A., D. Coon and M. Recchia. 2000. *Writing the Rules of Ecological Fisheries Management in the Bay of Fundy.* Saint John and Digby: Bay of Fundy Marine Resource Center, Conservation Council of New Brunswick and Bay of Fundy Fisheries Council.

Butler, M. 1998. 'Some History on Time Fisheries', in L. Loucks, T. Charles and M. Butler (eds), *Managing Our Fisheries, Managing Ourselves*. Halifax: Gorse-brook Research Institute for Atlantic Canada Studies, Saint Mary's University, 69–74.

Cole, H. 2003. 'Contemporary Challenges: Globalisation, Global Interconnectedness and That 'There Are Not Plenty More Fish in the Sea'. Fisheries, Governance and Globalisation: Is there a Relationship?' *Ocean and Coastal Management* 46: 77–102.

Escobar, A. 2001. 'Culture Sits in Places: Reflections on Globalism and Subaltern Strategies of Localization', *Political Geography* 20: 139–74.

Evans, S.M. and A.C. Birchenough. 2001. 'Community-based Management of the Environment: Lessons from the Past and Options for the Future', *Aquatic Conservation: Marine and Freshwater Ecosystems* 11: 137–47.

Finlayson, A.C. and B. McCay. 1998. 'Crossing the Threshold of Ecosystem Resilience: The Commercial Extinction of Northern Cod', in F. Berkes and C. Folke (eds), *Linking Social and Ecological System: Management Practices and Social Mechanisms for Building Resilience*. Cambridge: Cambridge University Press, 311–37.

Foster, E.G. and M. Haward. 2003. 'Integrated Management Councils: A Conceptual Model for Ocean Policy Conflict Management in Australia', *Ocean and Coastal Management* 46: 547–63.

Gibson, C.C. and T. Koontz. 1998. 'When Community Is Not Enough: Institutions and Values in Community-based Forest Management in Southern Indiana', *Human Ecology* 26(4): 621–47.

Graham, J., S. Engle and M. Recchia. 2002. *Local Knowledge and Local Stocks: An Atlas of Groundfish Spawning in the Bay of Fundy*. Antigonish, Nova Scotia: St. Francis Xavier University and The Center for Community Based Management.

Graham, T. and N. Idechong. 1998. 'Reconciling Customary and Constitutional Law: Managing Marine Resources in Palau, Micronesia', *Ocean and Coastal Management* 40: 143–64.

Holm, P., B. Hersoug and S.A. Ranes. 2000. 'Revisiting Lofoten: Co-managing Fish Stocks or Fishing Space?' *Human Organization* 59(3): 353–64.

Johannes, R.E. 1998. 'Government-supported, Village-based Management of Marine Resources in Vanuatu', *Ocean and Coastal Management* 40: 165–86.

Leach, M., R. Mearns and I. Scoones. 1999. 'Environmental Entitlements: Dynamics and Institutions in Community-based Natural Resource Management', *World Development* 27(2): 225–47.

Li, T.M. 1996. 'Images of Community: Discourse and Strategy in Property Relations', *Development and Change* 27: 501–27.

———. 2002. 'Engaging Simplifications: Community Based Resource Management, Market Processes and State Agendas in Upland Southeast Asia', *World Development* 30(2): 265–83.

Lindsay, J. 1998. 'Designing Legal Space: Law as an Enabling Tool in Community-based Management'. Plenary presentation, International CBNRM Workshop, Washington, D.C., 10–14 May 1998.

Lobe, K. and F. Berkes. 2004. 'The *Padu* System of Community-based Fisheries

Management: Change and Local Institutional Innovation in South India', *Marine Policy* 28: 271–81.

Loucks, L. 1998. 'Sambro Community Quota Fisheries Management: A Case of Innovative Community Based Decision-making', in L. Loucks, T. Charles, and M. Butler (eds), *Managing Our Fisheries, Managing Ourselves*. Halifax: Gorsebrook Research Institute for Atlantic Canada Studies, Saint Mary's University, 54–58.

Loucks, L., T. Charles and M. Butler (eds). 1998. *Managing Our Fisheries, Managing Ourselves*. Halifax: Gorsebrook Research Institute for Atlantic Canada Studies, Saint Mary's University.

Milsom, S. 2003. 'Fishing for Community Benefit', *Coastal Community News* 9(1): 5–7.

Mnookin, R.H. and L. Kornhauser. 1979. 'Bargaining in the Shadow of the Law', *Yale Law Journal* 88: 950–97.

Müller, C. 2003. 'Knowledge between Globalization and Localization: The Dynamics of Female Spaces in Ghana', *Current Sociology* 51(3/4): 329–46.

Perlman, D. 2003. 'Scientists Surprised by Findings in Certain Regions of Pacific Ocean', *Fredericton Daily Gleaner*, 24 February, D3.

Pinkerton, E.W. 1989. 'Attaining Better Fisheries Management through Co-management – Prospects, Problems, and Propositions', in E.W. Pinkerton (ed.), *Co-operative Management of Local Fisheries: New Directions for Improved Management and Community Development*. Vancouver: University of British Columbia Press, 3–33.

———. 1992. 'Translating Legal Rights into Management Practice: Overcoming Barriers to the Exercise of Co-management', *Human Organization* 51(4): 330–41.

Potter, B. 2002. 'Predatory Politics: Group Interests and Management of the Commons', *Environmental Politics* 11(2): 73–94.

Pretty, J. and H. Ward. 2001. 'Social Capital and the Environment', *World Development* 29(2): 209–27.

Ruddle, K. 1998. 'The Context of Policy Design for Existing Community-based Fisheries Management Systems in the Pacific Islands', *Ocean and Coastal Management* 40: 105–26.

Singleton, S. 2000. 'Co-operation or Capture? The Paradox of Co-management and Community Participation in Natural Resource Management and Environmental Policy-making', *Environmental Politics* 9(2): 1–21.

Stokowski, P. 2002. 'Languages of Place and Discourses of Power: Constructing New Senses of Place', *Journal of Leisure Research* 34(4): 368–82.

Wiber, M.G. 1999. 'Caught in the Cross-hairs: Liberalizing Trade (Post M.A.I.) and Privatizing the Right to Fish: Implications for Canada's Native Fisheries', *The Journal of Legal Pluralism* 44: 33–51.

———. 2000. 'Fishing Rights as an Example of the Economic Rhetoric of Privatization: Calling for an Implicated Economics', *Canadian Review of Sociology and Anthropology* 37(3): 267–88.

———. 2005. 'Mobile Law and Globalism: Epistemic Communities versus Community-based Innovation in the Fisheries Sector', in F. von Benda-Beckmann, K. von Benda-Beckmann and A. Griffiths (eds), *Mobile People, Mobile*

Law: Expanding Legal Relations in a Contracting World. Aldershot: Ashgate Publishing, 131–51.

Wiber, M.G. and J. Kennedy. 2001. 'Impossible Dreams: Reforming Fisheries Management in the Canadian Maritimes after the Marshall Decision', *Law and Anthropology* 11: 282–97.

Wingard, J.D. 2000. 'Community Transferable Quotas: Internalizing Externalities and Minimizing Social Impacts of Fisheries Management', *Human Organization* 59(1): 48–57.

7

Project Law – a Power Instrument of Development Agencies
A Case Study from Burundi
Markus Weilenmann

Introduction

With my case study from Burundi I would like to focus on an often neglected but particularly important field of law production: the field of
development politics. Development agencies are certainly front-runners
in the ongoing globalization process, but at the same time they also work
closely with rural 'target-groups', trying to empower identified victims
or marginalized groups and strengthen societal institutions. Hence,
they strive for a social balance that comes closer to their own notion of
social justice. All political interventions of development agencies can
thus directly or indirectly influence existing legal relations and change
the conditions under which people are able to use their rights. This is
especially true for all those projects or programmes that explicitly aim
at the promotion of the rule of law and good governance, the promotion of justice and human rights, crisis prevention and peace-building,
as well as for all those topics that are subject to the conditionalities.

In some developing countries, as for instance Malawi or Burundi, the
role of the state as guarantor of sovereignty, the rule of law and territorial control is thus often contested by powerful development agencies
that might even achieve a 'quasi-state status'. The term *Parastaatlichkeit*,
or quasi-state status, refers to a particular problem linked to this observation, namely the growing 'referral of sovereignty rights and fundamental tasks (to) groups and institutions' (Rösel and von Trotha 1999:
10) that compete with the postcolonial state for political leadership in
rural areas. Both authors stress the unconstitutionality of such kinds
of power-sharing, since this cession of sovereignty rights and principal tasks of public administration takes place stealthily, by processes of
'informal decentralisation' and 'privatisation'. Typically, those groups,
institutions or organizations involved in such processes are often lob-
bying for the advantages of competitive development patterns such as

'shopping for justice',[1] alternative forms of conflict resolution and the like. In addition, all development bureaucracies refer to a whole series of models and techniques in order to achieve more or less well defined progress. However, all these models and techniques are subject to a growing standardization, whereby a particular kind of law, so-called 'project law', plays a significant role because it structures the development political consulting process by normative means and intervenes in those sociopolitical contexts that are subject to any social change whatsoever. In the recipient countries, project law might thus clash with local customary law, religious law or the prevailing state law. Particularly in Sub-Saharan Africa, there are only a few actors who are as well networked, locally and internationally, as international development agencies are. Thus development agencies there become not only very important 'global players'; they are also increasingly regarded as important legal pluralistic actors in a cumulatively fragmented field of competing normative systems.

My chapter deals with these kinds of relationship between the 'global' and the 'local' and highlights the particularly precarious link between law, power and control. The study relies on the programming of a conflict transformation project in Burundi and focuses on the critical role of women. The project's programming will be discussed using an analysis of applied 'project law'.

What Exactly Is Project Law?

Project law is a new term and there is no intrinsic doctrine. In the literature, the term project law has been understood as having two different meanings, namely (1) as a planning instrument and (2) as an implementing tool:

1) There are, on the one hand, all those legal rules that guide the planning and conceptualization phases of a development project, their monitoring and the transfer of the project responsibilities to local implementing organizations. According to Günther and Randeria (2001: 70), such legal rules emanate from 'regulations and procedures of bilateral or multilateral development agencies, either made by these (organizations) or borrowed from their own national legal system'. They thus regulate a distinct understanding of development aid and shape the stated policy objectives and their reasoning. While such project law comes into existence and is reproduced within the development organizations and/or in interaction with their partners

in developing countries, project law of a different kind also emerges during the phase in which development projects are institutionalized and implemented.

2) Project law can thus also refer to those legal rules formed by the project personnel during the implementation process and in interaction with the so-called target groups (see Thomson 1987). Such project law lays down behavioural demands for the local population, devises new structures for decision making and the allocation of resources, and also regulates the various relationships between the project personnel and their target group(s) (see F. von Benda-Beckmann 1989). It is linked to the budgeting of the various projects and its components and also contains important criteria for the inclusion and/or exclusion of relevant parts of the total population.

Indeed, many of these concepts and principles are 'formally speaking ... not yet law, but in effect obtain the same level of obligation' (K. von Benda-Beckmann 2001: 38; see also Kingsbury 1999). Günther and Randeria (2001) use the term project law explicitly for those regulations and procedures that are the subject of bilateral or multilateral development cooperation. They focus mainly on 'memoranda of agreement, terms of references, management systems, administrative and budgeting procedures, accounting and auditing procedures and standards, regulations of purchase, benchmarks for evaluating the progress of the projects and the attainment of project goals, operational policies and operational directives of the donor organizations which are binding on the credit or loan recipient' (Randeria 2005: 154).

A controversial subject concerns the question whether the term 'project law' could also be used for the analysis of the normatively coloured relationship between development agents and their target-groups, as Thomson (1987) originally proposed. In particular the disputed question is whether the term also contains behavioural demands and normative concepts and goals such as 'poverty reduction', 'gender equality' or the 'recognition of human rights'. Keebet von Benda-Beckmann (2001) emphasizes the already existing normativity of such different terms as 'good governance', 'participation', 'co-management', 'sustainability', 'liberalization', 'privatization', etc. She argues that such normative concepts are already part of international law and therefore part of project law, too: 'These principles and concepts have been developed and elaborated in various parts of international law but they show little internal coherence. To some extent they are still proto-law, not yet fully developed principles. For another part they float around in development circles as abstract goals of development co-operation. These agencies of development co-operation … play an intermediary role in concretizing rights and obligations and in implementing international law.' (2001: 38)

Randeria (2005: 154), however, argues that the term 'project law' would lose 'its analytical purchase if the entire gamut of Western norms and values diffused within the architecture of international aid is subsumed under project law'. She suggests including such directives within the policy process, which in recent years has been largely dominated by international development bureaucracies: 'Development projects, for example in the area of family planning and reproductive health, certainly diffuse and even impose contraceptive practices, the acceptance of a small family norm … But these disciplinary practices, which are often institutionalized through policy frameworks … are better understood as techniques of governmentality rather than project law' (2005: 155). However, I cannot understand why project law and techniques of governmentality should be dichotomized. Though I certainly would not refer to the entire gamut of Western norms and values diffused within the architecture of international aid as project *law*, it is still important to stress that the role of project law is also a very important governance technique. With Foucault (1966) in mind, one should never forget that much of governmentality is also legally organized.

This difficulty requires a clarification between law and power. According to Franz von Benda-Beckmann, emphasis must be laid on the typical ambiguity of law, namely that it not only refers to the regulation of those social processes that have to solve concrete problems, but also provides 'the substantive criteria which are to be considered in the resolution of the problem' (F. von Benda-Beckmann 1986: 96). Behavioural demands – which in the case of project law are formed at different social and political levels and refer to the underlying problem definition of development projects – are thus a very typical mark of law, too. Clifford Geertz directs attention to a further quality of law, namely that 'law … propounds the world in which its descriptions make sense … The point here is that the "law" side of things is not a bounded set of norms, rules, principles, values, or whatever from which juridical responses to distilled events can be drawn, but part of a distinctive manner of imagining the real' (1983: 173). Law as 'statute' or 'general law' can thus also be seen as a projective cosmology. The containing values are values that allow the regulation of 'possible' – and this always means specific imagined – social problems. Therefore, it is not the images as such, but the *qualities* of these images that point at the underlying power constellations. The various qualities of normative behavioural demands could thus also be labelled witnesses of the underlying policy process.

Franz von Benda-Beckmann points at the development-political models that stand behind such behavioural demands and justify the chosen interventions. However, these models, which all contain statements about how the world is and how it should be, are not usually based on empirical studies. In fact, they point at the corresponding power constellations and bear the mark of normativity as they derive not only chosen rules of behaviour and target definitions from assumed social consequences, but also the legitimacy they are based on. In accord with F. von Benda-Beckmann (1989: 134), I therefore assume that development projects have the form of law.

Project Law in Practice: A Case Study

Under the broad title 'crisis prevention', a northern NGO launched several development programmes in Burundi, including programmes on the promotion of the rule of law and good governance, and a programme on gender. But all these programmes contain a peculiar, twofold bias. Except for the gender programme, where only women were engaged, the programmes were largely dominated by men (institutional gender bias). Moreover, until recently, all development programmes focused solely on the urban and educated elite (institutional class bias). While in recent times the institutional class bias has increasingly come to be perceived as an important problem that entails a series of strategic solutions in order to include the agrarian and in most cases illiterate population of the countryside as well, problem consciousness has not yet touched on the gender bias. On the contrary, the gender programme is still regarded as a particularly original answer to customarily regulated gender relations in Burundi. Since women, as the rationale goes, would remain silent in the presence of men and thus have no say, a development project should take these patriarchal framework conditions seriously and work exclusively with women. The gender bias is thus strategically justified and also applied by the Burundian partner organizations. This programme is the focus of my analysis.

In development political circles, crisis prevention programmes such as this gender programme are often regarded as very promising. They may have a remarkable impact on the organizational capacity of women's organizations in the recipient countries, and in difficult conflict constellations like Burundi's ethnic blockages, it is frequently observed that women could be addressed as an important, indirect target group in order to reach the armed rebel groups, the national army or the political opinion leaders and their strategic consultants (direct target group).

All the more interesting, then, is the rationale of this approach, as well as the results such a gender programme produces.

The Rationale of a Development Agency in a Chain of Translations

In development political practice, both variations of project law – project law as planning instrument and project law as an implementing tool – are closely intertwined and result in what Rottenburg calls *Übersetzungsketten* ('chains of translations'). In his book entitled *Weit hergeholte Fakten* (2002),[2] he describes the complex problems that emerge when development bureaucracies try to control the distribution and impact of their subsidies by the international transfer of policy objectives, development plans and rules of procedure. Eloquently, the author demonstrates how development agencies follow this path towards a deep ongoing contradiction of their own principle goal of self-determined development. Rottenburg argues that both the developers and their counterparts are systematically looking for a communicative consensus on the level of objectified solutions. Therefore, they are much engaged in technical and organizational questions, whereas the cultural dimension is largely classified as politically delicate and disregarded. In outlining some key elements of this rationale I found it very helpful to refer to Rottenburg's chains of translations, since not only the interpretation of the problem, but also the norms to which personnel have to refer, differ greatly depending on the professional function and hierarchical position of personnel within such a development agency. My case study shows how specific translations, carried out by distinct persons or groups of persons, finally meet such chains of translations, how these translations correspond to the role- and status-related interests of the translators, and how they conflict with diverse behavioural expectations and their corresponding behavioural tendencies. These chains of translations emerge at the conflicting lines that mark each development project, and they have normatively constitutive consequences for the direction of the various methodical steps.

Translations of the Executive Board

The top level of the responsible NGO is mainly engaged in fundraising matters. Their rationale refers largely to what is popular within the donor community. Here, we find only a slightly modified form of the current gender discourse. Thus, the management mentions that its so-called 'conflict analysis' has revealed 'that in the current context, Burundian women are often denied voice and agency. They frequently lack the confidence and skills to participate effectively in national life, and in peace-building processes' (Weilenmann, 2003, Appendix II: 2). Therefore, the northern NGO seeks first 'to assist women to develop women's confidence to engage as stakeholders in the peace process' (2003, Appendix II: 2) and to 'strengthen and develop linkages between women peace actors at grassroots, middle and top levels' (2003, Appendix II: 1) of Burundian society. In addition, the NGO obviously also has to offer a set of distinct properties for Burundi's conflict resolution, so-called 'skills' and 'tools'. It presents itself not as a development agency but as a so-called 'catalyst' that provides its own 'skills and tools so that [the Burundian women] can then contribute to finding some effective solutions to Burundi's conflict' (2003, Appendix II: 2).

This set of arguments, which refers to the discriminated position of women rather than to the political conflict potential between the Abahutu and the Abatutsi, changes the direction of impact of the crisis prevention programme at a decisive point. Women are declared a direct, not an indirect, target group. With the help of some properties of the northern NGO, they should thus be qualified to make a substantial contribution to conflict resolution in Burundi. However, this is particularly striking because Burundi's recent political history is very much marked by ethnic struggles (the so-called Hutu-Tutsi conflict) not directly linked to gender tensions. Burundi's ethnicity made political headway with the refugees from the first genocide in Rwanda in 1959, with the end of the monarchy in the early 1960s and with the final takeover of political power in 1966 by a particular Umututsi-branch, called Umuhima-tutsi, which comes from Burundi's south. Together with Thomas Laely (1995) and René Lemarchand (1994a), I interpret Burundi's ethnic clashes as a consequence first of the breakdown of the precolonial power relations, which were more or less destroyed by the former colonizers Germany and Belgium, and second of the noncompliance of bureaucratic directives of decision-making with actual living conditions and claims for a political legitimacy (Weilenmann 1997, 2000).

In order to justify this shift of arguments, the executive board of the northern NGO refers to a side issue: gender-related patterns of inclusion and exclusion common to every society, including Burundi. Yet it contains a deliberate partition of social reality. Since this set of arguments is about fundraising matters, it overemphasizes mainly those points that are directly linked to the perceptions of the donor community and could thus largely count on arousing sympathy: According to this rationale, Burundian women are excluded and discriminated against, they are lacking in self-confidence, they have skills not found elsewhere and they are potential bearers of peace. NGOs are (politically) passive development organizations, so-called catalysts, which merely put the interests of the (poor and discriminated) women first. However, in Burundi, voice and agency are not only denied to (most of all) women. As mark of an aristocratic society, the degree of access to voice and agency is also determined by social position within Burundi's hierarchical order: In front of a high-ranking person, every lower-ranking person is expected to be silent – common citizens in front of governmental personnel, Abahutus in front of Abatutsis, common farmers in front of public officers, uneducated in front of educated people, etc. From a more political viewpoint, however, it is this absence of a general right to voice and agency – and not the gender question – that is one of the most important issues.

Translations of the International Project Personnel

The international experts and project managers stay in continuous contact with a whole network of Burundian women's NGOs and therefore have to travel several times a year to Burundi. There, they must negotiate with the responsible ministries, justify the necessity of the programme in public, supervise the amount of the total expenses, discuss project implementation matters with the local staff, initiate new project components and coordinate the networking with other development agencies. In this context, the topic becomes more politicized, since the patterns of social inclusion and exclusion now become embedded in what I would call a strategic exploitation of 'victim roles': in discussions with political opinion leaders, who questioned the specific contribution of a gender programme to Burundi's actual problem configuration, two keywords in particular were stressed: the 'feminization of poverty' and 'rape'.

Both keywords cement the direction of the executive board's arguments. At the same time, the subject matter seems to have a political tone once more. But this is not very difficult in a country where the large majority of the total population has been severely affected by ethnic massacres and their far-reaching economic, legal and political consequences.[3] While one could now argue that from the point of view of the recipients, the production of such keywords may be a creative act to mobilize new funds,[4] I prefer to stay with the analysis of the complex power processes within the network of the development agency and to point at the problematic consequences of the normative clustering of society. While the project personnel of the northern NGO now stress that 'the Burundian women and children continue to constitute the majority of the total population' and add that 'women have borne the

brunt of the human, social and economic costs of the war and feminization of poverty remains a major issue' (Weilenmann, 2003, Appendix
II: 3), a couple of years ago exactly the same pattern of arguments was
common within development agencies overtly engaged in the Hutu-
Tutsi conflict. They stressed the '"hutu-isation" of poverty', pushed the
spin on ethnic discrimination forward and also advocated quotas and
empowerment – not for women, but for disadvantaged ethnic groups.
Typically, in both cases, the crude arguments of the population majority
are referred to,[5] the classification is not subject to further consideration,
and no distinctions and/or further differentiations are made. It seems
as if all Abahutus, that is to say all women, are victims and would have
borne the brunt of the after-effects of the conflict, even though there is
now more than enough literature available to provide for a more differentiated view.[6] If one goes one step back into the political history
of the country, one comes across the normative clustering of the colonial powers. Using different, mainly legal means, they tried in particular to overturn the complex states of rural dependency, as well as
the corresponding property and succession rights. Their goal was to
consolidate their own power claims, first with the aristocratic minority
of the Abatutsi and, when this attempt failed, they exacerbated ethnic
polarisation and turned to the Abahutu. In this way, they contributed
essentially to the ethnic clashes of today.[7] What all these attempts have
in common is that they are based on a partial orientation towards large
human groups (women and men, Abahutu and Abatutsi, seigniors and
servants, victims and committers) who, thanks to external intervention,
have to be favoured or discriminated against in order to achieve any
social change whatsoever. However, it is questionable whether the
ahistorical and ultimately arbitrary singling out of distinct target groups
– which always implies the advocacy of distinct and very individual
interests – really complies with the general objectives of long-term politics for peace. Furthermore, it is also questionable whether the actual
project law, which always contains a target group orientation, can comply with the more political topics such as the 'promotion of the rule of
law', 'crisis prevention' or 'good governance'.

In addition, both keywords, the 'feminization of poverty' and 'rape',
could be denoted normative catchwords in this context. In April 1991,
Burundi signed with law decree 1/006 the 'Convention on the Elimi-
nation of all Forms of Discrimination against Women' (CEDAW). Burundi's government is thus required by law to introduce substantial
steps against all forms of discrimination against women. Therefore the
'feminization of poverty', as well as of course 'rape', are important key-

words. But unfortunately, these keywords do not lead to development projects in the corresponding fields of work: the project has mainly a political goal; it wants to improve the organizational capacity of women's networks. However, it carries out no specific poverty reduction programmes for women, nor does it implement projects that deal with the particular traumatizing experiences of raped women, such as programmes of psycho-social help. Rather, the focus is on conflict mediation training that exclusively targets women. In order to legitimize this gendered approach and to hold critical questions at bay, the international project personnel thus exploit a norm of international law that condemns gender discrimination.

Translations of the Burundian Partner Organizations

At the level of the Burundian NGOs that organize, in close collaboration with the project personnel of the northern NGO, conflict mediation trainings for women's associations in Burundi's countryside, one can observe how the feministic phraseology – like the former ethnic phraseology – leads in practice to the forming and/or cementing of new or already existing patterns of scapegoats. During my stay in Burundi I was, amongst other things, interested in their methods of collaboration with men, the male-dominated public officers and the courts themselves. The answers left no doubt: 'The men?? – Ha, they are just doing nothing! They have always their meetings and are too much engaged in political affairs!' 'The bureaucrats? – No, we do not want to collaborate with those who never leave their office.' 'And what? The local courts? Oh, they are at least macho!' (Weilenmann 2003: 26).

This chain of translations shows how a development-related topic, namely the promotion of peace and gender equality, changes its interpretation and has methodological consequences as a result: while the general statements of the top management are only there to give a rough idea of the issue and the general approach, so the use of the two catchphrases 'feminization of poverty' and 'rape' refers to a larger concept of the international project staff members, who try to establish a common ideology for 'their' women's peace organizations. They state that 'the challenges facing women in the region are still enormous. Women are divided along ethnic and political lines. The marginal participation of women in politics and the lack of a clear ideology on the part of women's peace organizations constitute major obstacles' (Weilenmann 2003: 26). This goal is reinforced by the 'decision to conduct training programmes [on conflict resolution] exclusively for women', while the political opinion leaders, mainly men, who are responsible for the diffusion of the ethnic ideology throughout the whole country, are not targeted (2003: 26). In the words of the international staff members, this 'represents a strategic choice, not motivated by a desire to promote one gender group per se but in the interests of greater inclusivity [of women] in the long term. We do not exclude the possibility of working with men in the future but in the medium term ... we feel it is more strategic to continue with our current approach' (Weilenmann, 2003, Appendix II: 7). At the level of the Burundian NGOs, whose arguments largely resemble common patterns of ethnic allegations by referring to generalizing images like the 'macho administration', one gets a first taste of the expected outcome. In order to de-legitimatize alternately the state administration and the governing class, it is still very common within politicized Hutu circles and circles of development agents to talk about the 'Tutsi administration'.

Cultural Patterns of Behaviour in a War-torn Society: Another Chain of Translations

It would, however, be too simplistic to stop here, since there are other chains of translations emerging from the context of Burundian society. One of these chains refers to the cultural understanding of gender roles as it has developed in Burundi's national language, Kirundi. The idea of running a gender programme in Burundi could be particularly interesting if the programme really referred to a conflict analysis of such role attributions, because Burundi's folk concept of culture states that the so-called 'ethnic' identity is the bequest of the male line (from the father to the son) and that the female line has no ethnic identity: as a daughter, a woman has the 'ethnic' identity of her father, whereas as a wife, she is attributed with the 'ethnic' identity of her husband. And since in Burundi there are some very rough and misleading categories to distinguish Abahutus from Abatutsis,[8] the Abarundi usually differentiate according to the physical (biological) side of ethnic attributions[9] and the social side. While physically, women are regarded as what they are born as, they can shift socially from one ethnic group to the other by attaining another ethnic identity. In recent times, however, one can observe some changes within the urban middle class.

While well-educated and reform-oriented middle-class women have started to stress publicly the possibility of switching deliberately from one ethnic group to the other, rural and traditional opinion leaders (mainly men) cling more and more to the Kirundi connotations of emancipation. In the national language Kirundi, 'courage', 'masculinity', 'social recognition' and 'penis' are all indicated by a single term: *'bugabo'*. But the root of this term, *gabo*, is also part of the expression *'kugira igabo'*, which means not only 'to boast (about something)', 'to spread oneself' or 'to strut or prance around', but also 'emancipation' (Rodegem 1970: 95). In conflicting situations, women who have a good educational background (like a high-school degree or even a university degree) or hold socially important posts could therefore also be regarded as if their sex had *(bu)gabo*, too. So what we observe here is a slightly changing constellation of the female identity relating to new conflicts and general processes of urbanization and modernization.

During the hot phases of the war in the mid 1990s in particular, many women tried to cut across ethnic borderlines by supplying food and health services to hostile groups. They took many risks and became particularly active in the most contested fields of political separation (exclusion). Of course such life experiences, which are of high political value, open the chance to bring another perspective into the ongoing political debate. During the long absence of their husbands, they reorganized their households, created common forums for the exchange of information and material goods, started to fill posts within the abandoned local administration and so on, while well-educated women from Bujumbura-ville became more concerned with processes of institution-building, such as the foundation of national networks or NGOs.

While the catalogue of these activities refers closely to the cultural gender role in times of crisis, the northern NGO took a liking to such a cultural mechanism and developed a conflict mediation course for rural women. There, the women 'should recognize their own partiality – conditioned by their past, social context and current experience. The programme encourages women to develop an awareness of the different perceptions of those involved in the situation (including their own) and to develop strategies to manage these conflicting perceptions' (Weilenmann, 2003, Appendix II: 1). But at the same time, the northern NGO held its own interpretation of Burundi's ethnicity and was not ready to accept Burundi's folk concept, according to which Abarundi-women do not necessarily have an ethnic identity. The international project staff simply considered this rule a classical symptom of gender discrimination. Therefore, it challenged 'actively any assumption that women have no ethnic identity: both in training programmes and in discussions with partners' (2003, Appendix II: 1) and in this way started to ethnicize large parts of its own target groups.

Results: Chains of Translations as a Medium of Project Law

While this case study also has a very emotional side, as one wonders why such misunderstandings are possible at all, it also contains some typical characteristics of the functioning of project law. Behind the two chains of translations that interact with each other and continuously shape the process of project implementation, we can easily discover many behavioural demands and other so-called 'ought to be–statements' that refer to general visions of a 'better world'. Development aid is in fact a permanent negotiation process based on such 'better world–visions' that determine problem descriptions. According to Rottenburg (2002: 92–93), within development agencies we can observe a peculiar mechanism: during the processes of problem definition, Western societies and their organizational forms become idealistic models. These models then contour the problems of developing countries. But what is in the beginning just a figure of thought shifts in the course of time to become an objectified assumption. In the end, one often believes that the idealistic models of Euro-America, such as 'civil society' or 'gender equality', are concrete realities that often entail a missionary eagerness.

At this point, the process-related dimension of project law enters the game. The observed mechanism, the shifting of a figure of thought into an objectified assumption, is also related to the task of inserting, under tight time constraints, highly interpretative facts into a normative pattern that determines the subject matter of the goals and the project plan. If, however, international development agencies start to move into such highly contested fields as 'crisis prevention', 'good governance' or 'gender', the data often remain confusing, even for those specialists who know the region very well. Often, a reasonable (or seemingly reasonable) target system can be outlined only by employing a great deal of fantasy and creativity. Therefore, the danger is to fail to take into account the planning officer's personal value orientation, which starts to play a decisive role because it tends to be shifted into objectified assumptions.

This process facilitates compliance with all the normative instructions that regulate the relationship between the big donor agencies and the implementing organizations and fix the parameters of each development project, for project law also defines the ways a project topic has to be identified, what a project plan has to look like, how project implementation is to be executed or general policy objectives standardized. Most development agencies have thus developed a catalogue with guiding ideas and a general project model (see Weilenmann 2005b). All these rules refer to the Cartesian antagonism between '[irrational] culture' and '[rational] plan',[10] demonstrate the inner degree of institutionalization of development agencies and structure not only development agency networking in developing countries but – more importantly – also the design of their projects. However, the relationship between these rules and real project implementation remains an indirect one, since of course many other factors also remaining in the game have more to do with economic, political or personal constellations. A proper analysis of the chains of translation is thus imperative. They enable us to go all the way back from the project practices to the normative regulations that form these practices.

Formative for the individual translations on the part of NGOs are certainly the institutional regulations, like the already mentioned gender bias of the northern NGO that refers to a simplistic interpretation of customarily regulated status relations and results in the complete 'feminization' of gender projects. In addition, on the one hand one has to deal with questions of competency that are all legally regulated and that prescribe who[11] is responsible for which type of steps and when. In order to justify the proceeding vis-à-vis the different interest groups or – as in the case of the handling with the CEDAW – give credence to the proceeding as justified ('window dressing'), the individual NGO-translations refer thereafter to the standardized goals of the donor policies. On the other hand, the various translations also interpret the needs and interests of the various Abarundi representatives and point to the local networks of legal regulations that generate such models of behaviour. Therefore, the various NGO-translations not only belie their own self-image as 'catalyst'; they also solidify, turning into new definitions of reality that all also contain statements about how the world is or should be. But contrary to the problem definitions that refer in a first step to the same processes of translation but are – due to project law – then institutionally fixed (see Weilenmann 2005b), these types of translations and re-translations continue to form new patterns of interpretation of the development political network of norms, to dominate in this way the everyday life of projects, and to mark the competition with the postcolonial state for political leadership in rural areas.

The second chain of translations, which comes from the project environment, refers to the cultural context and the particular living conditions of Burundi as a war-torn society. It is geared to the customarily regulated and correspondingly legitimated patterns of social roles. Depending on living space (rural, urban), social status (ethnicity, education), gender and living circumstances (peace/war), these roles envisage another assignment of duties and offer different patterns of interpretation. The project personnel tie well in with these patterns of interpretation; however, they have only limited sympathy for the Burundian folk concept of ethnicity that widens the space of action for women, particularly in comparison with the corresponding gender roles of men. Fixed on a very narrow and also simplified interpretation of 'gender justice', the project personnel follow a property-oriented notion of equality according to which women must *possess* all that men have, including an ethnic identity.

The impasse the project got into was thus related to the complex problems that arise when development bureaucracies try to control the distribution and effects of their subsidies via the international transfer of their political goals, their development plans and process rules. Correspondingly, the argumentative patterns employed to mobilize funds turn out to be donor-driven, too. Of course, this impasse is also characterized by an undemocratic control of project law (see below). From a more practical viewpoint, one could argue that such a project is also lacking legal anthropological advice. Such advice could, for example, critically accompany the whole process of required translation activities. It could point at the circumstances that the different actors use – for instance for purposes of legitimatizing their competing claims – and the strategies used by the different legal bodies (customary law, state law, religious law, etc.). It could as well, at each stage, make the different options for action and the corresponding implications for all stakeholders transparent, so that such a project really contributes to its primary goal of crisis prevention.

Conclusions

To conclude, I would first like to stress the influence of Western development agencies on the design of project law. Project law is largely defined by the staff sections of these agencies; it guarantees the dominant influence of donor countries in decisions on what rules are to be applied when a development plan has to be set up. And because project law is a very important tool for the transfer of Euro-American behavioural demands, the donors have a considerable political impact on the social life of developing countries. In recent times, this process has been largely supported by the Anglo-Saxon paradigm of civil society that assumes a structural contradiction between the State[12] and society. This paradigm allows Western development agencies to cash in on the ideology of the 'free and independent civil society' and to denounce each attempt by the planning ministries to supervise and control development plans as a setback to the democratization process as such. But when one comes to terms with the application of project law, a democracy deficit emerges on the side of development agencies: problem definitions that also determine the development agencies' patterns of argument and position them politically are fabricated within the structures of project law. Instead of involving local actors in 'real' participation, these actors are ordered to participate according to the conditions set by the donor agency. In so doing, the donors thus remain far removed from what their own propaganda says about real participation. It is thus imperative to demand that the donors – not only for the application of ethical benchmarks, but also for the general principal of political inclusion – accept local political participation during the forming of rules and processes so that the democratic control of project law is assured.

Secondly, it is important to point to the degree of coordination between the various multi- and bilateral donor agencies. This coordination has already achieved previously unknown levels, but unfortunately, this does not hold true for the application of their internal rules and procedures or their corresponding behavioural demands. In addition, because project law is always tailor-made for the substantiated development projects, it can only be applied in the project region of the responsible development agency and only during the effective period of the corresponding project. Randeria (2005: 155) thus rightly points at the limited spatial, temporal and institutional validity of the individual project laws. For recipient countries like Burundi, different development agencies implement separate projects with different, partly even contradicting objectives, and therefore also particular groups or types of project law are applied. In addition, the big donors tend to subdivide the recipient countries into different spheres of influence and intervention.[13] The various development projects might thus conflict not only with distinct sets of local customary law, but also with state law and international law.[14]

Finally, I am coming to terms with the phenomenon of *Parastaatlichkeit* or quasi-state status, since project law also contains the potential to fragment the prevailing legal and political orders in the recipient countries and in this way to weaken their rule of law. This process occurs stealthily, as a result of the actual design of many project laws, and belies the State's required adherence to notions of sovereignty and territoriality. It demonstrates the negative consequences of increasing competition for political leadership in rural areas and questions the former concepts of law, power and control that referred to the State as the decisive power centre. However, given an understanding of law that connects the existence of law only to a state-controlled organization of power, it will not be possible to register the increasing legal fragmentation of the political and social landscape in developing countries. In these fields of action, project law is considered a very important power instrument, in large measure because it avoids the otherwise ordinary measures of democratic control. It thus empowers and encourages the different development agencies to follow, in a very fragmented manner, their own interpretation of the Euro-American vision as the best way of life, even though it is completely inadequate for the actual situation of those it is intended to assist. In this way, project law becomes an extremely powerful yet highly questionable power instrument of development agencies.

Notes

1. The term 'shopping for justice' stems from several discussions I had with some development agents in Malawi. They argued that 'since we are now living in a democracy, people have a choice. While under the former president Banda all and everything was controlled, people can now "vote with their feet" and "shop for justice"' (Weilenmann 2005a: 16).
2. Literally translated 'Facts collected from far away'.
3. Since independence more than half a million people have lost their lives during the endemic and repeated ethnic massacres.
4. Shalini Randeria proposes, for instance, speaking about 'creative misunderstandings' in order to get access to the funds: 'Creative misunderstandings are enabling fictions inherent in any development project and are unavoidable given the ambiguity of meaning of key terms in policy documents, and their local appropriation by various actors. Global policy shapes, and is in turn shaped by, the coalitions of interests around a certain policy language and set of goals.' (2005: 1)
5. In this context the 'majority argument' makes sense only if one can assume a far-reaching cultural homogeneity within the larger human groups. But precisely this point is highly disputed in Burundi. The same goes also for the subsumption of women and children into one large single human group. In such cases the role pattern of women is reduced to their motherly role (education of children). But this is not the point of this project. It is thus a purely tactical argument.
6. See Lemarchand (1994b); Reyntjens (2000); Chrétien and Mukuri (2002) Chrétien and Prunier (2003); and many others.
7. See Chrétien (1970); Lemarchand (1970, 1989, 1990, 1994a); Reyntjens (1994); Weilenmann (1997, 2000); Vansina (2001) and many others.
8. These are mainly based on the colonial anthropometric categories of body size, nose and lip formation.
9. These are oriented towards the contours of the ribs, the heel and the neck.
10. Ernest Gellner describes Descartes as the Samuel Smiles of the branch of insights: 'Misunderstandings are culturally based and culture is a kind of

systematic and cooperatively created set of misunderstandings. The important aspect of the misunderstandings is that they are commonly created and that over time they increase in number. Through companionship and history we sink into error and we escape from it through individual projects and plans' (1992/1995: 11, translated from the German).

11. As a rule, this is a highly specialized but relatively closely defined person subgroup.
12. The State as public authority and therefore capitalized, not the state as a synonymic category of a nation-state, and thus identical to society as a whole.
13. In Burundi's northeast the Americans are implementing a human rights programme largely influenced by Anglo-Saxon case law, while the Belgian General Direction of Development Cooperation (DGCD) plans a reprint of the old (colonial-based) *Codes et Lois du Burundi* and the already discussed northern NGO exclusively trains women in conflict mediation techniques, teaches them to have an 'ethnic identity' and denounces the official state courts as macho-driven etc., both in Burundi's capital Bujumbura-ville and in the countryside.
14. Randeria (2005) mentions projects on family planning, which, depending on the ethical and political orientation of the donor(s), might conflict with the national abortion laws of the recipient countries. Another conflict area concerns the different understandings and interpretations of human rights (cf. K. von Benda-Beckmann 2001; Weilenmann 2005b).

References

Benda-Beckmann, F. von. 1986. 'Anthropology and Comparative Law', in K. von Benda-Beckmann and F. Strijbosch (eds), *Anthropology of Law in the Netherlands: Essays on Legal Pluralism*. Dordrecht, Holland; Cinnaminson, NJ: Foris Publications, KITLV Press, 90–109.

———. 1989. 'Scapegoat and Magic Charm: Law in Development Theory and Practice', *Journal of Legal Pluralism* 28: 129–48.

Benda-Beckmann, K. von. 2001. 'Transnational Dimensions of Legal Pluralism', in W. Fikentscher (ed.), *Begegnung und Konflikt: Eine kulturanthropologische Bestandsaufnahme*. Munich: Verlag der Bayerischen Akademie der Wissenschaften, 33–48.

Chrétien, J.-P. 1970. 'Une Révolte au Burundi en 1934: Les Racines Traditionnelles de l'Hostilité à la Colonisation', *Annales, Economies, Sociétés, Civilisations* 25–26: 1678–717.

Chrétien, J.-P. and M. Mukuri. 2002. *Burundi, la Facture Identitaire: Logiques de Violences et Certitudes Ethniques*. Paris: Karthala.

Chrétien, J.-P. and G. Prunier. 2003. *Les Ethnies Ont une Histoire*. Deuxième édition avec une nouvelle introduction. Paris: Editions Karthala.

Foucault, M. 1966. *Die Ordnung der Dinge*. Frankfurt am Main: Suhrkamp.

Geertz, C. 1983. *Local Knowledge: Further Essays in Interpretative Anthropology*. New York: Basic Books.

Gellner, E. 1992/1995. *Descartes & Co. Von der Vernunft und ihren Feinden*. Frankfurt am Main: Junius.

Günther K. and S. Randeria. 2001. *Recht, Kultur und Gesellschaft im Prozess der Globalisierung*. Schriftenreihe der Werner Reimers Stiftung, Heft 4. Bad Homburg: Reimers.

Kingsbury, B. 1999. 'Operational Policies of International Institutions as Part of the Law-Making Process: The World Bank and Indigenous Peoples', in G.S. Goodwin-Gill and S. Talmon (eds), *The Reality of International Law: Essays in Honour of Ian Brownlie*. Oxford: Oxford University Press, 323–42.

Laely, T. 1995. *Autorität und Staat in Burundi*. Berlin: Dietrich Reimer.

Lemarchand, R. 1970. *Rwanda and Burundi*. London: Pall Mall Press.

———. 1989. 'The Killing Fields Revisited', *Issue* 18(1): 22–28.

———. 1990. 'Burundi: Ethnicity and the Genocidal State', in P. van den Berghe (ed.), *State Violence and Ethnicity*. Niwot, CO: University Press of Colorado, 89–111.

———. 1994a. *Burundi: Ethnic Conflict and Genocide*. Cambridge, New York, Melbourne: Cambridge University Press.

———. 1994b. *Ethnocide as Discourse and Practice*. Cambridge: Cambridge University Press.

Randeria, S. 2005. 'Mutual Complicity and Project Law in Development Cooperation – a Comment', *Entwicklungsethnologie* 14(1–2): 149–57.

Reyntjens, F. 1994. *L'Afrique des Grands Lacs en Crise: Rwanda, Burundi: 1988–1994*. Paris: Karthala.

———. 2000. *Small States in an Unstable Region – Rwanda and Burundi: Political Evolution in Rwanda and Burundi (Current African Issues)*. Uppsala: The Nordic Africa Institute.

Rodegem, F.M. 1970. *Dictionnaire Rundi-Français*. Tervuren: Annales du Musée Royal de l'Afrique Centrale.

Rösel, J. and T. von Trotha. 1999. *Dezentralisierung, Demokratisierung und die lokale Repräsentation des Staates*. Cologne: Rüdiger Köppe Verlag.

Rottenburg, R. 2002. *Weit hergeholte Fakten: Eine Parabel der Entwicklungshilfe*. Stuttgart: Lucius & Lucius.

Thomson, J.T. 1987. 'Land and Tree Issues in Three Francophone Sahelian Countries: Niger, Mali and Burkina Faso', in J.B. Raintree (ed.), *Land, Trees and Tenure*. Nairobi and Madison, WI: Land Tenure Center and International Council for Research in Agroforestry, 3–40.

Vansina, J. 2001. *Le Rwanda Ancien: Le Royaume Nyiginya*. Paris: Karthala.

Weilenmann, M. 1997. *Burundi: Konflikt und Rechtskonflikt. Eine rechtsethnologische Studie zur Konfliktregelung der Gerichte*. Frankfurt am Main: Brandes und Apsel.

———. 2000. 'Reactive Ethnicity: Some Thoughts on Political Psychology Based on the Developments in Burundi, Rwanda and South-Kivu', *Journal of Psychology in Africa* 10: 1–25.

———. 2003. 'Conflict Transformation and Peace-building in Burundi: A Consultancy Report with IV Appendixes'. Unpublished Paper, Bujumbura and Zürich-Rüschlikon.

———. 2005a. 'The Primary Justice Pilot Project of Malawi: An Assessment of

Selected Problem Fields from a Legal Pluralistic Viewpoint. A Consulting Report'. Unpublished Paper, Lilongwe and Zürich-Rüschlikon.

———. 2005b. 'Project Law – Normative Orders of Bilateral Development Co-operation and Social Change: A Case Study from the German Agency for Technical Cooperation', in F. von Benda-Beckmann, K. von Benda-Beckmann and A. Griffiths (eds), *Mobile People, Mobile Law: Expanding Legal Relations in a Contracting World*. Aldershot: Ashgate, 233–55.

8

HALF-TOLD TRUTHS AND PARTIAL SILENCE

Managing Communication in Scottish Children's Hearings

Anne Griffiths and Randy F. Kandel

Introduction

This chapter explores the power of law through an examination of the management and control of a legal process, the Scottish Children's Hearings system that was set up to deal with children in need of compulsory measures of supervision.[1] Based on a study that was carried out in Glasgow, our essay highlights the complex mix of differing normative orders that impinge on law in practice and that reflect the outcome of social interactions that take place during a hearing. It traces how international and global human rights law, including the United Nations Convention on the Rights of the Child (UNCRC) and European Convention on Human Rights and Fundamental Freedoms (ECHR) has shaped national legislation dealing with juvenile justice in Scotland and how a 'local' constituency (in the form of children's hearings in Glasgow) has responded to the challenges raised by applying transnational and global concepts in the context of a specific, local forum designed to meet the needs of its community. It reveals the multifaceted nature of power that is not just the product of unequal social relations but also reflects the dynamics of bureaucratic forms of governance.

In this process panel members (trained volunteer decision-makers at the hearings) struggle to reconcile global provision with Scots law in balancing children's and parents' rights from a welfare perspective based on the child's best interests. Parents and children, however, focus on assessing risk/benefit calculations that balance their obligations at hearings with informal codes governing neighbourhood and family life outside hearings. In addition, social workers and other personnel wrestle with balancing the system's formal legal requirements against the demands placed on them by the bureaucracies in which they work. Thus the hearings system represents a space where 'interlegality' (Santos 1985, 2002: 85) shapes the social interactions that inform the decision-making process, for it creates an opaque rather than a transparent forum, one that relies on partial withholding of knowledge of law and fact (what we call half-told truths and partial silence) to deal with the tensions of various overlapping, competing and sometimes even contradictory normative orders that make up the world in which participants and personnel operate.

Our discussion focuses on two procedural provisions of the Children's (Scotland) Act 1995, section 46 (clearing the room) and section 41 (appointment of a safeguarder), because they vividly demonstrate the way that the panel members scrutinize, parse and interpret the statutory language to square new global due process rights with their understandings of children's best interests, while simultaneously striving to maintain a smooth, well-informed hearing. Although intended to garner information from the child and the child's family, the usefulness of these two provisions, paradoxically, depends on panel members engaging in half-told truths and partial silence for reasons that will be outlined below.

Sections 46 and 41 were implemented to align Scots law with international approaches to due process promoted by the UNCRC, especially Article 3 (dealing with the child's best interests) and Article 12 (dealing with the child's right to be heard in judicial or administrative proceedings). They were also enacted to meet the requirements of the ECHR, principally Article 6 (dealing with the right to a fair hearing) and Article 8 (dealing with respect for private and family life), now embodied in domestic law under the Human Rights Act 1998.[2] While doing research on Glasgow hearings between 1997 and 2000,[3] it became clear to us, through interviews with forty of the four hundred active panel members in the Glasgow area[4] and attendance at initial and subsequent training sessions, that panel members were very aware of these international standards and focused on changes to the system brought about by the 'new' Act (as panel members referred to the 1995 Act) and its impact on their practice. Simultaneously, organizations like the Centre for Child Law and government departments that were to later form part of the new Scottish Executive (now Government), were also promoting public awareness of these issues. Our study is based on one area and cannot, therefore, be taken to represent the hearings system throughout Scotland. Nonetheless, it reveals how the relationship between formal law and institutional and bureaucratic norms was handled by various professionals in Glasgow at the time of our research.

Our analysis relies primarily on interviews and only secondarily on the 'spontaneous conversation' of our observed hearings, for several reasons. First, as researchers observing a hearing, we obviously could not interrupt to ask about withheld or secret information. Second, the statutory interpretation we elicited from the panel members is not overtly stated at hearings, or, in fact, anywhere else, unless asked about, although it constitutes a framework for their hearing management strategies. Third, section 46 requires everyone to 'clear the room' except the panel members and the child. It would have been impossible for the researchers to hear the conversation or compare what was said afterward. However, as will be seen below, the interviews and the hearings are contextually intertwined.

The Hearings, the Panel Members and Their Tasks

Established in 1971 and now regulated by the Children's (Scotland) Act 1995,[5] the hearings system engages vulnerable children under sixteen and their families in decision-making processes about the child's future in a nonjudgmental and supportive environment. State intervention covers a wide range of circumstances under section 52(2), including the neglect/abuse of children, offending behaviour and children who are 'beyond the control of a relevant person' or who fail 'to attend school regularly without reasonable excuse'. Although a legal forum with extensive powers under section 70, including power to remove a child from the home, it eschews adversarial court proceedings and formal legal rules of evidence and procedure in favour of an alternative forum, the children's panel, where all parties sit round a table exchanging their views about what is in 'the best interests' of the child. Based on a welfare, nonpunitive model of justice, it relies on disclosure and participation to achieve its objective. Thus transparency is central to it.

The children's hearings system thrives on a 'long and proud' tradition of Scottish volunteerism (Morrison 2001). Panel members are trained, unpaid volunteers who sit in panels of three. Although drawn from all walks of life in theory, our sample reflected a middle-class profile[6] of longstanding service (mean length 8.45 years) with a strong esprit de corps among them. They are highly and regularly trained. Although most disavow having technical legal knowledge (apart from the few who are lawyers), in practice they operate like professional judges who are knowledgeable about the law and regulations pertaining to the system and adhere to them. They interpret the legal framework that shapes the milieu within which participation and dialogue take place, and they engage actively in statutory interpretation as one of their most serious and significant tasks because it legitimates what is done, or is not done, in the name of law. Such interpretation plays a key role in establishing law's power and control over the process by setting the context in which social interaction is managed during hearings.

Panel members' other equally significant tasks are managing the hearing with participants who are often truculent, volatile or scared, and gathering as much information as possible in a short time span (usually under an hour) in order to reach a decision about the child according to three overriding principles. These are (1) that the welfare of the child is paramount (s.16(1)); (2) that children must be able to express their views and have them taken into account, where sufficiently mature (aged twelve or over (s.16(2)); and (3) that there should be minimum intervention, that is, that a hearing should make an order only if it is better for the child that such an order is made than to make no order at all (s.16(3)).

There are three parts to the hearing: (1) the rather formal reading of the grounds of referral – which the child must accept or which must be proved in the sheriff court before the hearing can commence; (2) discussion about what action should be taken; and (3) the decision and disposal that is based on a majority vote, after each panel member, independently, gives a decision. As parts 1 and 3 are relatively formal and brief, most of the hearing revolves around discussion about what action is in the child's best interests. This is intended to reflect an open and productive exchange. However, the class divide that exists between panel members and families (Waterhouse et al. 2000; Waterhouse and McGhee 2002) inhibits egalitarian discussion. Acquiring the crucial component of the children's and families' views often proves elusive (Hallett et al. 1998). Thus the social interaction at hearings does not occur on an equal footing because of panel members' social standing[7] and, more directly, because of the power they wield, which includes the ability to remove a child from the family home. Although such power is rarely exercised, children and families remain fearful that it will be in their case.[8]

Many children who come from poor, dysfunctional families cling to notions of privacy, loyalty and autonomy, resisting the state's power of intrusion into their lives by employing strategies that embrace silence, compliance and autonomy/defiance (Griffiths and Kandel 2005). They reveal as little as possible except where disclosure is advantageous, for example, to acquire the services of a home help. Thus children assess participation against what might happen after the hearing. They balance the potential benefits (school change, safety or protection) against the risks of incurring punishment, bullying or removal from home. Knowing this, panel members attempt to overcome children's reticence to speak.

Panel Members' Interpretations of the 'Clearing the Room' Provision: Section 46

Given their remit, panel members are perpetually in search of information. This is generally provided by professional reports, such as social workers' background reports that are circulated to the panel, family and other relevant persons before the hearing. However, panel members rely on verbal and nonverbal communication during hearings as a means of forming an independent assessment that may be measured against the recommendations contained in the reports (Griffiths and Kandel 2000).

One means of acquiring information that is open to panel members is to apply section 46 of the 1995 act. This section, implemented to conform to the due process requirements of the UNCRC (Articles 3 and 12) and the ECHR (Articles 6 and 8), is intended to foster children's participation by allowing the panel to speak to the child alone. Section 46(1) gives panel members authority to clear the room, 'in order to obtain the views of the child' or where 'the presence of the person or persons in question is causing, or is likely to cause, significant distress to the child'. However, panel members do not have control over the flow of information, and the chair must, in the interests of fairness, explain later 'to any person who was so excluded the substance of what has taken place in his absence' (s.46(2)). Most of the panel members we interviewed do not believe that children's and parents' rights should be equal at hearings. They balance rights according to their remit to make a decision that is in the child's best interests and resist incompatible due process incursions (Griffiths and Kandel 2006: 138–40). In our observation of hearings, section 46 was never utilized. However, all forty panel members that we interviewed found this legal requirement counterproductive and felt it undercut their primary focus on the best interests of the child. In order to deal with it they developed varying interpretations of the statute that correlated directly with their diverse views on competing rights regimes, enabling them to legitimize and use the provision for their purposes. Of the twenty-nine who talked about interpretation, their strategies appear to us to divide into three categories that we term literalism, gisting (which is how panel members refer to their interpretative practice) and loopholing.

Literalism

The ten literalists interpreted 'substance' to mean all substantive information on the conversation, but not necessarily stated verbatim. In their words, they glossed the provision to mean 'disclose any information that they've divulged' or 'sort of review what the discussion was and so on'. They considered the provision ineffective because children can see through it and do not talk. As one observed: 'In my experience, it has not helped because the child is not stupid, he or she knows that my Dad is in the next room and he's going to come back afterwards.' All in all, this group perceived disclosing the substance as a practice that 'defeats the purpose' of the section, making it 'relatively useless' or a 'false thing'.

Gisting

Another approach, referred to as 'gisting', involved the practice of providing 'the minimum to give an idea of what is being said'. For the twelve panel members who employed this strategy, as long as a parent is 'made aware of what went on' or has it 'explained generally what had happened', the requirements of the section are met. For this group, substance amounts to summarizing with a broad brush, engaging in generalities and, if they think it appropriate, deleting or downplaying certain matters or mentioning others elliptically. Unlike the literalists, they adopt a liberal approach to the section as being protective of children and interpret it accordingly, as one opined: 'I think this is part of what we are required to do. Although we are required to repeat the substance I think we have to protect the youngster's interests ... so it can't be a verbatim account of what has been said.' This approach enables panel members to ignore specifics that might put the child at risk without being dishonest to the parent.

Loopholing

The most liberal interpretation of the section is embraced by the 'loopholers', who virtually turn the section's intent topsy-turvy by guiding children to speak about emotions and desires (rather than facts) and using this information to get parents to reveal what is going on in the family. Rather than interviewing the child, panel members interrogate the parents, using hunches and their perceptions of parents' fears and concerns to bring out the facts that parents believe children might have divulged to the hearing. They do this by bringing up leading questions like 'Do you and your boyfriend drink a bit of beer in the evening?' rather than making assertions, so that the child is not directly implicated in anything the panel members say.

These varying approaches closely resemble judicial approaches to statutory interpretation that involve the literal rule, the golden rule and the mischief rule of construction in Scotland (Walker 2001: 415–18; Busby et al. 2006: 39–40) and the plain meaning, holistic textuality or intent construction in the U.S. (Solan 2005: 427; Eskridge 2006). They represent panel members' efforts to manage the hearing and control the flow of information that is central to the process in difficult circumstances.

Panel Members' Interpretations of Verbalizing the Decision Whether to Appoint a Safeguarder: Section 41

Implementation of section 41 is another aspect of the hearing that members perceive requires careful handling. This section deals with the appointment of a safeguarder, who is an independent person appointed to make recommendations about what is in the child's best interests. Prior to the 1995 act, a safeguarder could be appointed only by the chair and only if there was a conflict of interest between the child and family and/ or social work. The 1995 Act expanded the safeguarder's potential role so that hearings are required to consider 'if it is necessary to appoint a person to safeguard the interests of the child in the proceedings'. If made, an appointment is 'on such terms and conditions as appear appropriate' (s.41(1)(b)), and it is made by all three panel members. The circumstances in which appointments are made now cover a range of issues (Hill et al. 2002) including conflicts between parents and social work, or within the extended family or between the different agencies working with the child.

In order to fully explain the panel members' interpretation of the section, we now touch on other hearing personnel and their professional and institutional constraints, for sometimes the reporters' and social workers' roles inadvertently collude in a conspiracy of silences and holdings-back that leave the panel members puzzled, wary or uncertain as to what the disposal should be because of lack of information.

Reporters

Reporters are employed by the Scottish Children's Reporter Administration (SCRA), a national body charged with the management and deployment of reporters throughout Scotland under section 128(4) and (5) of the Local Government etc. (Scotland) Act 1994. They may but need not be legally qualified. Some have backgrounds in social work or education. Reporters (acting independently from local authorities) operate as gatekeepers to the system. They investigate cases brought to them by agencies such as social work departments, schools and the police, or even by the public. After reviewing the situation the reporter decides whether to drop the matter, or encourage a child and family to work with social services on a voluntary basis, or proceed to a hearing. While reporters attend hearings, their remit is not to participate in decision-making but to ensure that panel members follow appropriate procedure and comply with legal requirements.

As reporters compile the grounds for referral, they play a crucial role in framing the hearing. However, they may find themselves keeping silent or telling 'half truths' in two ways. Firstly, they sometimes restrict referral grounds to those that are easiest to establish, in order to get the child into the system, although they are aware that other, more serious grounds may exist. Secondly, they may not divulge to the panel information they have acquired through their broader contact with the family because they do not wish to influence the panel members' decision.

This situation arises because the hearings system is premised on reaching a disposal that is in the child's best interests. Thus the child's welfare lies at the heart of the system. However, a hearing cannot commence until the grounds are admitted. The more complicated the grounds, the more difficult it may be to elicit acceptance of them from the child and family. Contested grounds require referral to the sheriff court for proof. This requires adjournment of the panel with postponement of the hearing until proof is forthcoming. All this takes time. Given that the hearing's ethos is to get beyond grounds to discussion of the child's welfare, reporters may decide to use the lightest, simplest grounds of referral, for example truancy, to get the child into the system. In this case admission is easier to obtain, as is proof, since all that is required is the school's attendance record for the child.

However, while this provides an easy entry point into the system, truancy is often a manifestation of underlying symptoms that can range from abuse, neglect or helping a sick granny, to bullying and child prostitution. As one safeguarder, formerly a reporter, explained: 'One of the reasons for children coming before a hearing for truancy is that that's the easiest option for the reporter. There's nothing easier. There can be all sorts of problems which are in my view the real reason for the child appearing at the hearing which are not stated because they are difficult to prove ... whereas truancy is dead easy [to prove] ... I consider that to be underhand and unacceptable ... I used to have to prevent people doing that [when I was a senior Reporter]. However, this is not so much of a problem; it is done much less nowadays.'

Yet, the change of verbiage – from the narrative context in which the reporter receives the child's information, into one or more formulaic charges – inevitably leads to a recontextualization of the child's situation through the panel members' different perspectives. At the same time, reporters refrain from discussing matters that are not addressed by the panel or the participants, as they are not entitled to participate in the hearing except to clarify legal or resource issues. For example, after one truancy hearing we observed (Griffiths and Kandel 2005: 281) the reporter revealed that a young boy had not been attending school because he felt under pressure to support his nonmobile mother, who was on a three-year waiting list for a hip replacement operation. Although concern for his mother appeared to be the boy's main motivation for nonattendance at school, the hearing never discussed this.

On another occasion, the reporter revealed dissatisfaction with the social worker's statement to the panel that all was in order because the young woman in question was 'at a new school and she's been attending for the last three weeks'. This was because the reporter knew that 'attendance at school was not the only issue' that was affecting the young woman's behaviour: she had had a pregnancy terminated a few months earlier. The social worker, who was new to the case, was either unaware of what was going on or reluctant to disclose details to the panel. Social work's failure to submit a written report to the hearing meant that it had to be continued.

Social Workers

At the hearing, the role of the social worker is to speak to and update the social background report and its recommendations. From panel members' perspectives, social workers are frequently involved in partial silence or half-told truths for the following reasons. Firstly, their departments have limited and shrinking resources, which may lead them to have minimal contact with and knowledge of the child and family concerned. In such cases their reports are based on an incomplete picture of the family that nonetheless forms the basis for their recommendations about disposal. As panel members observed, social workers' reports may well be silent about issues that are of importance to them, which is why they may appoint a safeguarder.

In ten out of the thirty-four hearings we attended we observed social workers informing the panel that they had only recently been appointed to the family and that they had either never met the family before the hearing (and were thus speaking about another social worker's report)[9] or had only had one meeting with them prior to the hearing. In addition, limited resources place constraints on how social workers operate, forcing them to prioritize their efforts, which may place them at odds with panel members about what action should be taken. For example, in one truancy case that we observed (Griffiths and Kandel 2005: 279–81), the social worker opposed the panel members' desire for a supervision order on the basis that given his department's priorities, the boy was not 'appropriate for group work or a befriender or family work' because '[h]e doesn't fit the "care package" criteria ... Prioritization is the name of the game ... and [he] is not a priority' (2005: 280). Everyone recognizes that the insufficiency of resources to fit needs is perpetual. Even with the Scottish Executive's recent funding to ameliorate the problem, it is not clear that funds are reaching their appropriate targets, and some needs remain more important than others.

Secondly, by virtue of their job description, social workers may have long-standing relationships with children and families over many years. The need to work with their clients over time often constrains what they say both in social work reports and at hearings. In this situation, their option is either to 'tell all' to the panel members at the risk of alienating the families they work with, who are now entitled to copies of these reports, or, alternatively, to make vague statements that skate over relevant facts in an attempt to maintain an ongoing relationship with their clients.

Many panel members, reporters and safeguarders spoke about the consequences of increasingly conservative fiscal policy that make it hard for them to work with children and families due to lack of resources, as well as the increasing intrusion of due process transparency rights that sometimes backfire. They commented that some social workers are deliberately vague in social background reports, employing phrases such as 'the mother felt unable to cooperate at this time' without any further elaboration, and rationalized these practices on the grounds that social workers are reluctant to upset families or damage relationships with them, lest that prove counterproductive to their work.

Safeguarders

Safeguarders were introduced into the system in 1985. Their remit is to compile a report for the panel making recommendations about what is in the child's best interests. Their role is one of an independent investigator,[10] with no attachment to social work or to SCRA. According to the *Guidelines for Practice* (1999) issued by the Safeguarders Association, there are three core responsibilities in safeguarding a child: (1) ensuring the child's rights are protected; (2) ensuring the child's views are established and communicated to the hearing; and (3) ensuring any proposals made are in the child's best interests.

Safeguarders study case papers and reports, speak to social workers and carry out several interviews with the child(ren) and parents. They also interview any other relevant people such as extended family, teachers or doctors while investigating the child's daily environment. Although they have authority to interview relevant persons, they have no compulsory powers; thus interviews are consensual and usually occur in private without legal representation. Afterwards the safeguarder writes a comprehensive but succinct report for the panel that is also made available to the child (if aged 12 or over) and family. This report embodies the child's views, those of the parent(s) and/or family and the safeguarder's recommendations about what is in the child's best interests. Overall, a good safeguarder should create a contextualized snapshot of the child's situation at the date of interview. This contrasts with the type of longitudinal reports produced by social workers that may be constrained by limited resources or affected by social work's ongoing relationship with the family. Although it is not legally required, best practice as advocated by the Safeguarders Association requires that a safeguarder attend the hearing.

Safeguarders consider themselves to have two advantages over social workers. First, they can recommend what is in the child's best interests without regard to institutional constraints on resources. Second, as they have no ongoing contact with the child and family they are more disposed to speak frankly to them than to social workers. As one safeguarder observed: 'The social worker that you're dealing with doesn't have the power to make the decisions … and I think nowadays what are clear, obvious solutions, they can't support because of finance or misconstructions from above … [as a result] … very often social workers will agree with me when I'm taking an opposite view and say thank God you're going to be able to say that because I can't.' Another commented on how children and families often reveal less to social workers because 'there is a kind of fear that once you've got involved … with social work, you can't get them off your back … I'm very anxious to say, once this is all over you'll never see me again.'

However, the snapshot approach has the disadvantage of time limitations as well as limitations on knowledge acquired. Many safeguarders stated that some cases were so volatile that they had changed their recommendations between the submission of their reports and the hearings themselves.

Panel Members

Our data demonstrate that in addition to children's and families' reticence, panel members have to contend with the institutional roles, regulations and constraints under which reporters and social workers operate. Hence, panel members have to manoeuvre around blind spots in the information they receive.

In applying section 41, panel members supported the expanded remit of safeguarders as useful in certain cases. The Scottish Executive (2002) documents an increase in safeguarders' appointments from occurring only rarely to featuring in about 10 percent of cases after 1995. However, our panel members almost unanimously disliked discussing the possible appointment of a safeguarder in every case (which they considered to be mandatory although it was not expressly stated in the statute).[11] The panel members felt it made families unnecessarily anxious and disrupted the management of hearings.

Our interviewees considered safeguarders as potent yet unpredictable information gatherers, for the following reasons. Differences in safeguarders' and social workers' recommendations may create complexity and dissension. Panel members' assessments of safeguarders' work vary widely, from 'worth their weight in gold' to 'dross'. Safeguarder training, say the panel members, is correspondingly variable and patchy.[12] Further, if a safeguarder is appointed, the hearing is continued and that decision-making passes to another set of panel members on the duty roster. Safeguarders have the power to appeal against the panel's decision on the child's behalf, although they rarely do so. Though safeguarders' pay is minimal, panel members are mindful that safeguarders are a resource that has cost implications. Panel members are also concerned about the intrusiveness of appointing yet another person to investigate the child and family. From the panel members' perspective, the sum of these factors makes a safeguarder both a valued and an uncertain resource.

In their role as managers and decision-makers, panel members want to refer to safeguarders only when they want to appoint them, or where a rare request for appointment is made by a social worker or parent. Nineteen of the panel members we interviewed employed clever legalistic interpretations of the statute to meet their dual purposes – minimizing unwanted attention of the provision without flouting what they believed to be required. They used four fairly formalized routines to deal with the issue, which we term 'the full explanation', 'the split explanation', 'discussion among panel members' and 'the adequacy of reports approach'. Some panel members used more than one of these routines.

The Full Explanation

Six panel members used the full explanation approach, which is usually adopted at the start of a hearing. It explains to those present that a safeguarder is an independent person who will provide a report on the child and family to the panel and make recommendations on what is in the child's best interests if this is considered necessary. It then sets out the safeguarder's role. As one panel member explained:

> It really has to be strictly speaking mentioned during the hearing, so that you can 'put in your report that you have considered a safeguarder'. However, how it's done depends on the case. [In] some cases it's quite clear and your colleagues are in total agreement that there is absolutely no need for a safeguarder. So how I would say it as a Chairman then, is that there is also a further resource available which is known as a safeguarder where an independent view of the whole situation can be determined and they're not panel members, they don't work for the social work department, but in this case my colleagues and I are in agreement that there's no requirement for that.

The Split Explanation

In contrast, four panel members advocated the split discussion approach, which generally consists of a cursory mention of the safeguarder at the beginning followed by a fuller explanation of what the safeguarder is and does at some appropriate time later in the hearing, or by a statement that the appointment of a safeguarder is not necessary. Out of this group, one of the panel members explained: 'I mention it before we get into a discussion and I say that at any time any of the panel members can say, I think at this stage that we want to appoint a safeguarder and if that comes up then we will discuss it further with them at that time.' These panel members believed that they should mention the appointment of a safeguarder at the beginning of the hearing, but also felt that a full explanation at that point was unnecessarily disruptive of the hearing and should be left in abeyance until it featured as a possibility in later discussions. One commented that he gives a minimum 'presentation at the beginning [for] covering myself, but during the hearing then I'll go on to say more [if it is necessary]'. As another observed: 'You can mention it at the beginning and you usually say as we go along there is a person called a safeguarder and at every hearing we must consider one and that's not to say we need one but if we should, we will stop and say do you want to consider a safeguarder ... because at any time during the hearing you can totally change your mind you know, there can be something disclosed and you think no, I do want a safeguarder's report here.'

Discussion among Panel Members

Four panel members adopted an approach that deals with the issue of a safeguarder through panel members' discussions of whether or not to appoint one during the hearing. This approach draws upon the immediate and unverbalized mutual understandings of the three panel members on any case, so that if 'there's something not right about the whole case and you're going to need some more information very quickly [then] as panel members you should be able to say: "If we just stop for a minute I'm going to consult with my colleagues to see if we feel we have enough information."' If there is no need for further information nothing more is said, so that a safeguarder is never directly mentioned. Sometimes, however, when the matter is raised directly but colleagues agree that an appointment is unnecessary, no more is said, so that the issue receives minimum exposure.

Adequacy of Reports Approach

Another version of this type of approach, adopted by six panel members, involved references to the adequacy of reports. This generally occurs at or near the end of the hearing, particularly where the panel see no reason to appoint a safeguarder. In this situation the chair asks panel members 'whether the existing reports are adequate, and whether or not any other reports are needed, including a safeguarder's report'. If panel members agree that no more reports are needed, no more is said about a safeguarder. This is done so that 'the family don't get frightened by the word safeguarder'. Some panels go even further by not using the word 'safeguarder' but just speaking about 'reports' so that the chair simply asks, 'Are we ready to make a decision? Do you feel you require any further reports or information?' and leaves it at that if no further reports are required.

In considering the appointment of safeguarders, panel members once again must assess how much to say and when to say it, bearing in mind that problematic communication with children and families requires careful handling. Redundant references to third parties such as safeguarders, who represent yet another potential intervention into family life, can promote unnecessary anxiety that inhibits participation. As one panel chair observed: 'It only confuses families who are already tense.' Hence, panel members have adopted the above ways of strategically balancing the legal requirements of section 41 with their management of the hearing.[13] These strategies are also in accordance with the judicial approaches to statutory interpretation discussed above.

Working the System: Participation, Operational Constraints and Diverging Agendas

Children's hearings in Scotland are based on a welfare-oriented approach that strives to reach consensus in proceedings about what is in the child's best interests. In upholding this aim they promote the concept of transparency through disclosure and participation. Our research, however, reveals that what is intended to be an open form of dialogue turns out to represent a more complex and concealed process of communication that derives from partial silence, secrecy and half-told truths. Power in this context is not just confined to the unequal social relations that exist between panel members and the children and families that come before them but also manifests itself in the bureaucratic forms of governance that shape other professionals' engagement with the system. Constrained by their institutional and professional positions,[14] panel members, reporters, social workers and safeguarders, speak from different perspectives, with different priorities and to differing effect within the hearings system.

Panel members, who need to garner information, control hearings and make decisions, interpret sections 41 and 46 so as to balance welfare and participatory rights in ways that they consider to be consistent with the system. We found that panel members had three different styles when using section 46, the 'clearing the room' provision, but all the styles' adherents (literalists, gisters and loopholers) draw upon traditional judicial canons of statutory interpretation. Furthermore, the three groups called upon these techniques in different ways that accorded with their views on how much should be said or relayed to whom. Similarly, in dealing with section 41, panel members adopted different styles of interpretation involving the full explanation, the split explanation and the adequacy of reports presentation. These approaches also reflect panel members' attempts to interpret the law in accordance with the hearings' needs.

Reporters, given their position as gatekeepers to the system, some-times select the simplest ground for referral, such as truancy, as a 'hook' to bring in the child, even where more serious grounds may exist.[15] They may also feel obliged not to share previous knowledge of children and families lest they exert undue influence on the panel's decisions, for the system is oriented towards the child's future rather than dwelling on the child's past. For this reason, hearings were designed to accept the grounds of referral first, before proceeding to a consideration of 'needs not deeds' (Kilbrandon 1964; Waterhouse et al. 2000: 1).

On the other hand, social workers, whose social background reports provide the most information to panel members, often find themselves in long-standing work relationships with the children and families. The need to continue working positively can constrain both them and their reports at hearings. Also, their focus and remit on families may differ from that of panel members fixed on the child's welfare as a paramount consideration. Some panel members expressed dissatisfaction that chil-dren often come to hearings because of their families' shortcomings but that the panel had no direct power over such families at the date of our research.[16] Also, because many social workers are overstretched because of conservative fiscal policy, they may have insufficient knowl-edge and contact with the child and family to know what is going on or make a solid recommendation. Similarly, because of fiscal policy, social workers may have to recommend action that they do not perceive to be in the child's best interests because of lack of resources.

Safeguarders can, when appointed by the panel, carry out an inde-pendent investigation into what is in the child's best interests and pro-duce a report that does not have to take account of the kind of restraints that face social workers. The safeguarders we interviewed, largely re-cently retired reporters, panel members or social workers with expe-rience of the hearings system, find they know how to challenge the system's professionals and see past institutional blind spots. They also stated that children and other family members divulge more to them because they know a safeguarder will be gone from their lives after the case. However, the safeguarder's value depends upon his or her ability to carry out the role. Panel members found this to be very variable.[17] Furthermore, however well done, the safeguarder's report can provide only a partial picture of the child and family, being based on a limited snapshot of them in time and space.

After looking at these factors, the apparent openness and transpar-ency of hearings is revealed as an illusion veiling a more opaque side, founded on partial silence and half-told truths (Tiersma: 1995) that arise not only from participants' competing perspectives and agendas but also from the tensions that personnel have to handle within their own domains. These include squaring law with the institutional demands that are placed on them. In this process withholding information turns out to be an effective tool for managing the ambivalence of interlegality. Panel members must reconcile the welfare justice regimes of children's hearings with the international and global autonomy rights regimes deriving from the UNCRC and the ECHR, while social workers must reconcile the hearings system with social work departmental policies and the practical needs of getting along with their clients. Even children and families who attend hearings must assess their participation in the light of the local informal law of loyalty and strong discipline that shapes their lives outside the hearing. Although reporters and safeguarders may find themselves less conflicted, the constraints of their positions entail some secrecy nonetheless. Even safeguarders may be grounding their reports inadvertently on evanescent snapshots of what is going on.

The trade-offs and the tensions that these positions embody result from trying to negotiate welfare and autonomy rights of children while also taking account of other parties' due process rights. The fact that such negotiation takes place within a more informal, alternative legal setting than a court renders it more susceptible to bureaucratic demands that are placed on it through the differing institutional roles and professional affiliations of those who service it. In navigating this universe, holding back information that is not regarded as suitable and emphasizing what is, proves for all concerned to be a much more powerful tool than transparency and openness in providing for management and control of the process.

Acknowledgements

The authors wish to thank Clair McDiarmid, Janice McGhee, Kay Tisdall and Alison Wright for their insightful comments on a draft version of this chapter. The text as it stands, however, is the authors' sole responsibility. We would also like to thank the Annenberg Foundation and the British Academy for funding the research on which this chapter is based.

Notes

1. The Social Work (Scotland) Act 1968 that established this system originally referred to compulsory measures of care, but the word supervision was substituted for care under reforms implemented by the Children (Scotland) Act 1995.

2. For the tensions that exist in dealing with Articles 6 and 8 in terms of balancing children and parents' rights see Griffiths and Kandel (2006: 138–40).

3. This research, funded by the Annenberg Foundation in the U.S. and the British Academy, formed part of a comparative study on children and legal proceedings in the U.S. and Scotland.

4. These were selected by the Glasgow Panel Chair. Our data also include interviews with 25 social workers, 25 safeguarders, 65 young people with experience of panels and 67 without, 25 parents and 34 observed hearings.

5. For details see Lockyer and Stone (1998); McDiarmid (2001); Norrie (2005); Edwards and Griffiths (2006); Thomson (2006).

6. Our panel members generally came from professional/management backgrounds. Only one was a taxi driver and one was a secretary.

7. The Scottish Executive (2005) recognizes this disparity and plans to rectify it in future.

8. Even children who have no experience of panels expressed the view that they existed to remove bad children from their home.

9. This involved two cases. In one case the social worker only received the papers and met the family on the morning of the hearing.

10. Although no formal relationship exists with those servicing hearings, 14 safeguarders interviewed had worked previously as a social worker, reporter or panel member. Of those remaining, 10 had had careers that brought them into close contact with hearings. Such links are in keeping with findings from the Scottish Executive (2002).

11. While it may be the case that national good practice guidance for panel members requires them to raise the matter of a safeguarder in every hearing, this was not the view of one of the panel chairs, who is a lawyer.

12. Since the date of research more extensive, national training for safeguarders has been introduced.

13. In reviewing the system the Scottish Executive (2005, section 2) 'invite views on whether the role of the Safeguarder should be maintained'.

14. See Griffiths and Kandel (2004, 2005) for children's and families' views of the process.

15. Since the Human Rights Act 1998 came into force, anecdotal evidence from panel members suggests that reporters may be less inclined to act in this way.

16. S.75A, which was inserted into the 1995 Act by s.116 of the Anti Social etc. Behaviour (Scotland) Act 2004, now gives hearings power to consider whether to require the Principal Reporter to apply for a parenting order.

17. Since the date of the research there is now mandatory training for new safeguarders.

References

Busby, N., B. Clark, R. Paisley and P. Spink. 2006. *Scots Law: A Student Guide.* Haywards Heath: Tottel Publishing.

Edwards, L. and A. Griffiths. 2006. *Family Law.* Edinburgh: Thomson/W. GREEN.

Eskridge, W. 2006. 'Book Review: No Frills Textualism: Judging Under Uncertainty', *Harvard Law Review* 119: 2041–75.

Griffiths, A. and R.F. Kandel. 2000. 'Hearing Children in Children's Hearings', *Child and Family Law Quarterly* 3: 283–99.

———. 2004. 'Empowering Children? Legal Understandings and Experiences of Rights in the Children's Hearings System', in S. Halliday and P. Schmidt (eds), *Human Rights Brought Home: Socio-legal Perspectives on Human Rights in the National Context*. Oxford and Portland, OR: Hart Publishing, 231–55.

———. 2005. 'Globalizing the Local: Rights of Participation in the Scottish Children's Hearings System', in F. von Benda-Beckmann, K. von Benda-Beckmann and A. Griffiths (eds), *Mobile People, Mobile Law: Expanding Legal Relations in a Contracting World*. Aldershot: Ashgate, 277–95.

———. 2006. 'Children's Confidentiality at the Cross Roads: Challenges for the Scottish Children's Hearings System', *Journal of Social Welfare & Family Law* 28(2): 135–50.

Hallett, C. and C. Murray, with J. Jamies and B. Veitch. 1998. *The Evaluation of Children's Hearings in Scotland*, vol. 1: *Deciding in Children's Interests*. Edinburgh: The Scottish Office Central Research Unit.

Hill, M., A. Lockyer, P. Morton, S. Batchelor and J. Scott. 2002. 'Safeguarding Children in Scotland: The Perspectives of Children, Parents and Safeguarders', *Representing Children* 15(3): 169–83.

———. 2002. *The Role of Safeguarders in Scotland*. Edinburgh: Scottish Executive Education Department, Education and Young People Research Unit.

Kilbrandon, L. 1964. *Report of the Committee on Children and Young Persons Scotland*, Kilbrandon Report, Cmnd. 2306. Edinburgh: HMSO.

Lockyer, A. and F.H. Stone (eds). 1998. *Juvenile Justice in Scotland: Twenty Five Years of the Welfare Approach*. Edinburgh: T. & T. Clark.

McDiarmid, C. 2001. 'Perspectives in the Children's Hearings System', in J. Scoular (ed.), *Family Dynamics: Contemporary Issues in Family Law*. London: Butterworths/LexisNexis, 29–48.

Morrison, J. 2001. 'Democracy, Governance and Governmentality: Civic Public Space and Constitutional Renewal in Northern Ireland', *Oxford Journal of Legal Studies* 21(2): 287–310.

Norrie, McK. 2005. *Children's Hearings in Scotland*. Edinburgh: Thomson/W. GREEN.

Santos, B. de Sousa. 1985. 'On Modes of Production of Law and Social Power', *International Journal of the Sociology of Law* 13: 299–336.

———. 2002. *Toward a New Legal Common Sense: Law, Globalization, and Emancipation*. London: Butterworths LexisNexis.

Scottish Executive. 2002. *The Role of Safeguarders in Scotland* by M. Hill, A. Lockyer, P. Morton, S. Batchelor and J. Scott, Glasgow: Scottish Executive.

———. 2005. *Getting it Right for Every Child: Proposals for Action*. Astron: Scottish Executive.

Scottish Safeguarders Association. 1999. *Guidelines for Practice*. Scone: Scottish Safeguarders Association.

Solan, L.M. 2005. 'Private Language, Public Laws: The Central Role of Legislative Intent in Statutory Interpretation', *Georgetown Law Journal* 93: 427–86.

Thomson, J. 2006. *Family Law in Scotland*. West Sussex: Tottel Publishing.

Tiersma, P. 1995. 'The Language of Silence', *Rutgers Law Review* 48(1): 1–99.

Walker, D.M. 2001. *Scottish Legal System: An Introduction to the Study of Scots Law.* Edinburgh: W. GREEN/Sweet & Maxwell.

Waterhouse, L. and J. McGhee. 2002. 'Children's Hearings in Scotland: Compulsion and Disadvantage', *Journal of Social Welfare and Family Law* 24(3): 279–96.

Waterhouse, L., J. McGhee, B. Whyte, N. Loucks and R. Stewart. 2000. 'Children in Focus', vol. 3 of the *Evaluation of Children's Hearings System.* Edinburgh: Scottish Office Central Research Unit, the Scottish Office.

RELIGION AS A RESOURCE
IN LEGAL PLURALISM

9

KEEPING THE STREAM OF JUSTICE CLEAR AND PURE

The Buddhicization of Bhutanese Law

Richard W. Whitecross

> Retrospection is a kind of sorcery that imagines, invites, and reinvents
> those losses that mark survival or that constitute, in its most ancient
> sense, the image of contemporary identity as person, institution, collec-
> tivity or law (Goodrich 1994: 1568).

In 1991 *National Geographic* carried a lengthy article on Bhutan entitled
'Bhutan: Kingdom in the Clouds'. The reader encounters a set of claims
about the essence of Bhutanese identity and the character of contemporary Bhutanese society and culture. 'In serene isolation ... after centuries of solitude', 'Shangri-la as it is – a land of pure air, fragrant pine
forests' (Bunting 1991: 78). Similar sentiments are expressed in other
writings, in particular travel writing and coffee table books on Bhutan.
These images have been and continue to be used by the Bhutanese state,
as well as Bhutanese and Western tour operators, to present a particular
image of Bhutan as steeped in Buddhism and environmentally aware,
a place where tradition blends with modernity, maintaining a 'balance
between tradition and development' (Ura 1997: 239).

Developing recent literature on Tibetan image-making in Diaspora, I
argue that these reflexive, politicized notions of Bhutanese culture and
identity are 'unprecedented and distinctly modern' (Huber 2001: 357).
We can understand these images as simultaneously the products and
the means of production of a complex transnational politics of identity
within which the Bhutanese, like other populations in the Himalayan
region, are 'increasingly both representing themselves and being represented by others' (Huber 2001: 357).[1] Reading the National Assembly
reports and resolutions, one can begin to trace a hint of these issues
arising in the late 1960s, but it is only in the 1980s that we can see the
crystallization and the impact of these images on government policies. In this chapter, I focus on the representational style and agenda
of this Bhutanese self-image as expressed and performed in the law
courts. Specifically, I examine the buddhicization of the representation

of the courts and the set of practices associated with them, as well as the emergent idea of a Bhutanese/Buddhist jurisprudence. I argue that this emergent discourse claims to be both grounded in 'the rule of law' sanctioned by the Buddha and, simultaneously, part of a broader transnational law tradition.

The chapter is in three sections. The first is a description of the new district court in Phuentsholing, southern Bhutan. Considered to be the blueprint for future court buildings in Bhutan, the new district court marks a major transition both in terms of the location and architecture of the law courts. In this section, I note the incorporation of certain iconographic images from a ritual dance, the *raksha marcham*, described briefly below. The second section begins to draw out the features outlined in the first section and specifically to examine the emerging discourse that associates contemporary court practices and legal principles with Buddhist teachings. Furthermore, I argue that there is a simultaneous attempt to link Bhutanese Buddhist court practices with a wider transnational law tradition. The final section argues that the conscious representation of contemporary court practices and legal codes has failed to gain popular credence or enhance popular confidence in the legal system. This moves away from law in everyday life, to its very operation, its normativity.

There is a ritual dance performed annually at the religious festivals (*tshechu*) throughout Bhutan called the *raksha marcham*, or the dance of the *raksha*. *Tshechu* act as both social events, drawing as they do people from the surrounding districts, and as an 'opportunity to be immersed in the meaning of their religion' (Pommaret 1990: 105). The *raksha marcham* is very popular in Bhutan – indeed, it may be unique to Bhutan – and serves a didactic purpose. The dance or ritual drama represents the impartial judgment of the Lord of the Underworld, Shinje Chosgyal, with the assistance of Black Demon as prosecutor and White God as defence, of two individuals. The first man, a hunter, had led a nonvirtuous life, and the second, a householder, had led a virtuous life. The hunter is found guilty of various sins (crimes) and sent to the hell realms, whilst the virtuous householder is found innocent and passes upwards to the Buddha realms (Anonymous 2000: 4–8).

Significantly, the visual imagery of the *raksha marcham* has been drawn upon by the Royal Court of Justice. Masks depicting the Lord of the Underworld, Black Demon and White God now appear in the courtrooms. During a recent interview I asked when the masks had first appeared there, and a senior official indicated that they were introduced in the mid 1990s. A clue to these recent additions to the symbolism of the courtroom is provided by a recent statement made by the chief justice. In an interview, he expressed his concern that ordinary Bhutanese did not respect laws that did not reflect wider social and cultural practices. Lyonpo Sonam Tobgye notes that 'laws are always strong only when they have social sanction and religious sanctity' (*Kuensel* 2003).

Building upon the chief justice's statement, I illustrate how the Bhutanese courts and their personnel seek to establish a particular vision of the moral bases of law. This imaginary of law, of justice, forms a complex interweaving of several discourses. On one level, it seeks to naturalize the wider processes of modernization brought about by the Bhutanese state and sponsored by a range of international bodies.[2] Simultaneously, it seeks to present Bhutanese society and culture as unique, under threat from worldly forces that would, if left unchecked, obliterate an ancient, Buddhist culture.

There are two distinct audiences for the various configurations of these discourses. The first is an internal audience of Bhutanese from a range of ethnic and religious backgrounds. It is important not to be distracted by the promotion of Bhutan as a Buddhist state or to ignore the large Hindu population that exists in the country. Within this local audience is a smaller audience of officials and policy makers with their own set of understandings, aims and objectives. This is perhaps illustrated by the recent increased promotion of the concept of Gross National Happiness in Bhutan and externally.[3] Beyond Bhutan are a number of external audiences comprising, amongst others, major donors and international agencies who want to see a recognizable legal system and procedures established as part of the process of ensuring equal access to justice. However, the external audience is much more complex, including non-Bhutanese who project certain desires and representations onto Bhutan. The varied Western reactions to the concept of Gross National Happiness illustrate this point. These two major discourses, each with their own dialectic and tensions, must be accommodated by the personnel of the law in the operation of the state laws. What I examine here is the dual role of the court in an active and highly publicized modernization programme and in its simultaneous promotion of a reified view of Bhutanese cultural values.

Phuentsholing District Court: A Modern 'Traditional' Court

Phuentsholing, the second largest city in Bhutan, is located 174 km southwest of the capital, Thimphu. Despite the various buildings that incorporate traditional design elements in mouldering concrete, it does not feel especially Bhutanese. Dujardin comments that Phuentsholing is 'of a more hybrid typology and architectural arrangement due to its contiguity with the Indian border town of Jaigaon' (1997: 65). A striking feature that one can hardly miss is a concrete wall approximately 2 m high running through the city, separating Jaigaon from Phuentsholing. The wall, erected by the Indian authorities, marks the frontier between the two countries. At various points the wall is broken by wooden planks and boards acting as small impromptu bridges between India and Bhutan. People mill about, crossing to and fro by leaping over the storm conduits draining the heavy monsoon rain water away from the city centre.

Passing through the 'Gateway to Bhutan' to Jaigaon, one is struck by the contrast. Despite the decaying concrete facades of the buildings and potholes, Phuentsholing has a sense of order. There is a uniformity and control over the physical appearance of the city. A few meters away this picture tumbles into chaos, a vibrant blend of styles with jostling crowds of shoppers, hawkers, rickshaw drivers and vehicles racing towards each other and the vulnerable pedestrian. Jaigaon has grown with the development of Phuentsholing, Bhutan's most important commercial centre. According to recent estimates the population of Phuentsholing is approximately 30,000, rising each day to about 50,000 as day labourers cross over from Jaigaon and the surrounding countryside.

The court in Phuentsholing is, strictly speaking, a subdistrict court below the district court located at Chukkha. However, due to the size of Phuentsholing and its status as Bhutan's main centre of commerce, the court is an important one. Until mid 2003, the court was located in cramped offices shared with the district administration. With funding from Danida, a new court building was designed, built and officially inaugurated in September 2003.

Drawing on research conducted by the legal research unit on Bhutanese architecture, the new court building represents the reformulation of 'state-religious' architecture of the *dzongs* that serve as the 'archetype of public, political and collective architecture' (Dujardin 2000: 164). Unlike the *dzongs*, the Phuentsholing court faces outwards rather than inwards, conveying a sense of openness. Internally it is spacious, light and clean, with separate offices for the clerks and judges, a rear entrance for prisoners being escorted to and from their court hearings, and separate holding cells for male and female prisoners. All this represents a marked contrast from the cramped quarters of both the local district offices and the *dzongs* in which many district courts are still located. However, the Phuentsholing court building does combine many elements of *dzong* architecture – for example, it has a tall, deep central tower reminiscent of *utse*, the central towers of *dzongs*. This tower is balanced by two lower wings to each side that house the courtrooms and offices, which like the tower draw on the architectural style of the *dzong*.

There are three key features that further evoke the architecture of the *dzong*. The first is the very large oriel window (*rapse*) on the central block, through which light enters the entrance hall and the second-floor shrine room. Two smaller oriel windows on the first floor allow light into the two main courtrooms. These windows and the open walkways on the ground and first floors are elaborately decorated. The second feature is a broad band of red around the top of the walls interspersed with 'mirrors', which copies the detailing of *dzongs* and temples. The final feature is the use of a special form of roof called *jabzhi*. Normally, or at least in the past, the use of *jabzhi* – which can best be described as a form of lantern, square with windows on all four sides – was restricted to palaces, temples and monasteries (Amundsen 2003: 80). These elements draw on a high register of architectural features reserved for religious or government structures and convey a strong message to those approaching the court. This is underscored by the presence of a *dar shing*, a tall pole with a long white flag, surmounted by a golden parasol indicating the need to observe *driglam namzha* (official code of conduct) both in the vicinity and inside the court building. The authority and almost sacral nature of its functions appear to blend with a modern, efficient building, separate from the older district offices and by inference independent from political and policy considerations.

Entering the courtrooms from the public entrance, one notes that the orientation is to the rear of the room. Separated by a low barrier and two pillars, the judge's dais is located at the rear. A side door allows the judge to enter directly from his private chamber. In front of the judge's seat on the dais is a low, intricately carved table with the court seal depicted on it. Behind the judge's dais are two national flags and, along the wall, framed photographs of the current monarch and the three previous monarchs. A large version of the court seal picked out in raised relief fills the wall above the judge's dais. Directly above the dais is a red mask representing Shingje Chosgyal, Lord of the Underworld, the main figure in the ritualized judgment of the dead, the *raksha marcham*, performed annually at local *tshechu*.

In front of the dais, two tables facing each other across the width of the dais are reserved for the clerks of court and prosecution. On the right and left pillars respectively are two further masks – one white,

White God, and one black, Black Demon. French notes that in central Tibet 'on the whole, legal spaces were free of decoration, religious objects, altars or pictures. Tibetans stated that upon entering they knew these rooms were not religious in nature. When empty of their actors, legal spaces looked like the interior of any administrative office' (1996: 150). Therefore, it is interesting to note the appearance of these masks as part of the court décor. In other courts, for example the High Court of Justice and the district court in Jakar Dzong, one finds the same. There appears to have been a move during the 1990s to introduce a variety of symbols into the decoration of the courts, notably the design and use of a court seal and the masks used in the *raksha marcham*. At the front of the court next to the public entrance are benches for the general public.

As with many of the offices of high officials, the space is ordered to move from less-honoured to more-honoured. This social ordering of space applies both horizontally and vertically. In the courtroom, this is reflected in the placing of the judge's dais against a solid wall, dominating the centre of the court space. The vertical hierarchy of the space is emphasized by the portraits of the kings hung on the wall above and behind the dais. Raised by the dais, the judge occupies the next level, followed by the clerk of court and legal representatives seated in front of the dais. Of course, litigants and accused individuals who stand before the judge may be looking directly at the judge, but having to stand was traditionally considered a less dignified posture socially. These comments apply also to the layout of both the district court in Jakar and the high court in Thimphu.

Looking at the new law court, we can begin to see the increased reliance by the Bhutanese judiciary on cultural symbolism. By noting the evolution of the architectural symbols, I argue we can gain an insight into the role of the courts in projecting several competing discourses that seek to present and naturalize a particular vision of the Bhutanese state. In part, the design of the building, drawing as it does on earlier, preexisting architectural models, tries to present a recognizably 'Bhutanese' appearance whilst striving to establish a link with great traditions of lawgiving. This is conveyed by the physical transparency of the building, which looks out on to an open area of ground rather than into a courtyard. The simpler architecture suggests a sense of efficiency, which is reflected in the provisions for the detention of prisoners and their separation from the public attending the courts. Indeed, many aspects of the design and layout of the Phuentsholing court would not strike a Western observer as noticeably unusual, with the décor held to be merely a reflection of local tastes.

Judicial Practices: Meaning, Practice and Buddhist Modernism

Kinley Dorji, the editor of the only national newspaper, stated in a paper presented at a conference in Bhutan in February 2004 that 'Buddhism is not just our religion; for most of Bhutan Buddhism transcends our culture and our daily lives ... the institutions that strengthen the faith, within and without the official monastic order, must be supported and upheld. Only then will we have the assurance that our guardian deities will continue to stand by us, and defend us, as they have done for centuries' (*Kuensel* 2004: 18). He goes on to argue: '[L]et us eschew this tendency to introduce new laws and requirements just because the rest of the world is doing it' (*Kuensel* 2004: 19).

Buddhism as the state religion has been made central to the process of image making in Bhutan since the mid 1970s.[4] Indeed, the last Vajrayana Buddhist kingdom in the world has served as a powerful trope – used in part to contain modernization, to promote cultural uniformity among the heterogeneous peoples living within Bhutan's territorial borders and more recently, to inform the appearance of the law courts.

The contemporary Bhutanese legal system is relatively new, emerging as it has since the 1960s. However, in a short text prepared by the Royal Court of Justice, we are informed that 'The history of Bhutanese legal system has a long and traditional background. Zhabdrung Ngawang Namgyal promulgated the first set of Bhutanese laws and codification of these laws was completed in 1652 during the reign of the first temporal ruler' (RCJ n.d.: 1). The text continues: '[T]he said Code was based on the fundamental teachings of Buddhism', noting that 'the principles of Buddhism and natural justice as originally set forth have not been changed and have always been upheld' (RCJ n.d.: 3). More specifically, 'Bhutanese laws have evolved over the centuries as a reflection of culture and lifestyle of people keeping the stream of justice clear and pure' (RCJ n.d.: 4). These claims and the language used set out a clear image of Bhutanese law as just, sanctioned by centuries of tradition and Buddhist principles. It does not distinguish the modern law codes and court practices from those of the earlier legal system, which was closely tied to the governance of the state with administrative and judicial power concentrated in the provincial governors. The text has a didactic purpose – to educate visiting advisors, and also to present and validate the contemporary legal system to literate Bhutanese. It is worth noting that the citations are from the *Pali vinaya*. It is generally agreed that there are three living *vinaya* traditions. Chinese and other East Asian monks follow the *Dharmagupta vinaya*, the Tibetan and other Central Asian monks the *Mulasarvastivada vinaya* and, finally, the Southeast Asian and Sri Lankan monks follow the *Pali vinaya*.[5] So it is significant that, rather than turn to well-known classical Tibetan texts on the *vinaya* (Tibetan *'dul wa*), the legal researchers attached to the law courts who prepared the text have drawn specifically from texts widely available in English. Secondly, it raises a related issue – are the authors of the text treating the *Pali* literature as a source of 'classical law'?

A telling feature in the language of the same text is the apparent creation of a language of jurisprudence, notably via the separation of natural law (*rang zhin gi khrims*) and positive law (*chay pai khrims*).[6] This interpretation is strengthened as we read of positive laws being based on a set of general legal principles, the first of which is 'the separation of power and responsibility'.[7] Certainly it could be argued that the Dual System established by the Zhabdrung Ngawang Namgyal represented a form of separation of power between religious and secular authority. However, since the process of modernization commenced in the 1950s, the actual separation of powers between the executive, legislative and judiciary in Bhutan is very recent. Indeed, a high proportion of Bhutanese I interviewed question whether this has yet been achieved.

The recent rapid modernization of the Bhutanese legal system, much criticized by international organizations in the early 1990s, has sought simultaneously to stress its openness to change and its role in upholding traditional, and uniquely Bhutanese, cultural practices. The computerization of court records, the training of police officers to use computerized charge sheets and the training of bench clerks, all of which have been funded by foreign donors, are often cited by court officials when discussing the innovations in the legal system. In response to concerns expressed by both Bhutanese and external observers about the quality of the judiciary, a legal course was established in 1992. The development of the first legal education course, leading to a National Legal Certificate, continues to draw heavily on the structure and subjects taught in the monastic curriculum. At about the same time the legal research unit not only became involved in drafting new laws and procedural codes, but also undertook research on matters concerning Bhutanese architectural styles, etiquette (*driglam namzha*) and legal terminology. As a result, the first full text on *driglam namzha* was written by a researcher attached to the high court in 1997.

The problem of translating new legal terms, often drawn from the Anglo-American legal traditions, prompted the high court to undertake research to trace suitable terminology culled from the corpus of

Buddhist writings. The legal researchers worked closely with respected monastic scholars to find Buddhist equivalents for the new legal terminology, and gradually a sizeable glossary was built up. I want to illustrate this process with one word – justice. How to translate justice into Dzongkha was one of the tasks facing the legal researchers. In an early version of the court text cited earlier, the term *drig trims* was used for justice (RCJ, no date). This compound word carries the idea of being in strict accordance with the written law. However, in the most recent draft version of the court text it has been amended to *drang trims* (RCJ). The word *drang* means straightforward, honest, sincere, trustworthy and carries a deep moral sense that is absent from *drig*, which refers to discipline and outward form. Notably, the term *drang po* appears in the Tengyur, the commentaries to Buddhist teachings, and means righteous.

This was carried further by the introduction in 2001 of the term *drang pon*. *Drang pon* replaces the word *thrim pon* for judge. The latter phrase literally means the 'lord of the law', with the word *thrim* associated with the administration and enforcement of secular law. There was marked resistance from many who could not understand why the Dzongkha word for judge had to be changed from *thrim pon* to *drang pon*. There is, in my opinion, a clear move to present through this change in language a particular image of the judge as impartial, upright and the source of justice rather than the mere enforcer of state laws. In response to public doubts about the term, a letter from the research division of the Royal Court of Justice was published in *Kuensel* in March 2002 stressing that the term was originally used in seventeenth-century documents. It notes that the term *thrim pon* 'neither had an exalted position nor noble responsibilities'. The anonymous writer argues that 'words must have inspiring values and appropriate meanings suitable to the particular context'. The letter ends by noting that the 'judiciary of Bhutan has undertaken extensive and intensive research for more than nine years and has consulted a number of scholars' and that 'the educated Bhutanese is the wheel of positive change. We are appreciative of the comments'.

As we can see, the relationship between Buddhism and Bhutanese law is being promoted. Yet at the same time, when asked if I found much Buddhist thought contained in the *Thrimszhung Chenmmo* (Supreme Laws) of 1959, I replied that I did not find any overt references to Buddhism, and this was accepted as accurate. There appears to be a contradiction or tension therefore amongst the judiciary. On the one hand, it recognizes the secular, often nonindigenous sources of law; on the other, it wants to legitimate these laws with cultural and religious references. There is a definite sense of introducing or revealing to both the Bhutanese and non-Bhutanese alike the Buddhist principles on which the modern legal system is based and thereby to impart a sense of historicity to the laws and institutions. This is clear in the presentation of an essay specifically drawing on the symbolism of the *raksha marcham* that was published in *Kuensel* (2003) in an abbreviated version.

Drawing on citations from the *Pali vinaya*,[8] the paper sets out at length how Bhutanese criminal court procedures are based on principles found in Buddhist teachings. The paper argues that 'almost all principles of a fair trial are enshrined' in the *raksha marcham*. Specifically, the right of '*habeas corpus* ... the right of being represented by a legal counsel, uninterrupted hearing, knowing the charges, prosecution of crimes, defence through rebuttal, production and establishment of evidence and *ratio decidendi*' (Dubgyur 2003: 3). Yet the terminology used to convey this interpretation is itself heavily influenced not by Buddhism, but by Western legal terms and concepts.

As he develops his argument, Dubgyur interprets each aspect of the ritual dance in direct relation to legal principles embodied in the set of court practices set out in the Civil and Criminal Procedure Code 2001. The *raksha* attendants are interpreted as demonstrating that the accused is receiving an open trial 'meant to check against judicial caprice and create public confidence in the fairness ... and impartiality of the administration of criminal justice' (2003: 4). However, this claim to open trial can be questioned. During a major criminal case concerning prostitutes and pimps in Phuentsholing that attracted a high degree of public attention, the trial was held *in camera* 'to protect privacy'. Furthermore, as many Bhutanese observe, public access to the law courts is itself very recent. Developing the right to counsel, the role of Black Demon and White God are directly associated with state prosecutor and public defender, though again the right to call on a *jabmi*, a legal representative, in a criminal trial was only extended in the 1990s following adverse criticism by the International Red Cross (Hainzl 1997).

One can gain a sense of the article from these brief comments alone. I do not question that the author does see the *raksha marcham* as incorporating legal principles. Rather, I want to highlight the conscious way in which the new court system, its vocabulary and procedures are being naturalized through the description of the ritual dance. Importantly, it seeks to make the changes appear indigenous, firmly rooted in the cultural, moral and religious values of Bhutan. The article purposefully links newly delineated legal principles, arguably borrowed from the Anglo-American legal systems, with popular, local-level understandings of virtue and non-virtue. Throughout fieldwork, people commented and assessed things on the basis of moral values. Discussing thefts from temples and stupas, Ngawang declared that the perpetrators did not know the 'Bhutanese alphabet' – by this he meant that they ignored the 'ten virtuous actions' (Whitecross 2000). By drawing on this value system, the legal system is seeking to establish its legitimacy by stressing its values and laws firmly located in Bhutanese values (as defined by the elite) whilst at the same time emphasizing that it is contemporary and able to adapt to changing social needs.

Each aspect of the criminal trial seeks to stress the propriety of the courts in providing the accused with a fair, impartial hearing. However, this desire to create a specific image of the law court appears to require not only legitimating by association with Buddhist principles, but also by providing a sense of historicity. Dorji questions the introduction of new laws and explicitly questions the integrity of the personnel of the courts. He argues that it is not the 'introduction of a whole set of foreign laws in order to ostensibly make things "watertight"', but rather the 'putting into these positions people of high integrity, whose common sense and sense of fair play are more likely to engender the all important public perception that justice is indeed being done' (2004: 19). What is revealing – a common link between Dorji and Dubgyur – is the desire to create public confidence in the law courts and their personnel. However, one argues for the need for judges of strong moral character, whilst the other seeks to present the legal system as embodying traditional, Buddhist values that naturally ensure that the practices of the courts are fair, untainted by personal interests. I believe this reflects a subtle re-presentation of the law courts and its set of practices that since the early 1990s has been accompanied by references to Buddhism. Just as images of environmental fragility and cultural uniqueness draw heavily on various global discourses and are aimed at creating a distinct community of sentiment among Western and non-Bhutanese audiences, appeals to a particular version of Buddhist modernism represents yet another strand of a complex set of discourses shaping Bhutanese identity.

Fashioning Identities: Legitimacy and Notions of Justice

Garfinkel describes courtroom ritual as a degradation ceremony in which 'moral indignation serves to effect the ritual destruction of the person denounced' by defining the accused as, in effect, an enemy of the people and their ultimate values (cited Garland 1991: 68). During the ritual drama of the *raksha marcham*, the audience is reminded of the importance of virtuous actions, of faith in the dharma and the fate that awaits those who do not live virtuous lives or lack faith in Buddhist teachings. Similarly, the court procedure seeks to evoke in its audience both a respect for the law and a rejection of the criminal. During the *'cham* the Black Demon is feared for his determination to secure the soul of the deceased. Yet in court, as the prosecutor, this role is validated as the protector of the community and as representative of the state, and the audience's ambivalence is directed towards the accused.

The rituals of the courts, especially though not exclusively in cases of criminal trials, operate within a particular community of belief, grounding their practices within the social relations, authorities and traditions of the community. The outward reception of 'Western'-inspired codes of court procedure may satisfy donor agencies, but once within the confines of the court, its spatial organization, its temporal routines and its linguistic codes all help to structure the status of the parties involved and the symbolic meaning of the event. In Bhutan, I argue, we are witnessing a significant attempt to present 'justice', and the operation and function of the courts, in recognizably Bhutanese terms. How far we can describe this as 'Buddhist' is debatable. I have, by focusing on the spatial organization of the courts and their 'rituals', sought to make three points. First, that in seeking to enhance their role, the courts are now open to the public and media reports. Second, the move to establish courts as physically distinct from other government buildings has altered the role of the courts as the place where 'justice is done'. The ritual aspects of the penal process are now confined to the courtroom and the process of conviction and sentencing. Third, just as Shingje Chosgyal is neutral, immune to all pleas or bribery, the use of the iconography of the Lord of Underworld seeks to project the image of a judiciary capable of rendering legal judgments free from bias and political motivations. This is the main intention – to legitimate the judiciary and to enhance public confidence in the formal legal process.

Mirroring the drama of the *raksha marcham*, the focus of public attention and the locus of ritual display is the declaration of punishment, rather than the process of punishment itself. This aspect, rather like the sinner being led away, is conducted in private, away from the public gaze. This creates a contrast with previous penal systems in Bhutan, prior to the modernization of the legal system, where punishment was public – M. Piessel visiting the Trongsar *dzong* comments on a man wearing a large wooden cangue and leg irons in the mid 1960s (1988: 171). The modern prisons, not dealt with in this paper, are removed from public scrutiny and are concerned more with management than governance. The rituals of court, which apply in criminal and civil cases alike, seek to prompt particular value commitments on the part of the participants and the audience, generating and regenerating a particular mentality and sensibility; this was often implicit in my discussions with members of the judiciary about the role of law in contemporary Bhutan. The physical layout and appearance of the courts create a setting in which the majesty of the law can be performed. There is a deliberate process of creating a spectacle that builds on cultural symbols and meanings as part of a spectacle. Of course, not every case becomes a spectacle, even though the procedures and rituals are involved in the most mundane cases. Rather, as we have now begun to see, showcase trials and hearings, whose decisions are relayed by the media to the public, represent the meaning and practice of justice. These have included a case concerning electoral corruption and the sentencing of 111 Bhutanese for treason in September 2004 (*Kuensel* 2004).

Reflecting on the various threads linking the ritual dance, the model court building and the recent connection made between the ritual judgment and the set of court practices and the apparent legal principles underlying them, I began to think more specifically about the contemporary Bhutanese state's use of the law courts, their practices and the symbols of 'justice' in promoting traditional values so as to naturalize major changes in structure and practice and to legitimate the authority of the Bhutanese state through both an indigenous discourse and an international discourse about the rule of law. The spectacle created by the new model court, court procedure and the symbolism incorporated in the courtrooms seeks to evoke awe and instil deference amongst the public.

Yet the majority of informants – small shopkeepers, monks, schoolteachers, minor government workers, students and farmers – do not, in my experience, recognize law in its buddhicized version being presented by the courts and their personnel. Rather, for them it remains secular, and they retain a deep scepticism about its claims of impartiality and the equality of those appearing before the courts. This was illustrated during a picnic with a large extended family from Punakha. Yeshe Lhamo sat preparing *doma* (betel nut) and informing her cousins of her latest battle with her aunt over a parcel of paddy land. She explained that she had been removed from the courtroom because she challenged the judge appointed to hear the case. Yeshe said, 'I told him, to his face, I thought he was being paid by my aunt. He became angry and had me thrown out. But, we all know how judges make their money. I wanted him to realize I would not just accept things.' Her family all agreed, and their comments about the judiciary were highly critical.

In promoting a certain version of being Bhutanese, the court assumes that it is an accepted discourse. There is a strong form of censorship that is fully operational in all new identity making. One can detect a strong tendency to edit out negative evidence that contradicts the image of the legal system being produced. There is a self-editing, a self-censoring that is manifested in discussions with court personnel along with an awareness of the need to present the courts and their practices in accordance with the current image – a legal system based on notions of equality and impartiality, open to all and founded on Buddhist principles – even though at times this is privately questioned by the very people seeking to promote this ideal image.

Conclusion: Images and Imaginings of Bhutanese Justice

I began this chapter with a series of images that serve to capture or represent the essence of Bhutan. Throughout the essay I have gradually sought to question, indeed challenge, the image of Buddhist law in Bhutan and to reflect on the role of the courts and modern Bhutanese legal system in presenting a particular vision of Bhutan – a unique legal system, based on age-old tradition and religious values, that has contained throughout its history the values and legal principles that can be found in wider law traditions. At the same time I have mentioned the increasing rationalization and bureaucratization taking place at every level of the Bhutanese legal process. The most characteristic development for the everyday application of law is the embrace of efficiency, highlighted by the emphasis on computerization and surveillance of the law clerks to ensure that they process their workload efficiently, and the promulgation of a doctrine of court process.

These facets of modern Bhutanese justice encouraged by donors, whether they are a way to make the courts more comfortable as described in a school text, or a focus of mediation, potentially minimize claims on justice in favour of improved process. Heydebrand and Seron concluded their discussion of the increasing rationalization of justice (in the U.S.) with the observation that 'what is squeezed out of the traditional form of law is a locale for a moral vision' (1990: 288). In Bhutan, we find an increased claim to a moral vision of justice based on the role of the courts and their personnel being linked to the normative practices of Bhutanese culture. Yet, for all the official claims, iconography and neologism, it is difficult not to feel that these claims are hollow, and that efficiency, form and process – rather than delivering justice – are the primary operational concerns and are linked to maintaining and upholding the Bhutanese state.[9]

Acknowledgements

This essay benefited greatly from discussions with Thomas B. Hansen, Francoise Pommaret, Anne Chayet and colleagues in the School of Social and Political Studies, University of Edinburgh, as well as the participants at the conference at which a very abbreviated version was presented. All errors are, of course, my own.

Notes

1. Adams (1996), Huber and Pedersen (1997) and van Beek (2001) write about these themes respectively discussing the Tibetans in exile, Sherpas and Ladakhi Buddhists. See also Lopez (1998).
2. A range of international agencies operate in Bhutan. Amongst the most prominent are Danida (Danish development agency), SNV (Dutch development agency), UNDP, UNICEF and the World Food Programme.
3. Gross National Happiness is a concept promoted by the current king in the late 1980s and early 1990s that stresses 'happiness' as being more important than Gross National Product. Recently, there have been concerted moves to develop this concept beyond the rhetorical with a series of conferences. Some present Gross National Happiness as an antidote to Western consumerism and materialism, whilst others see it as a rhetorical device appealing to exoticized images of Bhutan as a Buddhist (hence peaceful and serene) land and masking deeper social issues (e.g. Hutt 2003).
4. This is not to deny the historical role of Buddhism in the emergence of the Dual System. Rather, I want to point to a redefinition and politicization of Buddhism in contemporary Bhutan. The Dual System refers to the division of the state between spiritual and temporal rulers and the form of government introduced by the Zhabdrung Ngawang Namgyal, who unified Bhutan in the early seventeenth century.
5. See Prebish (1975), von Hinuber (1994, 1995) and Huxley (1996).
6. Tibetan/Dzongkha: *rang bzhin gi khrims* and *byed pa'i khrims*. I am only now beginning to examine how far these terms can be used in reference to Buddhism and law, especially the differences and similarities between Buddhist concepts of natural law and Western jurisprudential categories. It is important not to read these terms and assume convergence with Western usage.
7. *thri tse bum zher*
8. I think it is worth noting that that an English-language translation, rather than a Tibetan version of the *vinaya*, is being cited. One cannot help but wonder what this implies about the audience to whom the paper is addressed, as well as the possibility that ordinary Bhutanese would comment that the *vinaya* is not applicable outside the monastic setting. These issues will be examined in a future essay.

9. I have drawn loosely on the title and focus of an official publication entitled 'Accountability, Efficiency and Transparency – Promoting Good Governance' (RGB 1999).

References

Primary Source in Dzongkha and Tibetan

Anonymous. 2000. *'brug pa'i 'cham gyi go don 'grel bshad dang dgra med tse'i rnga 'cham gyi dmigs rim mdor bsdus.* (*A short explanation to the 'Cham and the Drummers of Dramitse 'Cham of Bhutan*). Thimphu: KMT Press.

Secondary Sources

Adams, V. 1996. *Tigers of the Snow and Other Virtual Sherpas: An Ethnography of Himalayan Encounters.* Princeton, NJ: Princeton University Press.
Amundsen, I.B. 2003. *On Sacred Architecture and the Dzongs of Bhutan: Tradition and Transition in the Architectural History of the Himalayas.* Oslo: Arkitekthogskolen i Oslo.
Beek, M. van. 2001. 'Public Secrets, Conscious Amnesia, and the Celebration of Autonomy in Ladakh', in T.B. Hansen and F. Stepputat (eds), *States of Imagination: Ethnographic Explorations of the Postcolonial State.* Durham, NC: Duke University Press, 365–90.
Bunting, B. 1991. 'Bhutan: Kingdom in the Clouds', *National Geographic* 179(5): 78–101.
Dorji, K. 2004. 'Gross National Happiness: Concepts, Status and Prospects', paper presented at the Conference on Gross National Happiness, 18–20 February 2004. Thimphu: Centre for Bhutan Studies.
Dubgyur, L. 2003. 'The Influence of Buddhism on the Bhutanese Trial System', paper presented at the Conference on Buddhism, November 2003, Thimphu, Bhutan.
Dujardin, M. 1997. 'From Fortress to Farmhouse: A Living Architecture', in F. Pommaret and C. Schicklegruber (eds), *Bhutan: Mountain Fortress of the Gods.* London: Serindia Publications, 61–83.
———. 2000. 'From Living to Propelling Monument: The Monastery-fortress (dzong) as Vehicle of Cultural Transfer in Contemporary Bhutan', *Journal of Bhutan Studies* 2(2): 164–98.
French, R.R. 1996. *The Golden Yoke: The Legal Cosmology of Buddhist Tibet.* Ithaca, NY: Cornell University Press.
Garland, D. 1991. *Punishment and Modern Society: A Study in Social Theory.* Oxford: Clarendon Press.
Goodrich, P. 1994. 'Doctor Duxbury's Cure, or: A Note on Legal Historiography', *Cardozo Law Review* 15: 1567–89.
Hainzl, C. 1997. *The Legal System of Bhutan: A Descriptive Analysis.* Vienna: Ludwig Boltzman Institute for Human Rights.
Heydebrand, W. and C. Seron. 1990. *Rationalizing Justice: The Political Economy of Federal Court Districts.* Albany: State University of New York Press.

Hinuber, O. von. 1994. *Selected Papers on Pali Studies*. Oxford: Pali Text Society.

———. 1995. 'Buddhist Law according to the Theravada Vinaya – a Survey of Theory and Practice', *Journal of the International Association of Buddhist Studies* 18: 7–45.

Huber, T. 2001. 'Shangri-La in Exile', in T. Dodin and H. Rather (eds), *Imagining Tibet: Reproductions, Projections and Fantasies*. Somerville, MA: Wisdom Publications, 357–71.

Huber, T. and P. Pederson. 1997. 'Meteorological Knowledge and Environmental Ideas in Traditional and Modern Societies: The Case of Tibet', *Journal of the Royal Anthropological Institute* 3(3): 577–97.

Hutt, M. 2003. *Unbecoming Citizens*. Delhi: Oxford University Press.

Huxley, A. 1996. 'The Vinaya – Legal System or Performance Enhancing Drug?' *Buddhist Forum* 4: 141–63.

Kuensel. 2003. 'The Influence of Buddhism on the Bhutanese Trial System', 6 December. http://www.kuenselonline.com/article.php?sid=3520 (accessed 10 December 2004).

———. 2004. '111 Sentenced for Collaborating with the Militants', 4 September. http://www.kuenselonline.com/article.php?sid=4457 (accessed 10 December 2004).

Lopez, D. 1998. *Prisoners of Shangri-la: Tibetan Buddhism and the West*. Chicago: University of Chicago Press.

Piessel, M. 1988. *Bhoutan: Royaume d'Asie Inconnu*. Geneva: Editions Olizane.

Pommaret, F. 1990. *Bhutan: The Odyssey Illustrated Guide*. Hong Kong: The Guidebook Company Ltd.

Prebish, C. 1975. *Buddhist Monastic Discipline: The Sanskrit Pratimoksa Sutras of the Mahasamghikas and Mulasarvastivadins*. University Park: The Pennsylvania State University Press.

Royal Government of Bhutan (RGB) 1999. *Accountability, Efficiency and Transparency – Promoting Good Governance*. Thimphu: Royal Government of Bhutan.

Royal High Court of Justice (RCJ). No date. *Introduction to the Bhutanese Legal System*. Thimphu: Royal High Court of Justice.

Ura, K. 1997 'Tradition and Development', in F. Pommaret and C. Schicklegruber (eds), *Bhutan: Mountain Fortress of the Gods*. London: Serindia Publications, 239–51.

Whitecross, R.W. 2000. 'Signs of the Degenerate Age: Desecration of Chorten and Lhakhang in Bhutan', *Journal for Bhutan Studies* 2(2): 182–99.

10

Balancing Islam, *Adat* and the State

Comparing Islamic and Civil Courts in Indonesia

Keebet von Benda-Beckmann

Introduction

Since the end of the Cold War, the public role of religion, in particular of Islam, has become a major focus of political debate and social scientific enquiry. Religion generally has become more prominent in most parts of the world, but there is great variation in the mode and extent to which it is part of public life.[1] Its social, political and moral role has to be understood in relation to the alternative normative universes with which it has to compete. In some countries, powerful forces entrench religion deeply within the state organization. Political elites that understand their country as having religiously mixed populations in particular are careful to strike a balance between secularism and religion. These processes are often also affected by decentralization policies, involving a renewed interest in (neo-)traditional institutions and customary law. Courts play an interesting role in these reconfigurations, because they are state agencies but cannot simply impose state laws, because citizens are free to make use of their services or not. They act as interfaces between state control and citizens' freedom, often not fully independent, subject to control by other state agencies and other actors, steering disputants' behaviour to some extent while at the same time being dependent upon them. Courts are especially illuminating because they serve as a prism through which the power of the state to change the disputing behaviour of its citizens may be observed, for here the state can change the options that are available to such citizens, giving them an element of choice rather than formally prescribing or prohibiting certain behaviour.

This chapter will discuss whether expanding the jurisdiction of Islamic courts in Indonesia actually redirects disputants from civil towards Islamic courts. Indonesia has a religiously mixed population that devotes an increasingly prominent role to religion and demonstrates a renewed interest in customary law. It has the largest Muslim population in the world, and because its colonial history stressed ethnicity and downplayed Islam, its constitution is based on religious and ethnic plurality. The state legal system reflects an ongoing balancing act between three types of symbolic universes – the state, religion and *adat*, the Indonesian generic term for local customs and customary law – assigning specific roles to religious law and to *adat*. For example, there is a system of Islamic state courts parallel to the civil court system. Other religions do not have a court structure of their own, though certain Hindu groups are currently calling for Hindu courts (Ramstedt 2008). Furthermore, Islamic law applies to marriage and divorce for the Muslim population, so Muslims have to go to an Islamic court for marriage and divorce disputes. The regulation of land is a complex of state law and *adat*, full of contradictions. For kinship and inheritance issues the state legal system leaves its population considerable freedom. Muslims have the choice of bringing their inheritance disputes to a civil or an Islamic court. Civil courts usually apply *adat* law in inheritance cases, while Islamic courts in principle have to apply Islamic law.

The position of Islamic courts has been contested, and their jurisdiction has changed over time. The latest change was the Religious Judiciary Act of 1989 that expanded the jurisdiction of Islamic courts.[2] Freeing them from the limited jurisdiction they had in the regions outside of Java since Government Regulation 45/1957, it brought them onto an equal level with civil courts. While courts in general enjoy low prestige in Indonesia and relatively few cases reach the court at all, they are nevertheless seen as important signposts in the developing relationship between the state, *adat* and religion. At its introduction, the Religious Judiciary Act was generally interpreted as an indication of the increasing prominence of Islam. However, the effects are by no means uniform, and the use of Islamic courts varies considerably throughout Indonesia, even among regions that are regarded as strongholds of Islam.

A comparison between West Sumatra and the Gayo Highlands in Central Aceh, representing two sharply contrasting examples of citizens' responses towards the change in jurisdiction, will serve to account for these differences. Both regions have a predominantly Muslim population and a plural legal constellation of state law, Islamic law and customary law, though Islam has become more visible in public life. In both regions, disputes over inheritance are primarily dealt with by *adat* institutions, according to *adat* procedures and substantive law. Only when these do not provide an acceptable solution will parties turn to state courts: Islamic courts in the case of Gayo Highlands, civil courts in West Sumatra. In this chapter it will be argued that the differences in court use result in part from the respective customary laws, in particular from the gendered character of kinship and inheritance rules and the main inheritance issues that claimants seek redress for in court. They also result from the relative status of Islamic and civil courts within the region, from the role of the specific histories of the regions' incorporation into the Indonesian state and its colonial predecessor, and from the place of Islam in the current constitutional reconfiguration of the central government and the regions.[3]

I will first give a brief outline of the political developments in the regions and their relationships with the central government. This will provide the context for the analysis of court use in the two regions. After a short discussion of the changes in jurisdiction of the Islamic courts, I will present empirical data showing the differences in use of civil and Islamic courts in Central Aceh and West Sumatra with regard to inheritance disputes. In a first step towards explaining these differences, I will look into changes in kinship, residence, property and inheritance patterns in the two regions and investigate the constellations and issues of the main inheritance disputes. In a second step I will focus on the courts, see how they are positioned within the region and look at their division of labour within the two regions. I will argue that these factors cannot fully explain the differences in court use. In a last step I will turn to political arenas in which the relationships between Islam, *adat* and the state are negotiated and suggest that this does account for the different choices disputants make. In my conclusions I will consider to what extent the expanded jurisdiction in fact has expanded the scope of Islam and then draw some conclusions about the power of the national state to steer disputants' court use by means of changing the jurisdiction of courts.

Relationships between Region and Centre

The two regions have very different histories of incorporation into the Dutch colonial state and the Indonesian state. This has had wide-ranging consequences for the political constellations between centre and region and especially for the political role of *adat* and Islam in the current policies of autonomy.

Aceh and the Gayo Highlands

Aceh was one of the last regions of the archipelago to be incorporated in the colonial Dutch Indies.[4] It came under colonial rule only at the beginning of the twentieth century after fierce resistance, and the Dutch never managed to pacify the region completely. After independence it remained a problematic region, and secession movements erupted repeatedly and have lingered just under the surface during more quiet periods. In contrast to the Acehnese majority that was politically very active in the emergence of the Indonesian republic, the district of Central Aceh, the homeland of two major groups of Gayo Highlanders, was a remote mountainous area that was incorporated into the Dutch colonial empire at a relatively late stage. Islamized in the fourteenth century, the Gayo have kept themselves linguistically and politically distinct from the Acehnese population that dominates the province, if not the district. In the 1950s, the Gayo sided with the Acehnese opposition movement against the central government although, fearing Acehnese domination, they remained more loyal to the Indonesian nation state than the Acehnese did. The period of isolation ended in the 1980s, when Javanese transmigrants settled in the region and introduced coffee. Today it is a prosperous agricultural region producing coffee, patchouli and gambir for the world market. Its capital, Takèngën, boasts all the administrative facilities of a district capital, including a civil and an Islamic court.

The political leadership of Aceh was one of the most active and assertive opponents of the Suharto regime. The region holds vast areas of primary forest, substantial deposits of gas and oil and an expanding industry on its territory, and its political leaders strongly resented the central government's control over these resources. Voices advocating secession from Indonesia increased under the harsh repression of the central government, leading to violent clashes also in the Gayo Highlands in which many Javanese transmigrants were killed and many Javanese and other migrants left the region, among them many non-Acehnese civil servants, judges and court personnel. It took a tsunami to stop the violence and start negotiations for a workable autonomy within the Indonesian state. Within the new constellation of decentralized government, the province of Nanggroe Aceh Darussalam (formerly Aceh) has a special status with a high degree of autonomy.

The Acehnese autonomy movement has strong Islamic underpinnings, and Islamic political parties have played leading roles in the movement towards independence. Of late, Shariah law was officially introduced for some legal fields. However, Islamic courts do not refer directly to the Koran but apply the Compilation of Religious Law, an adapted version of Islamic law produced by the Indonesian government.[5] The population and its leaders use Islam to distinguish themselves from the central government and other regions. Positioning itself as an Islamic region is also part of a transnational discourse, drawing both on international law regarding self-determination of indigenous peoples and on universal Islamic discourses. The movement is supported by many connections with Malaysia and with Arabic countries and Islamic centres in the Middle East, though the government of Malaysia looks with apprehension at the centrifugal forces of its gigantic neighbour. The Gayo population has been strongly influenced by this political development, and Islam and Islamic reasoning have gained overall prominence in politics and in disputing behaviour.

West Sumatra

The Minangkabau of West Sumatra have a quite different political history.[6] They became part of the Dutch colony in the early nineteenth century during the Padri war, waged between Islamist groups attempting to found a theocracy and groups in favour of traditional government based on *adat*. The *adat* faction won with the help of the Dutch, and the region became part of the colonial state.

From early on Minangkabau played an important political role in the independence movement. When the republic was founded, Minangkabau was strongly overrepresented in the new government. Even so, disillusion quickly set in. Like the Acehnese, the Minangkabau took part in the rebellion of the 1950s against Javanese domination and Sukarno's centralization politics, and they paid the same heavy toll after it was repressed. When Suharto took over in 1965, repression against everything that smelled of communism was harsh, and the Minangkabau once more were hit hard. These experiences were deeply traumatic.[7] Keenly aware of the dangers of opposition, the region developed into a rather uncritical and passive follower of the Suharto regime from the 1970s on. It has become a prosperous agricultural region, exporting goods to other parts of Sumatra, Singapore and Jakarta. However, having few subsoil resources and little industry, the region depends on the central government for redistribution of the country's vast resources and has profited from remaining loyal to the centre.

Islamic parties have strong support in West Sumatra, but in contrast to Aceh, Islam is currently not mobilized as a basis for regional autonomy. Contacts between the Minangkabau and Aceh were cordial, frequent and intense, yet nowadays many Minangkabau are very critical of the combination of separatism and political Islam in Aceh. Despite the fact that many Minangkabau disapprove of the separatist stance of Aceh, they always look to Aceh for developments in Islam. But in contrast to Aceh, where religion is used as a political resource to fight for autonomy, the focus of discussions of Islam in West Sumatra rests on the moral and legal role Islam is to play. During 2002 and 2003, there was some debate about whether or not Minangkabau should follow the Acehnese example and introduce Shariah. The majority of the population considers this neither a realistic nor a desirable scenario. Most Minangkabau are confident that their particular *adat,* based on matrilineal kinship and inheritance patterns, will keep them from following the Acehnese example.

For West Sumatra a major issue in the new relationships between the centre and the region concerns control over expropriated village property. This conflict goes back to the so-called Domain Declarations in the 1870s, by which the state claimed control over all uncultivated land. Much land that was under the traditional authority of villages was expropriated and given out to planters, corporations or logging companies. Today's Indonesian government has inherited this legacy. During the last two decades of the Suharto era expropriation for the public good rose exponentially, but the land was often in fact given to ex-military and other Suharto cronies to ensure political support. During that period *adat* authority was seriously weakened and could not be mobilized to oppose the expropriations.

Since early times, within West Sumatra as well as in relation to the political centre, political and economic disputes with the government have been played out primarily in terms of *adat.* The political attitude towards Islam has always been uneasy because many feared that too great an Islamic influence would destroy the matrilineal system. Still, Islamic political parties have always enjoyed considerable support. During the heyday of Suharto's Golkar, Islam was virtually the only force through which opposition against the regime was possible. However, after the demise of the Suharto regime, *adat* again became an important legitimating force to claim more autonomy – though squarely within the national state on which it remains dependent – and to recapture control over village property. Despite the evident tensions between *adat* and Islam, Minangkabau strongly identify with both and miss no occasion to emphasize this: 'ABSSBK', the short form for saying '*adat* is based on the Shariah and the Shariah is based on the Koran', is on everyone's lips.

Thus, the regions have quite different relationships with the centre. Aceh negotiates its relationship from a strong economic position, while West Sumatra does so in the conviction that it will continue to depend economically on the central state. Islam plays out very differently in these two regions. Most Minangkabau politicians continue to see a tension between Islam and *adat,* and would not want to follow Aceh by introducing Shariah law. The Gayo have a more relaxed conception of this relationship, but they are uncomfortable with the pressure from Acehnese politicians and judges to broaden the scope of Islamic law. Moreover, while Islam is mobilized in the current negotiations for regional autonomy by Acehnese politicians, Minangkabau politicians mobilize *adat* for their claims for more autonomy.

The Jurisdiction of Islamic Courts

When Government Regulation 45/1957 established a uniform structure for Islamic courts outside of Java, this was interpreted as a compromise between the Ministries of Justice and Religion that perpetuated the disadvantaged position of Islamic courts during colonial times.[8] It provided Islamic courts outside Java with ambivalent and limited jurisdiction over inheritance. They were mainly to deal with marriage and divorce, support for children in the case of divorce and with Islamic institutions such as *wasiat* (bequest), *wakaf* (endowment) and *hibah* (donation). Moreover, Article 4 of the regulation cryptically stated for inheritance issues that 'according to the living law they are resolved according to the law of Islam'.[9] Where *adat* law was the 'living law', *adat* law was applicable; if the living law of the parties was Islamic law, Islamic law was applicable. It was left to individual judges to assess whether the living law of the parties was *adat* or Islamic law. According to Lev, most civil judges in the 1960s were rather hostile to Islamic law and Islamic courts and tended to interpret living law as *adat*. In regions with a pronounced Muslim population such as Aceh, civil judges were more inclined to apply Islamic law and 'have consistently gone beyond their statutory mandate' (Lev 1972: 204). But while Acehnese judges have followed this trend, this did not happen in the Gayo Highlands. Bowen (2003: 89ff.) reports for the 1960s that judges from both the Islamic and civil courts in Central Aceh, even when trained outside the region, had always retained a close relationship with their homeland. They saw *adat* as the applicable law for inheritance cases for the majority of the population. This attitude had changed by the 1990s under pressure from the Department of Religious Affairs as well as the Islamic High Court in Banda Aceh, and under changed economic conditions. As a result the Islamic court in Central Aceh no longer took for granted that *adat* was the 'living law' for the rural population and tended more towards following Islamic rules. In West Sumatra the living law for inheritance, in particular family property, has basically remained *adat*.[10]

The Religious Judiciary Act of 1989 expanded the jurisdiction of Islamic courts. It was generally interpreted as part of a policy towards a more explicitly Islamic Indonesian state at the expense of *adat*, but also at the expense of a multi-religious or a more secular state. Many followed this move with apprehension. Others welcomed the change as a sign that Muslims had gained confidence, successfully claiming a more prominent position in public life. With full jurisdiction over inheritance, Islamic courts acquired the potential to actually become the main institution dealing with inheritance cases for the Muslim population, replacing civil courts.

Inheritance in Islamic and Civil Courts

The Gayo have responded positively, and Islamic courts are now deciding on inheritance disputes.[11] By contrast, my analysis of the court registers suggest that these changes have not occurred in West Sumatra and inheritance has squarely remained an issue for *adat* law and civil courts (see Figure 10.1).[12]

Islamic courts hardly deal with inheritance disputes. In fact, there is remarkable continuity over the past twenty-five years in the use of civil courts, including the use of these courts for inheritance disputes, as well as in the use of Islamic courts, despite their widened jurisdiction since 1989 (see Figure 10.2).

Islamic courts deal with validation of marriages, inheritance and divorce, including the division of marital property and support for the

Figure 10.1 Litigation Rate for Inheritance in West Sumatran Civil Courts 1981–2003

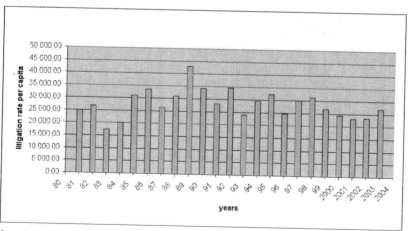

Source: Court registers.

Figure 10.2 Inheritance Cases in Islamic Courts in West Sumatra 1959–1965 and 1980–2000

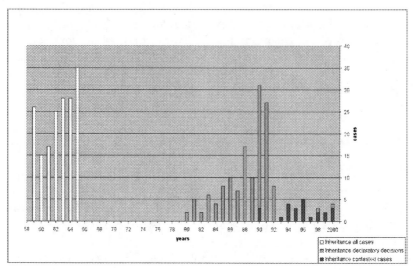

Source: for 1959–1965, Lev (1972: 211, Table 4); for 1980–2000, court registers.

children. Because Muslims are legally required to go to the Islamic courts to get a divorce, divorce cases make up the bulk in both regions. In both West Sumatran and Central Acehnese Islamic courts inheritance cases form only a small proportion of the caseload (see Table 10.1).

While the Islamic court in the district of Central Aceh treated twenty inheritance cases over three years, in West Sumatra nine Islamic courts decided on less than one case per court in the same period. Over a period of twenty years, only 133 inheritance cases were brought before the nine West Sumatran Islamic courts, and these cases usually concerned requests to confirm that a person is the legitimate heir to a deceased

Table 10.1 Inheritance Cases in Islamic Court of Central Aceh and in Nine Islamic Courts in West Sumatra.

	District Central Aceh* 1992, '93, '99	Province West Sumatra (9 courts) 1992, '93, '99	1980–2001
Total cases	680 *	1,164	36,530
Inheritance	20 *	8	133
Percentage of total	2.9 %	0.7 %	0.4 %

Source: Bowen (2003: 73).

Table 10.2 Per Capita Litigation Rates in Islamic and Civil Courts in 1999.

	Aceh Tengah*	West Sumatra	
Population	234,900*	4,500,000**	
Court type	Islamic Court*	Islamic Courts	Civil Courts
Total cases	1: 9,000*	1: 11,000	1: 15,000
Inheritance	1: 33,000*	1: 1,500,000	1: 27,000

*Source: Bowen (2003: 73). **Source: Badan Pusat Statistik Propinsi Sumatera Barat (2000: 33).

person, not the contested division of inherited estates. Most inheritance disputes are brought before the civil courts. Meanwhile, in 1999, litigation rates of inheritance disputes in the Islamic court of Central Aceh were almost fifty times higher than those in West Sumatran Islamic courts. By contrast, the litigation rates of West Sumatran civil courts resembled those of the Islamic court in Central Aceh (Table 10.2).

Unfortunately, Bowen does not give figures on long-term changes in court use in Central Aceh, so a more precise comparison cannot be made. We can, however, draw several conclusions. The litigation rate of inheritance issues has remained stable in West Sumatran civil courts and Islamic courts; disputants predominantly turn to civil courts with inheritance disputes. By the late 1990s, the inheritance litigation rate of West Sumatran civil courts resembled that of the Islamic court in Central Aceh. The increase in inheritance disputes that Bowen reports for the Islamic court in Central Aceh since the law of 1989 did not occur in West Sumatra.

Kinship and Inheritance

This section discusses kinship and inheritance patterns and shifts towards Islam in the two regions. Describing the constellations and issues that tend to give rise to disputes will allow us to investigate in the next section to what extent the shifts towards Islam and the issues and party constellations might explain the differences in court use.

Gayo Kinship and Inheritance

The Gayo trace descent primarily through the father's line; ties through one's mother are associated with spiritual power. They practice village exogamy usually combined with virilocal residence. Uxorilocal residence may be opted for when there are no sons in the village. Sons and daughters who marry out of the village lose their claim to ancestral land within the village. Inheritance is in principle bilateral, but there is no rule that specifies how wealth is to be transmitted. Because of the marriage patterns, there is a strong preference for sons, for the most important thing is that land remains within the village. Parents may allocate parts of their estate to each of their children. A daughter who lives within the village is more likely to get a house and perhaps some limited use rights over land, but sons receive fuller and more permanent rights over larger shares of productive land.[13]

The decision about the division of an estate has to be taken by consensus among the heirs. Initial agreement may be reached while the parents are living or upon their death, but the final agreement takes place when the estate is partitioned. Partition may occur immediately after both parents have died, but final partition often happens only much later. In such cases, the eldest son living in the village assumes the role of *wali,* the guardian of the estate, and has to organize the final consensual decision about partition. Upon partition, provisional allocations may be reallocated, and earlier agreements are often revoked or disputed at a later stage. In principle, the final allocation occurs on the basis of individual needs, but it is quite common that the guardian takes a larger share than the others, and sons often get more than daughters because they are seen as continuing the family 'trunk'. Quite often a son bullies his sister out of her part of the estate or greedily seizes the goods from his sisters when the final agreement for partition is to be taken. An in-marrying man from outside cannot fall back on long-established social relationships and therefore finds it difficult to defend the rights of his wife. Often local leaders take an active part in these deliberations to make sure that agreement is reached. However, neither the village head nor the imam can do more than talk intransigent brothers into lenience towards their sisters. Many couples in an uxorilocal marriage leave the village disillusioned after the parents have died.

Often a head of the family tries to avoid the tensions of intestate inheritance and prevent greedy sons from taking too large a part of the estate by making gifts to daughters during his lifetime. Gayo *adat* recognizes such gifts, but it is often not quite clear whether such a gift is permanent or an allocation during the lifetime of the head of the family. A gift under *adat* therefore provides insufficient guarantees for the daughter after her father has died. Alternatives are an Islamic gift (*hibah*) or bequest (*wasiat*), which are clearly defined as permanent transfers. However, whether a transfer was indeed a permanent gift or *hibah* becomes subject to manipulation when the giver is deceased. Once a son has taken the position of head of the family, he may want the property for himself and try to reinterpret such a gift as temporary. Thus, the majority of inheritance disputes concern disagreement among siblings about the division of an estate. There are also examples of junior brothers who do not get a fair share, but the more poignant cases pertain to sisters with in-marrying spouses.

Since the economic boom of the 1980s and the focus on cultivation of export products, the most valuable land is no longer ancestral land within the village that is used for rice cultivation. The valuable estates have instead become the coffee and gambir gardens, acquired since the 1960s, located at some distance from the villages. As a result, today many Gayo live in neolocal residence patterns, and often in two places: the village of origin and the settlements close to the gardens. Bowen reports that these new residence patterns and the economic importance of land that lies outside the village and is not ancestral property have changed the general attitude towards inheritance rules. The main bone of contention is still disagreement among siblings about the partition of an estate. However, neo- and duolocal residence patterns have dissolved the closed communities of the past. The reason for the former strong preference for sons and for passing on property to those who remain in the village no longer holds.

Notions of what is a fair partition have changed accordingly, and women have become more vocal in claiming a fairer division of the estate. Within the village setting, women have had some success in referring to Islam to claim a larger share of the estate. However, they do not invoke the specific Shariah rules for the division of an estate. While acknowledging that *adat* is to be applied, they invoke Koranic principles that stress the equality of women and foresee the entitlement of daughters to inherit. In the negotiations about partition, therefore, both *adat* and Islam are invoked to reach an agreement that is required by *adat*. Bowen reports that several Islamic judges are highly respected public figures in the region who are quite frequently informally approached by villagers to give advice in inheritance disputes. Thus, arguments derived from Islam are used in village settings to convince sons to allot their sisters a more appropriate share of the estate.

In the past, a woman who felt mistreated by her siblings had nowhere to turn. Both civil and Islamic courts tended to follow consensual decisions on partition reached among the heirs. If the court was satisfied that consensus had been reached, it would not question the outcome, however unfair it might have been for the daughter claiming redress. The Islamic court today is more inclined to question the justice of the negotiating procedures. If a woman receives a substantially smaller share than her other siblings, the court probes further and satisfies itself that the woman has not been pressed into agreement. Thus, the Islamic court uses arguments derived both from *adat* and Islam to question whether *adat* procedures have been properly followed. If the court is not satisfied that true agreement has been reached, it tends to follow (Islamic) principles of equality – though not the rules of Shariah – to decide on what it considers a proper division. It has become a common practice of courts to divide the land in front of the headman, rather than deciding on the size of the parts only (see also Lev 1972: 204). Individual women who have turned to Islamic courts of late have been successful in getting larger if not equal shares of the estate of their parents. However, Bowen also suggests that the wider effects of the Islamic courts and judges on inheritance decisions outside the court context seem to have remained modest. Sons, especially oldest sons who remain in the village, still tend to inherit a substantially larger portion of the estate than their siblings, especially sisters. And conflicts about the partition of an estate are rampant.

Minangkabau Kinship and Inheritance

West Sumatra, the homeland of the Minangkabau, is a prosperous agricultural region. But in contrast to the Gayo Highlands, where the most valuable agricultural land does not have the status of inherited land, agricultural land in West Sumatra is predominantly the inherited property of matrilineages, though much fragmentation and individualization has taken place.[14]

Minangkabau traditionally practised village endogamy, and residence was uxorilocal. Many live neolocally today, but this would still be within the village where the valuable land is situated. A married couple works on the inherited land of the wife. If a woman does not have sufficient land, her husband may be given some land by his family upon marriage, or the husband may buy or take additional land in pawn. Property rules make a fundamental distinction between inherited property (*pusako*) and self-acquired property (*pancaharian*). Inherited property devolves within the matrilineage and for all practical purposes is divided among the daughters who live and work on their family land. Minangkabau marriage and inheritance patterns thus provide women with a strong economic position. After a marriage is dissolved through divorce or death of the husband, a woman and her children remain entitled to house and land.

Up until the first half of the twentieth century, a man's self-acquired property also devolved to his sisters' children according to matrilineal principles. This became contested under both Islamic and modernizing influences, and inheritance practices changed. Some fathers started to bequeath their self-acquired property by means of a testament, or by *hibah. Hibah* was incorporated into Minangkabau *adat* as early as the nineteenth century, when it was transformed into a gift, revocable during the lifetime of the owner, which becomes operative after the death of the giver. Initially this required the consent of the matrilineal heirs, but by the 1930s courts acknowledged that a father could do this without the consent of the matrilineal heirs.

In the 1950s, the intestate inheritance of self-acquired property came on the political agenda again, and in two province-wide meetings of lineage heads and state officials in 1952 and in 1968 it was officially decided that property acquired by a man devolves according to Islamic law, while inherited property devolves according to *adat*. The civil courts did not follow this rule, however. In two decisions of 1968 and 1972 the Supreme Court of Indonesia decided that according to Minangkabau *adat* a man's self-acquired property is inherited by his children. In practice the issue has remained a source of conflict. Though it is generally recognized today that a man's self-acquired property devolves to his children, many conflicts arise between the children of a deceased man and his matrilineal relatives about the status of the property: high *pusako* that has been in the matrilineage for many generations; low *pusako*, which has been in the family since the grandparents; self-acquired property of the parents; or individual ownership (*hak milik*), which retains this status after it has been inherited. This determines which set of relatives is required for a sale or pawning contract to be valid. It is also relevant to the question of who will inherit the property. There is disagreement about the status of land given as *hibah* after it has been inherited. Most maintain that it becomes part of the pool of inherited property and from then on will be inherited by the matrilineal kin of the first heir. Others claim it becomes individual ownership and does not accrue to the pool of inherited property. Courts take the view that such property will eventually become part of the inherited property. Thus, as in the 1970s, the major disputes that reach court concern conflicts between a male heir's matrilineal kin and his children and turn around the status of disputed property.

Three Steps in Explaining Differences in Court Use

The first step in our comparison shows that the main inheritance disputes concern different sets of issues resulting from the respective kinship structure, residence patterns and related *adat* norms, as well as the different economic developments within the regions. In the Gayo Highlands the main issue was primarily to improve the inheritance position of sisters vis-à-vis their male siblings, and in particular the brother who acted as *wali* of the unpartitioned estate. In Minangkabau the focus of contention was to allow children, both male and female, to inherit self-acquired property from their fathers. Moreover, in both regions, classical *adat* inheritance rules have been challenged by means of Islamic law. In both regions, Islamic legal institutes, in particular *hibah*, have been used to avoid *adat* intestate inheritance regulations. Minangkabau have transformed it into an *adat* institution, while Gayo see it as an Islamic institute and follow its Islamic meaning as an irrevocable gift. In both regions *hibah* gives rise to many disputes. Gayo men may contest that the gift of property to a sister was indeed *hibah*, but there is no disagreement about the rules, while Minangkabau disagree about the rules pertaining to *hibah*. Thus, in both regions there has been a shift towards Islam in the most contested inheritance issues, though constellations of disputants and the issues about which they fight differ.

A second step in our comparison turns the perspective on courts. In Minangkabau the main inheritance issues are seen as an *adat* matter and therefore a case for civil courts. The changes in inheritance of self-acquired property and issues of *hibah* are seen as *adat* issues for which the civil court is competent. Civil courts regard themselves as the guardians of *adat*, while Islamic courts see themselves as competent in Islamic issues only, for which they would apply Islamic law. By contrast, the Islamic court in Central Aceh does not make a strict separation between Islamic law, in which it would be competent, and *adat* issues, in which it would not be competent. It still acknowledges that *adat* is in principle applicable in inheritance matters. If the heirs have reached an agreement about the division of an estate, the court follows this agreement. But in contrast to the past, the court today no longer accepts at face value a consensus over a particularly skewed division and puts the burden of proof on the shoulders of those claiming that consensus has been reached. To correct the unequal division of an estate, village leaders and the Islamic court refer to *adat* and Islamic principles of equality.

What emerges seems to be a paradox: in West Sumatra, Islamic influences within civil courts caused a shift in *adat* inheritance of self-acquired property of a man from matrilineal heirs to his children, while Islamic courts have consistently rejected dealing with inheritance issues altogether because they consider them *adat* issues. Meanwhile, the Islamic court in Central Aceh has redressed some of the problems women have according to Gayo *adat* with reference to Islamic principles of equality, but based on the understanding that inheritance is in principle an *adat* matter, in which it considered itself also competent. The differences in the respective customary laws – in Gayo based on a bilateral kinship and inheritance structure with a strong preference for men; in Minangkabau on a matrilineal kinship and inheritance structure – account for the kind of inheritance issues people fight about and for some of the adjustments that Islam has made in *adat*. But these cannot fully explain why the Gayo turn to the Islamic court while Minangkabau have continued to use civil courts. There are no inherent reasons why changes in inheritance rules could not have occurred in the civil court of Central Aceh, as they have in West Sumatra. Conversely, there are also no inherent reasons why the Minangkabau have not turned to Islamic courts as the Gayo have. The differences in *adat* or the broadened jurisdiction of Islamic courts and their more open attitude to gender equality cannot fully explain the differential use of Islamic courts. In fact, civil courts have been successfully used in West Sumatra to change *adat,* or to further interpretations of *adat* that were both closer to Islamic principles and to modern ideas of equality. Moreover, the Supreme Court has, in several famous decisions, improved the position of Islamic and Christian women in other regions, for example of Christian Karo Batak women in North Sumatra, whose kinship structure is very similar to that of the Gayo.[15] The Gayo could have followed the same strategy, but they turned to the Islamic courts instead.

The last step in the comparison concerns the overall political climate and the relative political weight and symbolic value of the relevant bodies of law (Lev 1972: 213ff.), including, I suggest, the political importance of the history of incorporation of specific regions. In the Gayo Highlands, emphasizing Islam and going to Islamic courts is politically correct *and* appropriate, given the gender discrimination in inheritance that is at issue. From the first, Islam has been a widely accepted mobilizing force against the national state. Islam symbolizes regional independence and at the same time serves to negotiate more regional control over natural resources. Because Aceh is well endowed with natural resources, it can negotiate its relationship with the centre from a far stronger position than Minangkabau. Islam marks an unambiguous and self-conscious identity in Aceh, including Gayo society. Going to the Islamic court is another expression of this Muslim identity and the political importance of Islam. It plays into the hands of those who regard Islam as an emancipating force in comparison to Gayo *adat:* Islam is seen not as a fundamental threat but rather as a correction to the Gayo kinship structure. Moreover, the Islamic court itself is well entrenched within Gayo society, and its Gayo judges are frequently asked for informal advice. Despite heavy pressure from the Islamic High Court and the Department of Religious Affairs, the Islamic court has consistently been of the opinion that it should apply *adat* principles in inheritance matters, but it also feels justified to invoke Islam to redress some of the injustices in *adat*. It does not insist on simply applying Islamic law, but carefully considers agreements that have been made according to *adat*, while recognizing that the economic developments have changed local *adat* considerably. Thus, disputants turning to the Islamic court follow the general trend towards a greater prominence of Islamic institutions without having to fear that these will undermine their *adat*.

Playing the Islam card at the expense of *adat* in West Sumatra would be politically contentious and potentially dangerous, and it would also be far less appropriate. Since the early history of incorporation, Minangkabau have drawn a sharp distinction between *adat* and Islam, and this relationship remains uneasy. The core of *adat* – matrilineal descent, embodied in the concept of inherited property – has been carefully insulated from Islamic influence. Most insist that changes in self-acquired property were changes within *adat*. For Minangkabau, Islam does not have the same emancipative ring that it has for Gayo because Minangkabau *adat* puts women in a rather strong position in matters of inheritance. Inheritance disputes do not pitch men against women but a man's matrilineal male and female kin against his sons and daughters.

In contrast to Aceh, Islam and Islamic law cannot help Minangkabau in their most pressing political ambitions for autonomy and control over village property either, for which they have to rely on *adat*. A stronger political focus on Islam might potentially support the small and as yet unimportant groups that strive for secession from the Indonesian state, a horror scenario for most Minangkabau. In view of these circumstances, Minangkabau tend to stick to civil courts, from which they expect support in the politically important issues of land claims, support Islamic courts might not provide. Looking at Aceh now and remembering their own violent past, most Minangkabau do not entirely trust their *adat* in the hands of Islamic institutes that, in contrast to Central Aceh, insist on applying Islamic law exclusively. And the trust that Gayo Islamic judges have built up among the Gayo population does not seem to exist among Minangkabau, where judges from the Islamic courts are not as well entrenched within the local community. Civil courts have proven to be amenable to change without threatening to destroy the foundations of their matrilineal *adat*, while Minangkabau, particularly women, are not confident that Islamic courts would be as compliant.

Conclusions

The analysis of the court use in two regions of Indonesia has shown that the degree to which the government can control the court use by changing the rules of jurisdiction appears to be limited. Even direct pressure from the provincial Islamic High Court and the Department of Religious Affairs on the Islamic court of first instance to apply Islamic law more systematically has had only limited effect. This is in part due to the fact that the courts themselves are differently positioned within the region and develop their own vision of which disputes they can deal with. In part it depends on the relationship between Islamic law and *adat* within the respective region and between the region and the central government. Additional factors are the alternative normative systems available to the local population, their specific kinship and inheritance structures and the kinds of issues disputants fight about. The analysis also shows that in arenas other than courts, the symbolic value of *adat* and Islam in negotiations carried out over autonomy within the national constitutional setting has an impact on the trust disputants have in the respective courts.

The fear that the broadened jurisdiction would bring a major shift towards Islamic dominance has not come true. To be sure, in both regions described above *adat* has undergone important changes under the influence of Islam, and the majority of the population has accepted this. Expansion of the jurisdiction of Islamic courts does automatically redirect disputants to Islamic courts. If anything, the analysis suggests that Islamic courts are successful in attracting inheritance disputes only if they do not apply Islamic law exclusively. Disputants continue to look for a careful balance between *adat* and Islam when turning to the state.

Notes

1. See e.g. Hefner (2000); Roy (2002); Bowen (2003); Watson (2005: 190f.).
2. See Lev (1972, 1973); Bowen (2003: 185).
3. See Lev (1972: 213ff.) for the influence of the overall political climate on Islamic courts.
4. This section is based on Bowen (2003).
5. Personal communication, President of the Islamic High Court in Banda Aceh Soufyan Saleh S.H., 25 June 2007.
6. See F. von Benda-Beckmann (2001, 2005, 2006b, 2007).
7. See Kahin (1979, 1999).
8. Lev (1972: 75ff.); F. von Benda-Beckmann (1979: 126ff.).

9. Lev (1972: 116). See for the debates on the term 'living law' Lev (1973: 21f); F. von Benda-Beckmann (1979); Slaats (1988); Bowen (2003: 53f).
10. F. von Benda-Beckmann (1979: 126ff., 268f.); K. von Benda-Beckmann (1984: 3, 44, 61); Tanner (1971: 230).
11. Bowen (2003).
12. My research on court use in West Sumatra started in 1974/75, together with Franz von Benda-Beckmann and with Narullah Dt. Perpatih nan Tuo from the Faculty of Law at Andalas University. See F. von Benda-Beckmann (1979); K. von Benda-Beckmann (1984). Recently, long-term data from the registers of all civil and Islamic courts in the Province of West Sumatra were collected in collaboration with Takdir, Tasman, Narullah, Yuliandri, Zulheri, Mardenis and many students at the Centre for Alternative Dispute Resolution at Andalas University. Barbara Lenz helped tabulate the raw data and Mirco Lomoth and Sung-Joon Park prepared the tables and charts for this chapter. For the Gayo Highlands see Bowen (2000, 2003).
13. This section is based on Bowen (1988, 1991, 2003).
14. This section is based on F. von Benda-Beckmann (1979); K. von Benda-Beckmann (1984); F. and K. von Benda-Beckmann (2006a).
15. Lev (1972); F. von Benda-Beckmann (1979: 126, 128ff.); Slaats and Portier (1986); Slaats (1988); Bowen (2003: 54).

References

Badan Pusat Statistik Propinsi Sumatera Barat and Badan Perencanaan Pembangunan Daerah. 2000. *Sumatera Barat Dalam Angka (West Sumatra in Figures) 1999*. Padang: Badan Pusat Statistik Propinsi Sumatera Barat BPS in cooperation with BAPPEDA Propinsi Sumbar.

Benda-Beckmann, F. von. 1979. *Property in Social Continuity: Continuity and Change in the Maintenance of Property Relationships through Time in Minangkabau, West Sumatra*. The Hague: Martinus Nijhoff.

Benda-Beckmann, F. von and K. von Benda-Beckmann. 2001. *Recreating the Nagari: Decentralisation in West Sumatra*. Working Paper No. 31. Halle/Saale: Max Planck Institute for Social Anthropology.

———. 2005. 'Democracy in Flux: Time, Mobility and Sedentarization of Law in Minangkabau, Indonesia', in F. von Benda-Beckmann, K. von Benda-Beckmann and A. Griffiths (eds), *Mobile People, Mobile Law: Expanding Legal Relations in a Contracting World*. Aldershot: Ashgate, 111–30.

———. 2006a. 'How Communal Is Communal and Whose Communal Is It? Lessons from Minangkabau', in F. von Benda-Beckmann, K. von Benda-Beckmann and M.G. Wiber (eds), *Changing Properties of Property*. Oxford: Berghahn, 194–217.

———. 2006b. 'Changing One Is Changing All: Dynamics in the Adat-Islam-State Triangle', in F. von Benda-Beckmann and K. von Benda-Beckmann (eds), *Dynamics of Plural Legal Orders: Special Double Issue of the Journal of Legal Pluralism and Unofficial Law Nrs. 53–54/2006*. Berlin: Lit, 239–70.

————. 2007. 'Ambivalent Identities: Decentralization and Minangkabau Political Communities', in G. van Klinken and H. Schulte Nordholt (eds), *Renegotiating Boundaries: Local Politics in Post-Suharto Indonesia*. Leiden: KITLV Press, 417–42.

Benda-Beckmann, K. von. 1984. *The Broken Stairways to Consensus: Village Justice and State Courts in Minangkabau*. Dordrecht, Leiden, Cinnaminson: Foris Publications, KITLV Press.

Bowen, J.R. 1988. 'The Transformation of an Indonesian Property System: "Adat", Islam, and Social Change in the Gayo Highlands', *American Ethnologist* 15: 274–93.

————. 1991. *Sumatran Politics and Poetic: Gayo History, 1900–1989*. New Haven, CT: Yale University Press.

————. 2000. 'Consensus and Suspicion: Judicial Reasoning and Social Change in an Indonesian Society 1960–1994', *Law and Society Review* 34: 97–127.

————. 2003. *Islam, Law and Equality in Indonesia: An Anthropology of Public Reasoning*. Cambridge: Cambridge University Press.

Hefner, R.W. 2000. *Civil Islam: Muslims and Democratization in Indonesia*. Princeton, NJ: Princeton University Press.

Kahin, A. 1979. *Struggle for Independence: West Sumatra in the Indonesia National Revolution: 1945–1950*. New York: Cornell University Press.

————. 1999. *Rebellion to Integration: West Sumatra and the Indonesian Polity 1926–1998*. Amsterdam: Amsterdam University Press.

Lev, D.S. 1972. *Islamic Courts in Indonesia*. Berkeley, Los Angeles: University of California Press.

————. 1973. 'Judicial Unification and Legal Culture in Indonesia', *Indonesia* 16: 1–37.

Ramstedt, M. (forthcoming). 'Regional Autonomy and Its Discontents: The Case of Post–New Order Bali', in C. Holtzappel and M. Ramstedt (eds), *Decentralization and Regional Autonomy in Indonesia: Implementation and Challenge*. Singapore: ISEAS.

Roy, O. 2002. *Globalised Islam: The Search for a New Ummah*. London: Hurst & Company.

Slaats, H. 1988. 'A Continuing Story: The Use of State Courts in Indonesia', *Review of Indonesian and Malay Affairs* 122: 133–53.

Slaats, H. and K. Portier. 1986. 'Legal Plurality and the Transformation of Normative Concepts in the Process of Litigation in Karo Batak Society', in K. von Benda-Beckmann and F. Strijbosch (eds), *Anthropology of Law in the Netherlands*. Dordrecht: Foris Publications, 217–39.

Tanner, N. 1971. 'Minangkabau Disputes', unpublished PhD diss., University of California, Berkeley.

Watson, C.W. 2005. 'Islamic Books and Their Publishers: Notes on the Contemporary Indonesian Scene', *Journal of Islamic Studies* 16(2): 177–210.

11

KINGS, MONKS, BUREAUCRATS AND THE POLICE
Tibetan Responses to Law and Authority
Fernanda Pirie

Tibetan groups at either end of the plateau maintain significant autonomy over their local order and processes of conflict resolution. In this
chapter I contrast a village in Ladakh, at the western end of the Himalayan mountain range, now part of India, with a nomadic encampment on
the grasslands of Amdo, in central China. I discuss the local experiences
of and reactions to legal control by the modern state. These two Tibetan
groups have been subject to the very different legal and governmental
regimes of a liberal democracy and a one-party state. However, each
maintains a measure of autonomy in a way that is not directly related
to the nature of the state's legal control. In the remote village in Ladakh
the state is distanced from the local political and legal order, while its
agents are treated with the utmost deference and respect. Amongst the
nomadic group in Amdo, by contrast, the state's agents are regarded
in almost wholly negative terms and scorned as mediators, yet the nomads actively seek out the state's representatives to determine boundaries and restrain violence.[1]

Oppositional models of domination and resistance of the type proposed by Scott (1985, 1990) and Escobar (1992) do not adequately characterize the relations between either of these subordinate groups and
the respective states of India and China. Nor can they account for the
differences between them. Ecological factors, the historical experience
of control over resources, the power of religious establishments and the
part they have played in the management of conflict have led these two
Tibetan groups to develop quite different understandings of the nature
of their own social order. These involve very different ideas about the
roles that outsiders can and should play among them, characterized
by deference and distance and by selective submission to authority, respectively. These attitudes continue to affect the exercise of legal control
and judicial authority within the structures of the modern state.

Ladakh

The Himalayan region of Ladakh has always been predominantly an agricultural area, its sparse population clustered into small, widely spaced
villages where irrigation makes subsistence possible in the high and
arid environment. The region lay, for long, at a crossroads of Central
Asian trade routes, and the main Indus Valley was host to outsiders,
traders and foreign influences. Its rulers waged wars with Kashmiri,
Tibetan and Mongolian forces, and the local population was frequently
mobilized both to fight and to provide labour and transport, as well as
to pay taxes.[2] External control over the villages was, and is, exercised
mainly from two sources: firstly the political regimes of the kingdom,
colonial government and modern bureaucratic administration, and secondly, the Buddhist monasteries.

The kings ruled for several centuries through ministers whose families came to form a small aristocracy, elevated in the social hierarchy.
Contact between these ministers and the villages was, however, infre-
quent, largely limited to tax collection. There is some evidence of judicial activity in the capital, Leh (Cunningham 1854; Carrasco 1959), and
the ministers were said to have 'given the law' in their areas, but the
villagers themselves told me that they generally remained far away in
the Indus Valley. The last Ladakhi king was conquered by the Kashmiri Dogras in 1843, and the region was incorporated into the princely
state of Jammu and Kashmir. Many of the aristocrats were employed
as administrators in the new government, and a certain amount of
bureaucratization took place, including expansion of the legal system,
but there is no evidence that judicial control extended far outside the
capital. During the Ladakhi kingdom and subsequent colonial period,
therefore, the villagers' experience of political control largely consisted
in the payment of taxes and compliance with labour obligations.

Buddhist monks and their establishments were patronized by the
kings from the earliest days and obtained considerable wealth, much of
it in land.[3] The monks are elevated in the social hierarchy, even above
the aristocrats, and are accorded the utmost religious respect. Gradual reform has seen the abolition of most monastic taxation, but these
establishments still receive considerable donations from the laity and
large numbers of boys, and a few girls, are sent to join the monastic
population. In return, the monasteries have established small temples
in each village, tended by caretaker monks who perform ceremonies
required by the villagers. Thus their influence, unlike that of the aristocrats and modern bureaucrats, extends right into the remotest villages,

and they are still able to command significant material resources from the lay population. However, there is no evidence that the monks have ever been allowed to interfere in village politics or in processes of conflict resolution.

Since Indian independence the region has been governed by administrators appointed in Jammu, while legal order is nominally upheld by the police force and regional courts. Taxes have largely been abolished and successive governments have pursued modernizing agendas in the region. The villagers now generally see the state as a force for good and a source of material benefits. They participate in state and national elections, and the new government officials have been incorporated into the social hierarchy in superior positions, alongside the aristocrats. Nevertheless, the government's administrative control is barely visible within the villages and the Ladakhis hardly touch the courts: 'The villagers just don't bring their conflicts to court', explained one Leh-based lawyer, 'they prefer to settle them within their villages'.

Until the mid twentieth century, therefore, the relationship between the villages and centres of power, both political and monastic, was characterized by the extraction of resources and granting of military and religious protection. This has now been replaced by a reversed flow of material benefits from the centre to the villages. However, neither has been accompanied by close control over village politics.

Village Practices

Photoksar is one of the remoter Ladakhi villages, still two days' walk from the nearest road and separated from its neighbours by high mountain passes. Its population of around 200 is divided into twenty-two households. To be a member of the village means belonging to one of these households, either by birth or by marriage. These households form various groupings for different purposes – life-cycle rites, agricultural events, festival organization and neighbourhood socializing – but for each type of event the group is different. These links thus form a web of cross-cutting ties, which unite the whole village into a network of alliances and effectively prevent permanent divisions from arising. Individuals are ranked, for all social purposes, in the *dral* (*gral*),[4] seating and dancing lines which place the monks, aristocracy and (now) visiting officials into higher positions. The villagers, who are all of the commoner class, are arranged solely according to age and gender. The system of hierarchical ranking that supports the status of the former power-holders also, therefore, represents relatively egalitarian relations within the village.

The headman of the village, the *goba* (*'go ba*), controls the community's funds and represents the village vis-à-vis outsiders. He organizes meetings, liaises with the astrologer and is responsible for settling disputes. However, this post rotates annually between all the full households of the village, and all important decisions are taken at the village meeting. This might involve the staging of festivals or a decision about the boys who should be sent into the monastery. The meetings are made up of the *yulpa* (*yul pa*), explained to me as being 'everyone', although in fact it is a body that consists only of the adult men and is firmly exclusive of outsiders. Within itself it is egalitarian; not even the age ranking is recognized. A ballot can be taken, with one vote counted from each household, but this is rarely necessary because in practice consensus is almost always reached. Certain men are actually more influential than others, but this is never acknowledged later. Those who attend always report what 'we' agreed, and the will of the meeting is expressed in the form of decisions said to have been taken by 'everyone'.[5] It is this internal group of the *yulpa* that has the ultimate political and judicial authority in the village, being the final arbiter in disputes, and it is the idea of absolute agreement among them that is the foundation of their authority.

The Resolution of Disputes

Village practices of conflict resolution are supported by a strong morality. All forms of fighting, arguing, quarrelling and the use of abusive language are disapproved of. People shake their heads over quarrels and shudder at the mention of fighting. Even the expression of anger is condemned in moral terms. These attitudes and, indeed, the whole scheme of village morality, are rooted in a firm sense of the importance and integrity of the community and the absolute need for cooperation amongst the individuals who constitute it. The social order is the responsibility of each individual.

Disputes do, nevertheless, occur: over straying animals, within marriages, or simply as a matter of bad relations between individuals. Overt quarrelling is a problem for the whole community and reconciliation is imperative. In minor cases the *goba* will attempt to resolve the problem by getting the protagonists to shake hands and promise not to fight any more, but in more serious cases a whole village meeting may be necessary. Fines will generally have to be paid, both to the perceived victim and to the *yulpa*, 'for the quarrel'. The object is always to achieve an agreement, rather than to determine individual rights and interests, and resolution is always marked by a ceremony of reconciliation, indicating that order has been restored within the community.

The authority enjoyed by the *yulpa*, in these cases, obviates the need for the villagers to appeal to external judicial sources. When describing their processes of mediation, people usually added that as a last resort they could call the police. In practice, however, such intervention is almost always avoided. 'When they are called, the police just demand money and beat people up', people complained. Even a suspicious death in a neighbouring village was resolved internally. The village meeting there decided that the families of the suspected culprits should be fined heavily and, in their view, unjustly. Nevertheless, they accepted this decision, rather than turning to the police.

This attitude to the resolution of disputes is intimately connected with the construction of the boundaries of the village community. People invariably use phrases meaning 'inside' or 'within' as the context in which disputes must be resolved. As I have argued elsewhere (Pirie 2007b), processes of conflict resolution are shaped by a sense of local order, an order that must be maintained within the boundaries of the immediate community. It is also an order that every individual is under a moral duty to maintain and which is ultimately enforced by 'us', the *yulpa*, acting through the village meeting.

Legislative Control

As well as distancing the police, the village boundaries also enclose a space that is insulated from the legislative control of the state. As far as the villagers are concerned, order in the village is maintained according to a variety of norms. Rules, described as 'taxes', *tral* (*khral*), are imposed on households by the *yulpa*, generally backed by the sanction of fines. There are also customs, *trims* (*khrims*), and a range of behaviour considered to be 'shameful'. The *trims* are simply things that 'we do'. Many of them govern fundamental matters, such as the devolution of property by primogeniture and the payment of taxes by each household. They may be flexibly applied but cannot be altered at will, even when they are perceived to work injustice. In one case, a widow was contemplating leaving the family home because of bad relations with her daughter-in-law. My informant was very critical of the girl, but there was no question about who would have to leave. It is an unalterable *trims* that the eldest son stays in the family home.

The people thus regard their village order as being internally generated by the *tral* and the *trims*, even when change has occurred in response to external influences. The Ladakhis talk about their practices of polyandry and primogeniture, for example, as the *trims* of having only one wife per generation. These practices were supposedly changed by state legislation in the early 1940s, and equal division of property between all children is now required by law,[6] although change only began to occur in the 1960s, when economic developments made the division of landholdings feasible. In Photoksar daughters still never inherit (save when they have no brothers) and land division is rare, but the people do recognize a change in their *trims*. One woman explained that now, if younger brothers want to be independent, the eldest son receives most of the land, the next about half that amount and the younger sons even less. 'This is our new *trims*', she said. Another man explained that these changes had occurred because some families could now afford to divide their land; he also acknowledged that they might have been influenced by changes occurring elsewhere. However, no one ever mentioned the existence of state laws.

Despite the democratization that has followed Indian independence, therefore, and the transformation of the state into a source of benefits, the Photoksar villagers continue to insist on the centrality of their own, internal, *trims* and to disregard the state as a source of judicial authority.[7]

The Moral and Religious Orders

A similar pattern can be seen in the villagers' relations with the monastic centres. Photoksar has two small temples, which are maintained by the monasteries of Lamayuru and Hemis, and their monks are accorded the highest social and religious respect. However, all monks are firmly distanced from involvement in village politics. Their status actually excludes them from the body of the *yulpa*, even if they are from village families, and they are never consulted in connection with disputes. Like the aristocrats and, now, local officials, they are accorded the utmost respect in the hierarchical seating lines, but this respect sets them symbolically apart from the cohesive group of villagers.[8] It is Bourdieu's (1990) 'habitus' acting negatively to avoid the encroachment of power into the internal spaces, over which only the internal body of *yulpa* has authority.

Anger is one of the 'three fundamental poisons' of Tibetan Buddhism, and the religion's texts incorporate a set of basic moral rules, the *mi gewa rchu* (*mi dge ba bcu*), which condemn killing, stealing, adultery and so on. However, there was never any reference to these within the frequent discussions of disputes and morality that I heard within Photoksar. My more literate informants knew of them but never elaborated on their content. In fact, people never made any explicit link between their moral judgments and any aspect of their religious or cosmological practices, Buddhist or otherwise. Even the educated urban elite, normally keen to emphasize the significance of their religious principles, would not attribute their moral attitudes or practices of conflict resolution to a religious scheme of morality.[9] The perceived significance and impact of religious and ritual practices is, rather, confined to the dictates of the law of karma and the cosmologically generated problems of physical misfortune. The villagers' moral universe forms a separate sphere, firmly linked to the sense of the community and the need to maintain order within it. A distance is kept between these spheres. Although the religious practitioners still command significant material resources from the population, and although their authority in religious matters is almost unquestioned, the ideological significance of their influence is limited. Both conceptually and structurally, therefore, the politico-moral order of the village is insulated from the influence of the economically and spiritually powerful religious practitioners.

Historic Relations with Centres of Power

The fiscal demands made of the villages by the kings' and colonial regimes were considerable. It could be argued that the villagers' strategies for maintaining local autonomy in other areas of their social and political lives were developed as a means of resistance to centralized control. As Laura Nader (1990) argues, the maintenance of harmony can be a counter-hegemonic strategy against a dominant centre. In this they were and still are assisted by the ecological conditions that allow them to maintain a distance from centres of power. However, it is not just the exploitative state that was distanced from the internal affairs of the village. The authority of the respected religious practitioners, many of whom reside in the villages, is also confined to a distinct ritual and cosmological sphere. Through the distancing mechanism of the social hierarchy and their narratives of disorder, which vest ultimate judicial authority in the internal group of *yulpa*, the villagers maintain internal spaces of political and judicial order, and they continue to isolate these spaces from power-holders within the structures of the modern state.

Amdo

Relations between the nomads of Amdo[10] and their leaders, kings and Buddhist monasteries have, historically, been more dynamic. The Amdo grasslands on the northeastern corner of the Tibetan plateau, an area roughly the size of France, support mobile groups of pastoralists who herd yaks, sheep and horses and trade their surpluses with the neighbouring agricultural populations. Like many pastoral groups elsewhere, these nomads have developed segmentary tribal structures, combining and dividing to avenge pasture encroachments by neighbours and livestock thefts or to engage in warfare with more distant groups. As Gellner (1988) has pointed out, displaying the readiness to take immediate and violent revenge is an effective form of defence when property is mobile. Such dynamics involve the formation of much larger social groups than the villages of Ladakh, tribes of several thousand people.

From the thirteenth century political influence in the area was exercised successively by Mongol, Manchu and Hui Muslim forces, who levied taxes, appointed rulers and controlled trade. This influence was always light in the pastoral areas, where Buddhist monasteries, hereditary ruling families and kings exercised more immediate control over tribal groups, largely by appointing the headmen to the tribes in their areas (Carrasco 1959; Fairbank 1978; Pirie 2005). The kings of Sokwo and Ngawa and the hereditary chiefs of the Golok tribes, it is said, could mobilize significant economic and military resources, both to support and protect the monasteries and also to challenge their neighbours (Ekvall 1939; Hermanns 1949: 231). Labrang, like other powerful monasteries in the region, likewise appointed the headmen to at least twelve tribes (Ekvall 1939: 68–69). It does not appear that the monasteries levied extensive taxes, but the nomads told me that the extent of their monastic donations was always, and remains, a source of pride amongst them.

After the Chinese occupation of 1958 all the monasteries were closed, the lamas were imprisoned, executed or forced to marry, and the power of the local leaders was removed, while the pastoral population was reorganized into groups for collective herding. A period of political, economic and social reforms that followed in the 1980s, however, has substantially allowed the nomads to revert to their old pastoral practices. They have also re-formed themselves into tribal groups, although with elected leaders in place of the old ruling families and monastic appointees.

The Segmentary Structures and Patterns of Feuding

The tribal groups are generally known as *dewa* (*sde ba*)[11] and are themselves divided into villages or encampments. In my fieldwork area, an encampment might consist of forty tents housing around 200 people, with relations between them being relatively egalitarian. Although in the past there were significant distinctions between rich and poor (servant) families, there was never an elaborate class structure. Each encampment is now under the charge of one or more headmen, *gowa*, selected by the people.[12] Their duties are to coordinate pastoral movements, allocate summer grazing land, negotiate with local authorities, organize ritual events and resolve local fighting and disputes. On important matters they convene a meeting, which should be attended by one man from each tent. To this extent, local organization has parallels with that of the Ladakhi village. Each encampment is also part of a *dewa*, however. Previously, some of the tribes in Machu were ruled by hereditary *gowa* and others by the monks sent by Labrang. These used to 'make all the decisions' in their *dewa*, people told me. The *gowa* would 'sort out all the problems' – fighting, killing and stealing – and everyone 'had to do what they ordered'. Today, however, it is a council consisting of the *gowa* of each encampment that performs these functions.

Group Dynamics

The nomads talk frequently and readily about both actual and potential violence. Everyone could tell me stories of fights and killings that had occurred within their families or villages within the last few years, and theft is a constant and real concern to them. In contrast to Ladakh, violence is not regarded as something that must always be suppressed. Rather, it has to be pursued when the norms of revenge demand. Men would tell me, for example, that they 'have' to get angry if a member of their family has been killed. Injury demands immediate retaliation. When there is conflict between two villages all the men of each must combine to take revenge on the other. It is the same in the case of fighting between *dewa*. A long-running dispute over pastureland between a tribe in Machu and the neighbouring Sokwo, for example, saw the outbreak of periodic hostilities, at which times the *gowa* sent round messages demanding that one man from each tent join the battle. Numerous similar cases were mentioned to me, and very similar patterns existed before the Chinese occupation.[13] Once a theft or physical injury has been inflicted retaliatory violence can be avoided only by invoking the well-established procedures of mediation and, in the case of a death, the payment of blood money.

The nomads always talk as if their neighbours are just about to attack or steal from them, but unprovoked violence or theft, particularly against a neighbouring encampment, is strongly condemned, and within the encampment the nomads disapprove of all serious fights; murder would lead to the permanent expulsion of the killer's family. When some young men were caught stealing yaks from tents inside the village I stayed in, for example, considerable outrage was expressed. They were caught and severely beaten, and the *gowa* called a meeting to make new rules. Thieves should always be beaten, they decided, and in the case of theft from a neighbouring encampment, the families would have to pay back the livestock twice over. Good relations had to be maintained with neighbours, they explained. Within their encampment, the *gowa* thus exercise considerable authority to restrain and resolve violence, which was reflected in the language they used when talking to me: 'we decided the young men should be beaten', 'we settled this case', 'we expelled that family'.

When thirty sheep were stolen from the family with whom I stayed, the elder son Jamku went with some friends to search for the thief (on the basis of divination clues given by a monk). When they identified him in another *dewa*, Jamku declared his intention to fight immediately, but was restrained by his friends. He was later persuaded by his family and relatives within the village to let the *gowa* intervene, and the whole affair was settled with compensation payments over the course of the following weeks. To some extent, therefore, the encampment resembles the Ladakhi village. Good relations must be maintained within it, and authority over wayward individuals is exercised by the headman and meeting.

When conflict occurs between two encampments within one *dewa*, mediation procedures are also relatively informal, usually carried out by the local *gowa*. Some years ago some animals from the encampment I stayed in had strayed onto the pastures of the next. When a young boy rode over to fetch them he was badly beaten by the men of that group, which angered those of his own, who, as they explained, determined to take revenge. In the ensuing fight they killed a man from the next encampment. However, further conflict was prevented by the intervention of the *dewa gowa*, who organized a mediation and determined that the killer's family pay blood money and also be expelled from the area for three years.

Conflict between two *dewa* is more difficult to settle, however. The feud between the tribes in Machu and Sokwo, for example, had its roots in a pre-1950s pasture dispute, and during battles in the late 1990s at least eighteen men were killed (Yeh 2003; Shinjilt 2007). Tribal loyalty demands that the whole *dewa* combine on such occasions. One of the Machu *gowa* explained to me that one encampment, near the border, was refusing to join in the hostilities, on the grounds that it had many kinship ties with Sokwo; therefore, it had effectively been excluded from activities within the *dewa*. In order to preempt such intractable feuds, external mediators, *zowa* (*gzu ba*), usually and very quickly intervene when a fight breaks out between two men from different *dewa*. These are often *gowa* from neighbouring *dewa* or senior monks from local monasteries, men who are thus external to the feuding groups. Their initial task is to establish a temporary truce so that mediation can take place. The object of mediation is then to calculate the appropriate level of blood money, *mnyö-rtong* (*mi stong*), after the deaths of each side have been set off against each other. They may also establish where boundaries should run according to the local history of land use. Crucially, the mediators have to convince the parties that the proposed compensation takes into account all the relevant factors. My informants referred to the *gowas* with 'good speech' as being those who could easily resolve such problems. In some areas, such as Golok, certain members of the former ruling families are renowned orators, said to be able to use special riddles in the task of persuasion.

Today, as previously, the Buddhist lamas are at the pinnacle of this system. They are seen as able to resolve conflict that is beyond the capabilities of local mediators. 'People always tell the truth in front of them', the nomads told me, and the lamas suggest just solutions, *jömdri* (*rgyu 'bras*), taking into account the history of the case. The authority of the senior lamas from the major monasteries in the region, such as Labrang, is clearly linked to the religious status of their establishments. However, the two are not entirely congruent. Lamas are reincarnations of Buddhist deities or other eminent historical figures, and are seen as possessing special powers to assist souls in the afterlife. They are also regarded as the most effective intermediaries between people and their *zhabdakh* (*gzhis bdag*), the local deities who grant protection and bestow strength and good fortune on the living. The lamas are thus potent figures, able to influence both the fate of souls in the afterlife and the activities of the powerful spirits. It is this charismatic authority that gives them the power to overcome the nomads' norms of violent retribution.[14] It is, however, significant that none of the nomads ever referred to Buddhist morality when discussing conflict resolution with me. The nomads always insisted that the lamas were successful because everyone 'believes in' and 'has faith in' them, but they settle the nomads' disputes according to the norms of revenge and compensation.

The Amdo nomads, like the Ladakhis, therefore, retain their own set of norms for the resolution of conflict, independently of religious principles. Unlike the Ladakhis, however, they endow their senior religious leaders with ultimate judicial authority. The role of religious leaders as mediators in tribal feuds has been noted in the Middle East, where the power of Islamic 'saints' has been described by Gellner (1969).[15] Such external figures act as a counterpoint to the leaders of the local groups, who may themselves be required to support the norms of retaliation. In such cases the norms of revenge and group loyalty give rise to patterns of feuding that cause their leaders to seek external sources of authority for the purposes of mediation. As I have described elsewhere (Pirie 2007b), these dynamics involve a constant tension between angry individuals bent upon revenge, and their leaders and external mediators, who take responsibility for restoring order.

The Effects of Change

The upper layer of leadership, that provided by the monasteries and the former hereditary families, was swept away by the arrival of the Chinese in 1958. The monasteries were all closed and their monks were either imprisoned or sent to work elsewhere, often being forced to take wives. Secular leaders lost all their authority as the nomads were reorganized into groups for collective herding. Members of these families were also singled out as class enemies during the Cultural Revolution (Goldstein 1994; Makley 2005).

The early 1980s saw considerable reform throughout China under Deng Xiaoping, however. In Amdo the monasteries were allowed to reopen, and the animals were gradually returned to the private ownership of the nomad tents under the 'household responsibility system'.[16] The nomads very quickly became almost fully autonomous again in their pastoral activities and have largely regrouped themselves into the encampments and *dewa* that existed before 1958. In fact, the Chinese administration has now brought considerable material benefits to the nomads through the establishment of new towns and a network of roads. These have brought trading points, supplies of food and household goods, education, health facilities and some employment opportunities within easy reach of most families. The collectivization and redistribution of livestock has also done much to equal out the previously great disparities in wealth. Nevertheless, in contrast to the Ladakhis, the nomads tend to characterize their state in wholly negative terms. In particular, they resent the strict control the government still exercises: levying taxes, obliging the nomads to vaccinate their animals, enforcing a population control policy and, most controversially, fencing the pastureland. Land division is much resented because boundaries mean possession of land and scope for disputes between neighbouring groups. All these policies are enforced through systems of punishments and fines. The nomads were rarely specific about the consequences of noncompliance, however. 'They make us fence the land', 'they force the women to have the operation', they would say, simply, and complain about the police inflicting beatings for minor transgressions.

As Potter (1991: 28–29) describes, the Chinese government regards judicial processes as a means to secure its own goals of social control.[17] When it comes to conflict resolution, however, the criminal law is treated by the nomads as completely irrelevant. 'The officials cannot produce just solutions (*jömdri*), they do not care about the history', people told me. The nomads still turn to their own skilled mediators and senior lamas in such cases. This occurs even if the police have already caught and punished an offender. In the fight mentioned earlier, for example, the killer was caught by the police and imprisoned for eight years, but his family still had to pay blood money to the victim's family. By maintaining these parallel forms of justice the nomads are submitting themselves to double punishment, but they are also denying the legitimacy of the government's system of criminal law. Significantly, the authorities, on the whole, acquiesce in these activities. They may even call upon senior *gowa* or lamas to become involved in problematic cases in the interests of resolving a feud.

On the other hand, when a boundary dispute arose during my fieldwork the local *gowa*, keen to avert escalating violence, sought out the local government officials to make a decision. Although my informants were insistent that their social organization has essentially returned to that of pre-Chinese times, the authority of the former tribal leaders has been removed and replaced by the meeting of *gowa*. Chinese rule and its relaxation have resulted in a certain amount of (unintended) democratization of nomad organization, but by undermining the authority of the tribal *gowa* it has removed an important element from the previous system of social control. What nomads are now doing is turning to the government administrators to provide them with an equivalent source of authority. Conflict, including that between the Machu and Sokwo tribes, has often been caused or exacerbated by the government's redrawing of boundaries. However, even in cases unrelated to new boundaries the *gowa* complain that the police could, and should, do much more to prevent and control nomad violence. They see them as having the power to enforce an initial truce in order to allow mediation to proceed and are resentful when they do not use their power in this way. In contrast to the Ladakhi villagers, the Amdo nomads, therefore, regard their generally despised rulers as a potential source of decision making and coercive power, power that could and ought to be used in what they see as the interests of order. Standing outside the tribal structures, like the Buddhist lamas and religious mediators of the Middle East, the police and administrators are (or are thought to be) in a position to play a role as peace-keepers; yet at the same time they are not credited with the authority to exercise direct administrative and legal control.

Historical Relations with Centres of Power

A certain amount of order is, as I have described, generated from within the nomads' encampments through social pressure and the *gowas'* efforts to restrain violence and persuade angry individuals to accept compensation. The council of *gowa* performs a similar function within the *dewa*. However, the nomads also look outside those structures, calling on the oratorical skills of external mediators and the charismatic authority of famous lamas in the event of major disputes. Unlike the Ladakhis, whose sources of judicial authority are primarily internal to the community, the nomads' norms of retaliation mean that order has always, in part, been imposed from the outside.

A similar pattern has been re-created under the Chinese administration. Locally selected leaders restrain and resolve conflict within their areas, and the nomads continue to look to the judicial authority of their charismatic lamas, denying that the police's punishment of criminals has any efficacy. However, government officials represent an additional and potentially useful source of decision making. Notwithstanding the rejection of their political legitimacy, the nomads regard these officers as being under an obligation to use their power to settle boundaries and restrain violence, in this way contributing to their overall map of social order.

Conclusion

The Indian and Chinese states have very different ideologies of law and government. In the Indian democracy the legal system is designed, among other things, to protect the rights of its citizens, while in China's one-party republic legal processes are regarded primarily as instruments of government, designed to serve the state and what it defines as the interests of society. Nevertheless, Tibetan groups within each state maintain considerable autonomy over local legal processes and react to the state's legal control in ways not entirely explicable by the nature of such control. In Ladakh's mountainous terrain, clear boundaries can be maintained around the isolated village communities, protecting an order based on unity, agreement and the maintenance of harmonious relations. The villagers have been able to develop relations of deference and distance towards external sources of power and continue to do so within the modern state. On the grasslands of Amdo, by contrast, both tribal groups and their property are mobile. The associated principles of segmentary opposition mean that cooperative relations between groups can quickly be transformed into a dynamic of opposition and violence, causing their leaders to turn to external sources of judicial authority in order to settle feuds.

Ecological factors cannot fully account for these contrasting dynamics of autonomy, however. In the Ladakhi kingdom aristocrats and monasteries levied burdensome taxes but exercised light administrative control over the remoter villages. In Amdo the monasteries were more reliant upon donations, but like the former hereditary rulers they exercised considerable authority to settle conflict amongst the nomads' tribes. These patterns of power and authority are reflected in the different ideas about order that have been developed by each group. In a Ladakhi village, order is regarded as being internally generated, enforced by the village meeting and supported by a local moral universe, according to which all forms of violence are condemned. In Amdo, by contrast, the ideology of revenge and group loyalty requires individuals to display anger and aggression in response to incursions onto property.

The interaction between these different epistemologies of order, moral norms and structures of power is played out in the continuing relations between these local groups and the power-holders in each region, both political and religious. In the Ladakhi village the norms of conflict correspond most closely to the Buddhist moral scheme and its condemnation of anger, but the villagers distance their religious leaders firmly from their judicial processes. Similarly, the judicial power of the Indian state, although its representatives are highly respected, is not allowed to penetrate from the centre down to the local level. The Amdo nomads, by contrast, require feuds to be settled on the basis of compensation and blood money, which has little or nothing to do with Buddhist moral principles, but they look to the Buddhist lamas as the ultimate source of judicial authority. At the same time, they reject the authority of the state's criminal law but regard the officials of the Chinese government as at least capable of playing a useful role within their complex dynamics of order.

Acknowledgements

Fieldwork was carried out in Ladakh between 1998 and 2003, largely funded by the Economic and Social Research Council of the UK, and in Amdo between 2003 and 2004, funded by the Max Planck Institute for Social Anthropology. I am also grateful to David Parkin and Marcus Banks for their invaluable help with the Ladakhi material and to Franz and Keebet von Benda-Beckmann for their comments and advice.

Notes

1. Recent economic development has brought about the expansion of towns and new economic opportunities in both areas (Pirie 2005, 2007a). For the sake of comparison, however, this essay concentrates on two rural communities relatively distanced from such developments.
2. Historical details have largely been drawn from Francke (1926, 1995) and Petech (1977).
3. Although the population of the Kargil area, in the west, was largely converted to Islam, the majority of the people in the eastern areas were and remain Buddhist.
4. Ladakhi and Amdo are Tibetan languages. I transcribed words according to local pronunciation, but I add the Wylie (1959) transcription in brackets to indicate the Tibetan spelling.
5. In the villages closer to the centre and to the modernizing influence of the town, factions and power struggles have emerged in recent years. I have discussed the issues of hierarchy and equality and the effects of modernity at length elsewhere (Pirie 2007a: chaps 3, 7, 9).
6. Abolition of Polyandrous Marriages Act 1941, Ladakhi Succession to Property Act 1943, Hindu Law of Succession Act 1956.
7. In villages closer to Leh new forms of power and status have had a greater effect on the structures of village politics, but conflict resolution still remains a largely internal matter, even in the urban centres (Pirie 2007a: chap. 9)
8. The rotating leadership in the village and the need for the *yulpa* to achieve unanimity in major decisions are also barriers to decisive leadership and innovation, as I have discussed elsewhere (Pirie 2002).
9. This is a complex issue which I have discussed at greater length elsewhere (Pirie 2007a: chap. 5; 2007b).
10. I use the term, 'nomad' when referring to the pastoralists because this is used by the few English speakers among them. The Tibetan *drok-wa* ('brog pa) means 'people of the pastures'. The term 'Amdo' is a fairly recent invention, the region never having had much more than linguistic unity (Makley 1999: 94; Yeh 2003: 508).
11. The use of the term 'tribe' has been much contested in the literature. However, following Tapper (1983) and Khoury and Kostiner (1990), I use it for these relatively egalitarian and distinct groups, whose leaders who are more like chiefs than heads of a state.
12. This is the same term as the *goba* ('go ba) of Ladakh, with the Amdo pronunciation.

13. Details of the pre-Communist period are drawn from Ekvall (1939, 1954, 1964, 1968) and Hermanns (1949, 1959).
14. Their power is 'charismatic' in the sense of having a spiritual element, although in Weberian terms it has been routinized to the extent that lamas, more or less senior, are recognized when very young. Nevertheless, people do attribute greater powers to particularly learned individuals. The emphasis on their 'good speech' echoes the discursive element of charisma discussed by Csordas (1997).
15. The Nuer's leopard-skin chiefs are an African equivalent (Evans-Pritchard 1940).
16. I have described this more fully in Pirie (2005).
17. As he describes it, the Chinese system of legal control is characterized by instrumentalism and formalism, enshrining the principles that civil relations must serve state and social interests.

References

Bourdieu, P. 1990. *The Logic of Practice*, trans. Richard Nice. Cambridge: Polity Press.

Carrasco, P. 1959. *Land and Polity in Tibet*. Seattle and London: University of Washington Press.

Csordas, T. 1997. *Language, Charisma and Creativity: The Ritual Life of a Religious Movement*. Berkeley: University of California Press.

Cunningham, A. 1854. *Ladak, Physical, Statistical and Historical: With Notices of the Surrounding Countries*. London: W.H. Allen & Co.

Ekvall, R. 1939. *Cultural Relations on the Kansu-Tibetan Border*. Chicago: University of Chicago Press.

———. 1954. 'Mi sTong: The Tibetan Custom of Life Indemnity', *Sociologus* 4(2): 136–45.

———. 1964. 'Peace and War among the Tibetan Nomads', *American Anthropologist* 66(5): 1119–48.

———. 1968. *Fields on the Hoof*. Long Grove, IL: Waveland.

Escobar, A. 1992. 'Culture, Practice and Politics: Anthropology and the Study of Social Movements', *Critique of Anthropology* 12(4): 395–432.

Evans-Pritchard, E.E. 1940. *The Nuer*. Oxford: Oxford University Press.

Fairbank, J. (ed.) 1978. *Cambridge History of China*, vol. 10: *Late Ch'ing, 1800–1911*, Part 2. Cambridge: Cambridge University Press.

Francke, A.H. 1995 [1907]. *A History of Western Tibet*. London: S.W. Partridge & Co. and (1995) New Delhi: Asian Educational Services.

———. 1926. *Antiquities of Indian Tibet*, vol. 2: *Chronicles of Ladakh and Minor Chronicles*. Calcutta: Superintendent Government Printing.

Gellner, E. 1969. *Saints of the Atlas*. London: Weidenfeld and Nicolson.

———. 1988. 'Trust, Cohesion and the Social Order', in D. Gambetta (ed.) *Trust: Making and Breaking Cooperative Relations*. Oxford: Blackwell, 142–57.

Goldstein, M. 1994. 'Change, Conflict and Continuity among a Community of Nomadic Pastoralists: A Case Study from Western Tibet, 1950–1990', in

R. Barnett and S. Akiner (eds), *Resistance and Reform in Tibet*. London: Hurst, 76–111.

Hermanns, M. 1949. *Die Nomaden von Tibet*. Vienna: Verlag Herold.

———. 1959. *Die Familie der A Mdo – Tibeter*. Freiburg/Munich: Verlag Karl Alber.

Khoury, P. and J. Kostiner (eds). 1990. *Tribes and State Formation in the Middle East*. Berkeley and Los Angeles: University of California Press.

Makley, C. 1999. 'Embodying the Sacred: Gender and Monastic Revitalization in China's Tibet'. PhD diss., University of Michigan.

———. 2005. '"Speaking Bitterness": Autobiography, History and Mnemonic Politics on the Sino-Tibetan Frontier', *Comparative Studies in Society and History* 47(1): 40–78.

Nader, L. 1990. *Harmony Ideology: Justice and Control in a Zapotec Mountain Village*. Stanford, CA: Stanford University Press.

Petech, L. 1977. *The Kingdom of Ladakh: c. 950–1842 A.D.* Rome: Istituto Italiano per il Medio ed Estremo Oriente.

Pirie, F. 2002. 'Doing Good Badly, or at All?' *Ladakh Studies* 17: 29–32.

———. 2005. 'Feuding, Mediation and the Negotiation of Authority among the Nomads of Eastern Tibet'. Halle/Saale: Working Paper of the Max Planck Institute for Social Anthropology.

———. 2007a. *Peace and Conflict in Ladakh: the Construction of a Fragile Web of Order*. Leiden: Brill.

———. 2007b. 'Order, Individualism and Responsibility: Contrasting Dynamics on the Tibetan Plateau', in K. von Benda-Beckmann and F. Pirie (eds), *Order and Disorder: Anthropological Perspectives*. Oxford: Berghahn, 54–73.

Potter, P. 1991. *The Chinese Legal System: Globalization and Local Legal Culture*. London: Routledge.

Scott, J. 1985. *Weapons of the Weak: Everyday Forms of Peasant Resistance*. New Haven, CT: Yale University Press.

———. 1990. *Domination and the Arts of Resistance: Hidden Transcripts*. New Haven, CT: Yale University Press.

Shinjilt. 2007. 'Pasture-fights, Arbitration and Ethno-narration: Aspects of the Ethnic Relationship between the Mongols and Tibetans in Qinghai and Gansu Provinces', in U.E. Bulag and H.G.M. Diemberger (eds), *Proceedings of the Tenth Seminar of the IATS, 2003 the Mongolia-Tibet Interface: Opening New Research Terrains in Inner Asia, vol. 9*. Leiden: Brill.

Tapper, R. 1983. 'Introduction', in R. Tapper (ed.) *The Conflict of Tribe and State in Iran and Afghanistan*. London: St. Martin's Press, 1–82.

Wylie, T.V. 1959. 'A Standard System of Tibetan Transcription', *Harvard Journal of Asiatic Studies* 22: 261–76.

Yeh, E. 2003. 'Tibetan Range Wars: Spatial Politics and Authority on the Grasslands of Amdo', *Development and Change* 34(3): 499–523.

Notes on Contributors

Upendra Baxi, currently (since 1996) Professor of Law in Development, University of Warwick, served as Professor of Law (1973–1996) and Vice Chancellor (1990–1994) at the University of Delhi. He has also served as Vice Chancellor, University of South Gujarat, Surat (1982–1985), as Honorary Director (Research), The Indian Law Institute (1985–1988), and as President of the Indian Society of International Law (1992–1995). Professor Baxi was invited to deliver a course of lectures by The Hague Academy of Private International Law, published in 2000 as 'Mass Torts, Multinational Enterprise Liability and Private International Law' (*Recueil des Cours* 276: 305–427). His most recent books are *Human Rights in a Posthuman World: Critical Essays* (Oxford University Press 2007) and the third, revised edition of *The Future of Human Rights* (Oxford University Press 2008).

Franz von Benda-Beckmann is head of the Project Group 'Legal Pluralism' at the Max Planck Institute for Social Anthropology in Halle/Saale, Germany. Since 2002 he has been Honorary Professor of Legal Anthropology at the University of Leipzig and since 2004 Honorary Professor of Legal Pluralism at the University of Halle/Saale. He holds a PhD in law (1970) and obtained his habilitation in anthropology at the University of Zurich (1979). Before 2000 he was Professor of Law in Developing Countries at the Agricultural University, Wageningen. He has done fieldwork and supervised research in Malawi, West Sumatra, the Moluccas and Nepal. He has written and co-edited several books and published widely on issues of property rights, social (in)security and legal pluralism in developing countries, as well as on legal anthropological theory. He co-edited, with Keebet von Benda-Beckmann and Anne Griffiths, *Mobile People, Mobile Law: Expanding Legal Relations in a Contracting World* (Ashgate 2005) and, with Keebet von Benda-Beckmann and Melanie G. Wiber, *Changing Properties of Property* (Berghahn 2006).

Keebet von Benda-Beckmann is head of the Project Group 'Legal Pluralism' at the Max Planck Institute for Social Anthropology in Halle/

Saale, Germany. Since 2003 she has been Honorary Professor of Legal Anthropology at the University of Leipzig, and since 2004 Honorary Professor for Legal Pluralism at the University of Halle/Saale. She has carried out research in West Sumatra, on the Moluccan Island of Ambon, Indonesia and among Moluccan women in the Netherlands. She has published extensively on dispute resolution, social security in developing countries, property and water rights, decentralization, and theoretical issues in the anthropology of law. She co-edited, with Franz von Benda-Beckmann and Anne Griffiths, *Mobile People, Mobile Law: Expanding Legal Relations in a Contracting World* (Ashgate 2005), with Franz von Benda-Beckmann and Melanie G. Wiber, *Changing Properties of Property* (Berghahn 2006) and, with Fernanda Pirie, *Order and Disorder: Anthropological Perspectives* (Berghahn 2007).

Jane K. Cowan is Professor of Social Anthropology at the University of Sussex. Her major publications include *Dance and the Body Politic in Northern Greece* (Princeton University Press 1990), *Macedonia: The Politics of Identity and Difference* (Pluto Press 2000) and, with Marie Dembour and Richard Wilson, *Culture and Rights: Anthropological Perspectives* (Cambridge University Press 2001). She has also published numerous articles and chapters on gender relations, ritual, popular music, the politics of language and 'tradition' and questions of identity and minority claims-making in northern Greece. Her current work explores the intertwined production of internationality and minority at the League of Nations, tracing encounters between petitioners, advocates, international civil servants and state diplomats around minority petitions.

Carol J. Greenhouse is Professor of Anthropology at Princeton University (U.S.). She is a cultural anthropologist specializing in the interpretive and experiential aspects of state law and law-making, as well as the discursive interplay between law and other social domains. Her major publications, which explore these issues in the context of the contemporary United States, include *Praying for Justice* (Cornell University Press 1986), *Law and Community in Three American Towns*, with David Engel and Barbara Yngvesson (Cornell University Press 1994), *A Moment's Notice* (Cornell University Press 1996) and *Ethnography in Unstable Places*, co-edited with Elizabeth Mertz and Kay Warren. (Duke University Press 2002). Greenhouse is past President of the Association for Political and Legal Anthropology, and the Law & Society Association.

Anne Griffiths has a personal chair in Anthropology of Law at the University of Edinburgh in the School of Law. Her major research interests include anthropology of law, comparative and family law, African law, gender, culture and rights. Over the years she has been a recipient of research grants from the ESRC (Economic and Social Research Council), Wenner-Gren Foundation for Anthropological Research (U.S.), the Annenberg Foundation (U.S.), the British Academy, the Leverhulme Trust, the Commonwealth Foundation, the Carnegie Trust and the American Bar Foundation. Her major publications include *In the Shadow of Marriage: Gender and Justice in an African Community* (University of Chicago Press 1997), *Mobile People, Mobile Law: Expanding Legal Relations in a Contracting World* (co-edited with F. and K. von Benda-Beckmann, Ashgate 2005), *Family Law* (co-authored with L. Edwards, Thomson/W. Green 2006).

Randy F. Kandel is an anthropologist and an attorney. She is an Adjunct Associate Professor in the Department of Anthropology at John Jay College of Criminal Justice and an administrative law judge in New York. She has done research on legal forums that focus on children in Los Angeles, Glasgow Scotland, Anchorage Alaska, a Tlingit community in Kake Alaska, and central New York State. She has written more than twenty published articles and chapters on children and law, and is presently revising *Family Law: Essential Terms and Concepts* (Aspen Law & Business 2000) to make it Family, Law, and Social Context.

John F. Kearney is a social anthropologist working in both community-based and academic settings on natural resource management, local knowledge mobilization and community capacity building. He published with Patrick Kerans *Turning the World Right-Side Up: Science, Community and Democracy* (Fernwood 2006).

Laura Nader is Professor of Anthropology at the University of California. She has done extensive fieldwork among the Zapotec of Mexico and among Shia Muslim villagers in south Lebanon, and has worked extensively in the United States on the revolution in alternative dispute resolution. Nader was both editor and contributor to *The Ethnography of Law* (American Anthropological Association 1965). The author of *Talea and Juquila: A Comparison of Zapotec Social Organization* (University of California Press, 1964) led to the production of a film, *To Make the Balance*, and later a PBS film, *Little Injustices*. Nader has taught at Yale, Harvard and Stanford law schools. Her most recent books are *Harmony Ideology* (Stanford University Press 1990), *Naked Science* (Routledge 1996), *The Life of the Law* (University of California Press 2002), and *Plunder: When the Rule of Law is Illegal* (Wiley-Blackwell 2008) with Ugo Mattei.

Fernanda Pirie is a University Lecturer in Socio-Legal Studies at the University of Oxford, where she undertakes research into the developing legal realm in China, focussing on issues of order, state-society interactions and the relations between law and religion on the Tibetan plateau. Her most recent books are *Peace and Conflict in Ladakh: The Construction of a Fragile Web of Order* (Brill 2006), *Order and Disorder: Anthropological Perspectives,* jointly edited with Keebet von Benda-Beckmann (Berghahn 2007), and *Conflict and Social Order in Tibet and Inner Asia,* jointly edited with Toni Huber (Brill 2008).

Markus Weilenmann is a legal anthropologist and head of the Office for Conflict Research in Developing Countries. Focal points are demand-oriented research and consultancy on legal and social politics in Sub-Saharan Africa. Since 1978 he has conducted several field researches in Burundi, at first on the political history of conflict denial from an ethno-psychoanalytical perspective, then on dispute settlement in state courts from a legal-anthropological viewpoint. He has published several articles on strategies of dispute settlement and problems of nation-building in the Great Lakes region and is author of the book *Burundi: Konflikt und Rechtskonflikt* (Brandes & Apsel 1997).

Richard W. Whitecross is a qualified lawyer and anthroplogist. He has conducted fieldwork in Nepal, Bhutan and West Bengal and completed his doctoral research in 2002. His thesis is the first anthropological study of law in the Himalayan kingdom of Bhutan, and in 2003 he was awarded an *Economic and Social Research Council (ESRC)* Postdoctoral Fellowship, which he held at the University of Edinburgh. Since completing his fellowship, he has taught courses on Political Anthropology and a range of undergraduate and graduate courses on Law and Society. He has presented his research at conferences at Oxford, Yale, Buffalo and *School of Oriental and African Studies* (SOAS) and presented seminars in Cambridge, Oxford, Paris and Florence. Before becoming a Senior Researcher in Civil Justice with the Scottish Government in 2007, he was engaged in a major research project funded by the ESRC on representation in tribunals in the United Kingdom. His current research interests include children and the law, youth justice and public legal education. In addition, he continues to write on Bhutan. Richard is an Honorary Fellow in Anthropology at the University of Edinburgh.

Melanie G. Wiber is Professor of Anthropology at the University of New Brunswick, Canada. She is author of the book *Politics, Property and Law in the Philippine Uplands* (Wilfred Laurier University Press 1993) and co-editor of *The Role of Law in Natural Resource Management* (Vuga 1996) with Joep Spiertz. Her recent research focuses on new forms of property such as milk and fish quota in the Canadian Maritimes.

Index